Signs of the Spirit

Signs of the Spirit

Music and the Experience of Meaning in Ndau Ceremonial Life

TONY PERMAN

UNIVERSITY OF ILLINOIS PRESS
Urbana, Chicago, and Springfield

1 2 3 4 5 C P 5 4 3 2 1
∞ This book is printed on acid-free paper.

Support for this publication was provided by
the Dean's Office at Grinnell College.

Library of Congress Cataloging-in-Publication Data
Names: Perman, Tony, 1973– author.
Title: Signs of the spirit : music and the experience of meaning in Ndau ceremonial life / Tony Perman.
Description: Urbana : University of Illinois Press, 2020. | Includes bibliographical references and index.
Identifiers: LCCN 2019052272 (print) | LCCN 2019052273 (ebook) | ISBN 9780252043253 (cloth) | ISBN 9780252085178 (paperback) | ISBN 9780252052132 (ebook)
Subjects: LCSH: Ndau (African people)—Music—History and criticism. | Ndau (African people)—Social life and customs. | Rites and ceremonies—Zimbabwe. | Dance—Zimbabwe. | Drum—Performance—Zimbabwe. | Music, Influence of—Zimbabwe. | Spirit possession—Zimbabwe. | Spiritualism—Zimbabwe.
Classification: LCC DT2913.N43 P47 2020 (print) | LCC DT2913.N43 (ebook) | DDC 781.620089963975—dc23
LC record available at https://lccn.loc.gov/2019052272
LC ebook record available at https://lccn.loc.gov/2019052273

Contents

Acknowledgments

To everyone who has helped this manuscript come to life, I say thank you. *Vanhu veshe vakandidetsera ndinoti tinobonga yaemho*. Once they are frozen in print, ethnographies are the most deceptive of icebergs, with a single author's name floating above the surface and communities of people spanning continents and generations veiled beneath it, bearing the weight. None of this would have been possible without the people mentioned so insufficiently here. I hope these offerings adequately reflect my appreciation.

In Chipinge, Valentine became a close friend and Baba naAmai Muranda surrogate parents. Njodzi, Sundawo, and Dhumizulu kept me going when research was a struggle. Down the road, Davison and Serena Masiza taught me drumming, mbira, and sope. Dan Pato, Kelvin and Teremai Sithole, Mai Sibanda, Andy Mashiri, Kuda Muguti, Chonapi and Peter Gwenzi, Father Jabongwe, Sylvester Mukwashi, Zivanayi and Temba Khumbula, Timothy Mabvuu, Wilbert Mumbanyiwa, Mr. Ruuswa, Charles and Eddie Hlakama, Aggriya Mhlanga, Simon and Mildred Sibanda, Claude Chizana, and Mr. Bhuku all helped in ways big and small. In Muzite, Moses Zharikira, Tendai Chitopo, Samson Mapfumo *ne mhuri yavo*, Vhukani Muzite, Edison Sithole, Ambuya Mazveshe, Rodwell Muzite, Zombiyi Muzite, Stanley Mhlanga, Gordon Mtisi-Boden, Hlatywayo Matakura, Nengere, Mr. Munyuki, Ngarife Matabuka, Pileni Dube, Shepherd Dhliwayo, and Panganayi Ndlovu all demonstrated the hospitality for which Muzite is known. Research in the turmoil of twenty-first-century Zimbabwe isn't easy, but they made it feel as if it was.

My Harare family was the Chigamba family. *Maita basa.* Sekuru Tute Chigamba and Ambuya Chigamba, their children, their grandchildren, and their great-grandchildren became a second family. At the U.S. embassy, Rebecca Ziegler-Mano and Charles Tomondo were essential.

In graduate school, my professors Donna Buchanan, Gabriel Solis, Bruno Nettl, Charles Capwell, Matti Bunzl, and Paul Zeleza shaped the scholar I still hope to become, but Tom Turino was a towering presence in the formative years of my ethnomusicological life. He taught me semiotics, brought me to Zimbabwe, made music with me, and became a true friend. Several friends and colleagues helped along the way, including Stefan Fiol, Jennifer Kyker, David McDonald, Anna Schultz, Eduardo Herrera, Sylvia Bruinders, Maggie Adams, Jenny Fraser, Denise Gill, Mary Hunter, Katherine Hagedorn, Joti Rockwell, and Gabe Chandler. My colleagues at Grinnell College have been fabulous throughout my work on this book. Charles Blakney graciously shared his materials from Chipinge. The Fulbright-Hays Program and Grinnell College funded most of my research.

Thanks also to Laurie Matheson and the staff at the University of Illinois Press, who were invaluable partners in this process. Sections of this text have been read by more people than I can name over the years, but Tom Turino, Dave McDonald, Jennifer Kyker, Elizabeth Branch Dyson, and Stefan Fiol all read the manuscript when its length and incoherence made that a selfless act. I owe each of them a debt of gratitude for taking the time. Thanks also to Jennifer Kyker for the great photo on the cover. Two anonymous readers also provided invaluable improvements to the text. Anesu Gamanya, my former student, provided the lion's share of transcriptions and translations, a herculean task. Tawanda Pasirayi, Tapiwanashe Zvidzwa, Bazil Mupisiri, and Casper Takodza also helped.

Thanks to my family. Grandmas Perman and Helgeson reinforced a love of music, left me the money to make my grant last twice as long, and even tried to read my dissertation! My parents Dale and Karen and my brother Sam provided support—technical, financial, emotional, and otherwise—through the whole process. My parents have always made my choices to follow music, the humanities, and my path to Zimbabwe seem worthwhile. My parents-in-law Yiwen and Yuanfang freely provided so much childcare for the wonderfully distracting Paavo that I wrote most of this manuscript in China.

And to Jacquie. More than anyone, she has tolerated the insecurities that publishing creates. She read when asked, prodded when needed, and loved no matter what. Nothing seems like it could have been possible without her.

Prologue

Music, Experience, Meaning

On my first trip to Muzite, a remote community straddling Zimbabwe's border with Mozambique, the *muchongoyo* instructor who'd been so generous with his time offered to accompany me to the Meikles bus stop.[1] It's a twelve-kilometer walk, so this was no idle gesture. We walked along tree-lined paths through the quiet hills and talked. I asked all the questions typical of a novice ethnomusicologist, and he answered with the open honesty of one with an ambition frustrated by political and economic insecurity. As we left the scattered houses on the hills behind us and neared the commercial center of the township, he decided that I should meet Samson Mapfumo. We went to Mapfumo's bottle store, and he invited us to his home. In his eighties at the time, Mapfumo was a dynamo. He shared stories about the history of the Muzite community and showed off one of his most cherished possessions, a *ndonga* walking stick with a hand carved into the knob. He was a proud former councilor in the Ndau opposition party Zanu-Ndonga, named after the Ndau walking stick by its founder, Ndabaningi Sithole, so this object marked his history of resistance, his service to his community, and his well-earned authority.[2] He punctuated his pride in this legacy by demonstrating the powerful stomp central to local muchongoyo dancing. It was an unexpected and eye-opening encounter. When we left and made our way to my bus stop, I had no expectation that we would meet again, not least because the muchongoyo instructor who introduced us quit his job and left for South Africa shortly thereafter to seek better financial fortunes.

Months later, I met Mapfumo again entirely by chance with another of Muzite Primary School's hardworking muchongoyo instructors. Within minutes he had taken it upon himself to help my research, which had expanded from muchongoyo to include questions of spirituality and ceremonial life. He became an irreplaceable catalyst for my research, going so far as to host a ceremony at his home specifically so that I could film ceremonial drumming and the spirits who possess local mediums. More than once he walked several kilometers in order to mollify the concerns of someone I was hoping to interview and convince them that, despite my being a *muyungu* who asked a lot of questions, I could be trusted.[3] He encouraged everyone to help me as much as possible. This was no small courtesy. After eighty years of colonial rule and the increased paranoia and political infighting that were by-products of the Mugabe regime, rural elders had grown wary of curious outsiders. Mapfumo's standing in the community meant that a single word on my behalf opened the homes and hearts of locals who otherwise would have been understandably reticent.[4] Most of my eventual consultants and interviewees either needed time to trust my motives or wanted money to allay their fears. Mapfumo required neither and asked for nothing beyond treating the information I received and the people from whom I received it with respect.

Almost two years to the day after that initial meeting, as my research was ending and I was saying goodbye, Mapfumo asked me if I knew why he had helped me. Did I know why he trusted my sincerity? He barely knew me, after all. My research in Muzite had begun primarily at the suggestion of people I met in the town of Chipinge who respected the quality of the musicians in Muzite, which in essence meant that I showed up unannounced with few credentials beyond my word and the official research permit from Zimbabwe's government, hardly a well-loved institution in these parts.

After I confessed my ignorance, he offered me two reasons, both of which stemmed from that initial encounter at his bottle store and had little to do with my efforts to be respectful, ethical, sincere, or diligent. First, he said, it was "because you are wearing those," pointing to the copper beads and bracelet on my wrist. I had only been wearing them for a couple of months, at the suggestion of an ancestral *mudzimu* spirit in Harare, but had never considered the impact they could have. The spirit said that as a mbira player doing important work, if I wanted to properly respect the spirits whose music I was learning and to be respected as a worthy performer of such music, then I would have to do several things. One of these was to find a copper bracelet and copper beads to wear on my wrist.[5]

Second, when my companion and I had left his home on the day we met, it had rained. At the time, Zimbabwe was in the midst of a three-year drought, which, coupled with inflation and the chaos of land reform,[6] had contributed to serious food insecurity in the country. Rain was a welcome sight, so welcome in fact that aside from offering to host a ceremony on my behalf, he had wanted to thank the spirits for my arrival and for the rain that had accompanied it.

Copper and rain, two tangible signs into which I had put little thought, had opened up research opportunities, social relationships, and enriching experiences in ways of which I had been entirely unaware. For me, each sign was a shallow signifier. I had entirely forgotten about the rain, and I wore the beads primarily as a sign of respect for the family whose spirit had spoken with me rather than to the spirits themselves. For Mapfumo, however, these had been signs of complex dynamics between the living and the dead emerging from generations of social encounter and history. The trust he had felt because I was wearing copper beads was actually trust in his spirits, not in me. He had interpreted the beads as evidence that my work would be sufficiently respectful and that his help would not be futile. Therefore, after knowing me for a matter of minutes, he had offered his home to me for a ceremony. Later in that conversation at the end of my stay, he told me that had I not been wearing those copper beads, he would not have taken such a chance and would not have helped me so quickly. My early reassurances that I could be trusted most likely would have fallen on deaf ears. For Mapfumo, his spirits were communicating directly with him, through those beads, that I was trustworthy. He ignored the signs that made many of his neighbors wary of me: my white skin, tape recorder, notebooks, and questions. He ignored the worsening odds facing his community's flourishing and simply tried to help. The objects behind these seemingly innocuous signs were spiritual and intentional. They were telling Mapfumo something about me, but only as a result of what they communicated about the spirits he trusted. The effects of these signs were many and are ongoing. One effect is this book, one more sign on the long chain of experiences that connect the living with their spirits and the future with connected pasts.

Music, Experience, Meaning

Musicking is a powerful means through which to experience life.[7] It moves people to tears, to laughter, to ecstasy, even to sleep. It can tear people apart but more often brings them together, augmenting relationships that matter and helping form new ones that will matter thereafter. Musicking can bring the divine to earth, the dead to life; it can heal the sick. That musicking is capable of such things rarely comes into question. Its ubiquity suggests that its utility is understood, even if that utility goes unexplained, and that's the rub. Despite flourishing in seemingly every community on earth for millennia and despite decades of thorough multidisciplinary attention, explanations of how it works, why it feels good, and what it means remain elusive and fragmented. Musicians, listeners, scholars, and critics have spent untold hours trying to put into words exactly what it is about music that moves us. Music's power is knowable, but seemingly unexplainable. Words fail.

Words fall short because musicking works differently. As the ethnomusicologists Charles Seeger (1977), Steven Feld (1974), and Thomas Turino (1999) have demonstrated so well, the ways in which nonlinguistic humanly organized sounds represent the world and elicit effects in that world are quite different from the ways in which language does. This does not make musicking shallower than language, nor less meaningful, nor an evolutionary spandrel (Pinker 1997). Rather, it just means that putting these modes of meaning into words is difficult and likely to fail. Just because someone can't quite explain why playing the mbira brings them to tears doesn't mean that they are not crying.

I wrote this book in order to push past the limits of language and explain how musicking contributes to powerful emotional and spiritual experiences. I use the ethnographic moment, what the ethnomusicologist Michelle Kisliuk calls the "magnified musicking moment," to clarify the impact that the past and the future have on the immediacy of the present (Kisliuk 2017). The tools I use and theoretical explanations I offer are not all drawn from the Ndau community or the people who helped me with my research. They don't use words to explain these moments because there is no need to do so. This is typical of musicking experiences the world over. But the tools and explanations offered here all emerge from the details of the ethnographic moment, whether articulated verbally by participants or not. I don't want to put words in others' mouths, and I hope it is clear throughout that the interpretation is my own. My "speculative" thoughts, to borrow the performance theorist Deborah Kapchan's (2017) approach, capture what I know about this particular soundscape based on how I've been taught by Ndau listeners and players over the years and how I engaged in this soundscape with them. My goal is "sound writing," as Kapchan terms it, that effectively describes why these fleeting musical moments matter so much in ways that demonstrate both how meaningful Ndau musicking can be spiritually, socially, and emotionally, and how effective a semiotic ethnomusicology can be in illuminating those powerful meanings. My hope is that these theoretical tools convincingly render the ineffable and transcend the limits of speech in explaining the lasting consequences of a transitory ceremonial experience.

It is this kind of experience with the practices I label musicking that makes them meaningful; thus the three key terms of these introductory remarks: music, experience, and meaning. As lived, these abstract categories do not exist in isolation. There is no meaning without experience, nor music without meaning. In what follows, I rely on the phenomenology and semiotics of C. S. Peirce to explore the way in which meaning is experienced during Ndau spirit possession ceremonies and shapes emotional life.

In the Ndau-speaking communities of the Chipinge District of southeastern Zimbabwe that rely on the spirits around them for guidance, protection, and collective flourishing, musicking with dancing is the most public way to engage with spirits, deal with heartache and struggle, or celebrate. Musicking is the means through which communities experience life together. This does not mean that music is ubiquitous or is woven through every thread in the fabric of life; far from it. Days can go by in Chipinge's rural communities without much active engagement with sound or music making. It is no more a "natural" feature of local life than it is elsewhere. But it does mean that if there are events in which the community is expected to gather—whether to celebrate a wedding, installation of a new chief, or a homecoming, or whether to cope with death, drought, or witchcraft—musicking brings people together.

Musicking in this region manifests in a variety of forms and for a variety of reasons. I focus on one genre of musicking, the dance-drumming songs performed for and with *madhlozi* spirits. Thus, in the chapters that follow I have two major tasks. One is to introduce and explore the madhlozi performance traditions of Chipinge's Ndau communities, situating them within the historical, spiritual, musical, and political contexts of contemporary Ndau life in Zimbabwe. The second is to develop a theory of emotional experience in music in terms of the active role these performances play in local people's lives using a semiotic toolbox that is, I hope, consistent with the ways in which anthropology, neuroscience, and musicology more broadly think about and understand emotion. Musicking and dancing are especially rewarding, if challenging, modes through which to explore emotion because their usefulness for expression and elicitation manifest themselves in ways that are less mediated than is language. Ultimately, musicking helps people in these Ndau communities uniquely and constructively navigate their emotional lives. This book, situated in the specific ceremonial moments of the Ndau communities in which I lived, is about music, experience, and meaning.

MUSIC

By now it has almost become a clichéd ethnomusicological rite of passage to point out that most sub-Saharan African languages "lack" a word for music. Like many of my students, I was surprised to learn this as I studied Shona. I corral the word *lack* in scare quotes because the linguistic poverty implied by such an absence is, in reality, much shallower and uninteresting than the observation might imply. What could it mean about musical life that the word *music* doesn't exist? Perhaps most obviously it means that people weren't speaking English. It is important to provincialize the word *music* as the narrow sign of a specific language. If I were to assert that most super-Saharan European languages lack a word for madhlozi, would that be surprising? None of these languages lack the linguistic tools to describe spirits or spirituality, but I have yet to find an efficient translation. Neither ChiShona nor ChiNdau lacks the linguistic tools to describe what I call musicking. Simply put, the symbols they use are different and are organized differently.

Despite my identity as an ethnomusicologist, the centrality of musicking in this book's title, and the focus I place on sounds that an English speaker would label as music, I am more interested in what music affords as it becomes the means toward other ends and is thus meaningful than I am in music itself. The anthropologist Michelle Bigenho (2008) provides an instructive caution against musical exceptionalism and the presumed implication that music is the object of ethnomusicology's inquiry. I similarly approach music as the lens through which to understand broader truths; however, musicking itself also affords scope for such dimensions of human life as creativity, communication, and community that stand apart from other kinds of human and nonhuman interaction. I prioritize the experiences related to sounds and the consequences of those sounds. I focus on musicking in order to understand emotion, in part, as a corrective to existing literature about emotion and affect that focuses almost exclusively on language or physiology. The other multisensory signs of experience indexically connected to sound matter as well, but I organize my inquiry around what English speakers would call music and the emotions to which it so frequently relates.

The field of sound studies helpfully draws attention to the arbitrary separation between sound and music (Sakakeeny 2015, 122), but there are other arbitrary separations that can equally complicate music's exceptionalism. In

Chipinge, as in many southern African contexts, the separation of music from dance is much less clearly defined than it is in historically English-language environments. One always accompanies the other. Likewise, in ceremonial contexts, sound and society are linked in such a way that when announcing a coming ceremony, people are less likely to say that they are striking the drum, singing songs, or dancing than they are to say that they are brewing beer. Music, much like beer, becomes a tool in the service of social and spiritual ends.

As the musicologist Kofi Agawu puts it, "'Musicking' in Africa is indexed by a variety of terms: we beat, shake, touch, and play; we say, recite, recollect, and sign; and we move, stir the body, look our way, and dance. In speaking of 'African music,' then, we do well to keep this expanded semantic horizon in mind" (2016a, 3). Sound is one aspect of music, just as it is one aspect of ceremonial action, but an overemphasis on either is a path towards partiality. To be clear, I am not writing about "African music" as a whole. Despite James Ferguson's (2006) legitimate critique of anthropologists for fetishizing the particular (the trees) to such an extent that they lose the ability to offer any commentary on the general (the forest), I'm not even writing about Zimbabwean music or Ndau music. Ndau music, like Ndau culture, is at the very least a heterodoxy; it is not a monolith. I write about a specific ceremony taking place on specific days in a specific community among a narrow cross-section of Chipinge residents.[8]

EXPERIENCE

Experience is another slippery term, but ideally it can define the kinds of musical life with which I engage. Just as the ethnomusicologists Martin Clayton, Byron Dueck, and Laura Leante (2013, 1) use experience to focus attention on the phenomenal, I use it to shift attention from the inert stability of objects toward the fluidity of "social experiences in solution" (Williams 1977, 133). Although the tools, methods, and conclusions of Clayton, Dueck, and Leante differ considerably from mine, their framing and phrasing suggest a growing consensus that these are the areas in which musical life's importance can be understood.[9] I am more interested in this fluidity of experience as process than in music as an object or text to be read by participants or analysts. Musicking is influential in part because it takes place in specific places and times, in the ongoing, immediate present. Musicking is merely one mode in which to be in the moment, in the here and now; language is another. There are different ways of experiencing music ranging from thoughtful, symbolically driven reflection to hyper-focused "flow" states fully engaged with the musicking on hand and to trance. In the pages to follow, I show that participants engage in each at one point or another.

My approach relies on a form of phenomenology in order to explain each of these disparate modes of engagement with the world through sound. I do not rely on the texts rooted in Husserl or Heidegger that canonically claim phenomenology as a discursive practice or tradition, but rely instead on the phenomenology of C. S. Peirce and his interpreters.[10] Peircean phenomenology, or phaneroscopy as Peirce eventually named his approach,[11] provides tools for examining the present in the present, to explore experiences and processes of interpretation that happen in the moment rather than structural relationships. In particular, I examine experiences of semiosis as they inform collective experience, spiritual engagement, and emotional response.

In *How Forests Think*, the anthropologist Eduardo Kohn writes, "Selves are signs. Lives are thoughts. Semiosis is alive. And the world is thereby animate" (2013, 99). Living thought is a powerful synthesis of a certain kind of experience, but it also limits experience to a certain kind of engagement with the world, as semiosis. Despite my embrace of it, semiotic theory cannot explain everything, and the breadth of instances covered by a word like *experience* makes that clear. For example, certain Ndau communities gather together to music for their spirits, in part, to generate certain kinds of purposeful experience. For mediums the purpose is possession by a spirit, often experienced through trance. In trance, almost by definition, thoughts are not alive; thought becomes scarce, and perhaps this is the reason why trance is the most effective mode of experience through which to facilitate spirit possession. For other participants the purpose is social, a shared sense of "flow" in which the aspects of life and of the world that aren't in one's immediate focus seem to disappear. For still others, the purpose is experience defined much as Kohn defines it: as living thought. Sign making becomes evidence of life itself; experience is driven and defined by meaning.

MEANING

Meaning's meaning enjoys perhaps the least consensus among the three terms I am discussing. Like music, its status as a symbol masks some conceptual and organizational differences between it, as an English term, and its analogues in other languages. Part of the challenge is that the word has come to mean so many things, and *kureva*, the most common ChiNdau translation for *meaning*, covers only a few of these alternatives. On one hand, its use value could appear diminished as scholars disagree about which meaning of *meaning* to employ. On the other, pedantic demands such as this one for definitional precision can obscure its valuable flexibility. The neuroanthropologist Terrence Deacon (2012b, 9) complains that the science of meaning lags centuries behind the science of tangible phenomena like hemoglobin molecules, though meaning is more familiar to most of us. One aspect of meaning that is essential to my argument, yet often is contradicted in work on emotion or music, is that meaning is not the exclusive domain of language, nor is language the sole means of representation. Turino (2014), Elizabeth Tolbert (2001), and Gary Tomlinson (2015), among others, make clear the damaging consequences of restricting representation and meaning to language. For Tomlinson, "Linguo-centric and symbolocentric approaches to deep histories of the human are ubiquitous, but they build barriers, posit revolutionary shifts, and encourage catastrophism where instead continuities are called for" (2016, 146). Among these continuities, which inform much of the material to follow, are those between meaning and emotional experience, spirits and humans, history and the ongoing present, and the multiple dimensions of meaning itself.

In his work advocating, summarizing, and celebrating the possibility of coherent ethnomusicological theory, Timothy Rice mentions three meanings often ascribed to the single symbol "meaning": the signified, the valued, and the intended (2001, 21). He excludes the one component of meaning that Turino's Peircean approach privileges: effect (Turino 2014). *Meaning* now has four definitions. Kohn (2013, 72) detaches the gerund to make *mean-ing*, describing no fewer than seven possible options: means-ends relations, strivings, purposes, telos, intentions, functions, and significance.

I look to the semiotic theories of Peirce that emerge from the phenomenology mentioned above. Peirce's most influential contribution, the fulcrum for the complex theories weighted on either side toward generality and specificity, is the sign, which is anything that has an effect in an interpreter based on its representation of something else. Signs mediate between objects and effects. A simple word with countless variations of this definition, Peirce's *sign* is famously triadic: sign, object, and interpretant or effect. Implied in the triad, but separate from it, is the interpreter. Each of the numerous meanings of *meaning* described by Rice, Turino, and Kohn address the sign in different ways, alternatively emphasizing the sign's relation to its object (significance, means-ends), its effect, or the interpreter (telos, purpose). Using one word to cover each of these relations is understandably confusing, but perhaps still valuable once clarified. Given that Peirce's three-part sign is irreducible, meaning *must* account for all three. Focusing solely on the object signified reduces the sign to Saussure's semiological signifier. Focusing solely on the effect or the interpreter relegates the sign to Derrida's sense of play, with little regard for reality (see Short 2007, 45). My approach to meaning relies on a series of assumptions with which I think the people represented in this book would agree: There are objective realities, signs have consequences, and meaning emerges from the way a sign relates its reality to its consequences.

Semiosis is processual and can seem ceaseless. Signs are rarely fixed, like objects, but rather thrive in ongoing processes of interpretation. In English, meaning has usually been reserved for language and for the processes that Peirce calls symbol, most prominently employed in language. Symbol is also the element of Peirce's semiotics that most closely aligns with the signifier in Saussure's semiology. Aside from the problematic exclusion of effects in semiology and other sign types from symbolocentric accounts, one contribution that ethnomusicology has made over the years is to assert and defend musicking as deeply meaningful in ways that are distinct from language. From a Peircean perspective, meaning and experience are indivisible. Each shapes the other, both informed by and informing the effects of signs, the habits of past interpretations, and the values that shape them. Meaning and community can also seem indivisible. For the French philosopher Jean-Luc Nancy, indeed, "there is no meaning if meaning is not shared" (2000, 2). As I turn my attention to spirituality and emotion, the dynamic intersection of semiotic possibilities, purposes, and signified realities becomes central to understanding ceremonial experience and the meaning of shared musicking.

Outline of the Book

I offer this text as both an object of ethnomusicological inquiry into the relation between performance and affect, and a gesture of appreciation and admiration for the communities and individuals who welcomed me. Its purpose is to explain how musicking in rural Ndau communities in Zimbabwe was meaningfully experienced during the Horus Farm ceremony held on July 2–3, 2005, which I compare to other events from my fieldwork. Each chapter in Part II emphasizes an element of semiotic theory—objects, signs, effects, and continuity—in order to build a model for exploring affect and emotional experience. The model begins with signs as interpreted in relation to habits and values grounded in one's sense of self during emotionally and spiritually moving and intersubjective experiences. Once I've explained my model and the terms and tools within it, I move from the roots of ceremonial action through action itself to the fruits of that action.

Part I introduces the communities, events, and theories involved. Chapter 1, "Introduction: Finding *Madhlozi* in Chipinge," identifies the communities, spirits, and ceremonial practices at the heart of the book. I focus on the actors, both living and dead, at the Horus Farm ceremony. In Chapter 2, "Moving

Signs: The Experience of Affective Semiosis," I introduce my model and the key terminology rooted in the semiotics of C. S. Peirce. This chapter, in a sense, lifts the lid on my own thinking to provide as much conceptual transparency as possible.

Part II narrates the sequence of events at Horus Farm by following four categories of spirits who arrived to dance, one after the other. Chapter 3, "Late Afternoon: *Madzviti* and the Foundation of Interpretation," introduces madzviti spirits and explores the role of ritual musicking in shaping local habitus and relationships. Emphasizing the reality of semiotic objects, I explore the histories of their emergence and the purposes with which the living awaken them. Chapter 4, "Evening: *Zvipunha*, Signs, and Transformative Experience," begins with events that took place minutes after those with which Chapter 3 ends, exploring zvipunha spirits and signs of transformative experience. I focus on the here and now and the efficacy of musicking in shaping the emotional and spiritual possibilities of experience. Chapter 5, "Overnight: *Mhongo* and the Effects of Performance," extends the approach to emotion by addressing mhongo spirits and the effects of performance in interpretants. I explore the way ceremonial conventions can be manipulated or undermined. Chapter 6, "Early Morning: *Zvaayungu* and the Shaping of Ndau Modernity," looks to the future and the possibility of shaping new habits and semiotic domains. Zvaayungu spirits are from the recent past, having emerged after independence in 1980. I use this chapter to explore the semiotic continuity of signs representing objects and eliciting effects that shape the ways in which future events might unfold as communities strive to flourish. Finally, the epilogue synthesizes the major points from the text as a whole and provides a broader view, asking, What does this all mean?

The goal in the ceremonies I describe and analyze is to transform possibility into actuality. I focus on music because it is uniquely suited to facilitate experiential transformations such as this. Spirits don't engage discursively with people but, rather, embody multiple tensions within a discursive context of the living that shapes how they are understood. I focus on semiotics because it is uniquely suited to interrogate the phenomenology of these transformative experiences. Ndau ceremonial traditions in Chipinge do not thrive simply because custom is resilient or because the so-called structures from which they emerge are fixed, but because they provide hope: hope that people in the present can use the experiences of the past to make a better future.

PART I

Foundations

CHAPTER 1

Introduction

Finding Madhlozi in Chipinge

Arriving in Chipinge

My first glimpse of the town of Chipinge as it emerges from the surrounding hills and fields brings comfort, anticipation, and awe. Even after fifteen years' worth of visits, I look forward to the moment when it appears. The town, though it seems sleepy from the distance of a bus window, teems with activity. It is a small island of urban commercialism in a sea of agricultural values; layers of history have shaped a landscape of complexity and contradiction. A relatively small, remote corner of Zimbabwe, tucked along the border with Mozambique, Chipinge District is home to a population held together by loosely shared senses of history, political affiliation, and language yet disrupted by wide-ranging geographic contrasts.

Moving south from the city of Mutare on the A9, our bus descends into the Save River Valley, a parched and barren terrain that remains fully populated, dusty, and dry, as an unannounced cue that we are entering the Ndau-speaking region of Zimbabwe: Gazaland. The heat penetrates the bus. Baobabs dot the landscape. Even the walls of the round houses scattered on the hills on either side of the road look thirsty, cracked with age, drought, and neglect brought with poverty and struggle.[1] Life here is as hard as the soil that is so difficult to farm. Drumming here is slow and deliberate, resembling the tempo of local life relative to the highlands to the east. To reach the town of Chipinge, we turn left just before crossing the Save River at Birchenough Bridge, quickly ascend the hills of the Eastern Highlands, and pass the inviting Chipinge Safari Area, lush and seemingly bereft of people.

Life emerges. The earth is greener as baobab and acacia are joined by *musasa, mutamba, mukute,* wattle, and pine. The gradations of brown in the earth, the homes, and the vegetation of the Save lowlands are transformed as the earth turns yellow and bright red, trees burst with diverse shades of vibrant green, and the brown of the homes becomes a contrast in color. Corporate tea estates that escaped the purge of land reform swell with vitality. We are entering Chipinge's well-known farmlands, lush with tea, bananas, and coffee. Were we to turn left again we would enter Chimanimani, a tourist haven famed for its national parks, waterfalls, and greenery, though devastated in March 2019 by Cyclone Idai. But we veer right, headed for the center of Zimbabwe's Ndau districts and the town of Chipinge. After our bus passes the banana fields and tea estates among the villages in the Mutema Chieftaincy, the high-density Gaza township emerges from the hills. By now the townships and wards of Chipinge have climbed their way up the hills, evidence of Chipinge's steady growth over the past few decades. Perhaps in response to the multiple challenges of life in twenty-first-century Zimbabwe, more and more people have moved to town. Economic, political, social, and environmental instability have made rural life less and less secure. The town bustles with activity as tomato sellers and wireless network airtime vendors crowd the narrow sidewalks. Churches, houses veiled by durawall, stores, and loiterers fill the space. The business district has grown so much that the bottle store that marked the edge of town when I first arrived in 2001 seems to have crept nearer the center of town.

But the Chipinge I came to know remains. The familiar faces drinking at the well-aged Chipinge Hotel, the dusty roads fanning out from the town center out to the residential areas, and the lush green that gives the highlands of Chipinge a welcoming feel all endure. They form the background for the hustle of locals trying to make ends meet during trying times. Day-to-day life can be consumed by struggle. Unemployment remains stubbornly high, as do school fees and the cost of daily necessities. These two truths, warmth and struggle, engender an endless campaign to maintain one's existence. Daily conversations continuously turn to U.S. dollars, shifting gasoline prices, and possibilities for employment or escape.

These conversations are often accompanied by the sounds of Christianity, as churches new and old sonically dot the landscape of Chipinge. Because the Gaza Township rests against a hill in the distance, the sounds of worshippers there resound off the highlands as though they were a band shell and fill the urban soundscape, reminding shoppers and salespeople alike of the spiritual effort going into the lives around them. Superficially, that is the only evidence of spirituality at hand. One might never know that behind the scenes, and beyond the town itself, numerous residents of the greater Chipinge District rely on their spirits to help them navigate the challenges of today. One could say, "still rely," but the role of the spirits shouldn't be a surprise. They have helped for decades, some for centuries. They are not an anachronistic remnant pushing against the inevitability of modernity; they help shape that modernity. But these spirits no longer speak to everyone, as so many in Chipinge's Ndau community have turned to God in his multiple Christian iterations, leading to the range of faiths typical of many postcolonial environments. But they are still strong; they are still necessary. For those in Chipinge who do rely on their spirits, these strange times demand a continued respect for, reliance on, and confidence in their outsider spirits, the *madhlozi*.

KUBIKIRA DORO IN THE TWENTY-FIRST CENTURY: JULY 2–3, 2005

On July 2, 2005, I was invited by Davison and Serena Masiza to attend an event hosted by a friend whose home was on the newly resettled Horus Farm nearby. This particular ceremony serves as the principal site of the ethnographic experiences and analysis presented throughout the chapters to follow. My experience that day redefined my research in Chipinge District. The sources of my appreciation and nascent understanding of ceremonial life are the spirits who define it. The narrative thread here follows my experience of this event, at which I encountered the four communities of spirit delineated in Part II. I was a guest that day when our hosts brewed beer (*vabikira doro*) as a way of letting everyone know that a ceremony was to be held. The living and the dead alike were invited. People danced and sang from mid-afternoon to mid-morning the next day. During this ceremony four types of spirit arrived, one after the other:

Madzviti: Gaza Nguni soldiers
Zvipunha: Young girls, "nannies"
Mhongo: Spirits primarily from the Danda region of Mozambique
Zvaayungu: Soldiers from the Second Chimurenga in the 1970s

This book is about these spirits in Chipinge, the mediums who bring them back, and the ceremonies in which they emerge. Collectively called madhlozi, they are the "outsider spirits" of distant social encounters that have come to define Ndau identity and history. I augment the events of this ceremony with material from other ceremonies that I was invited to attend and record by the communities who hosted them in the Chipinge District. In describing these events, I address the logic of the madhlozi spirits and the nature of mediumship.

EXPERIENCING MEANING IN CEREMONIAL PRACTICE: A MODEL

In the volatile conditions of twenty-first-century Zimbabwe, where land itself is the unsettled site of political maneuvers and historical wrongs (Alexander 2006), ritual becomes a space for making history, reinforcing relationships, and reifying new possibilities. Spirit mediumship drives ritual action, making emotion and spirituality central features of social life.

Zimbabwe has long been the site of outstanding ethnomusicological, anthropological, and historical scholarship, from within and without the country, with a strong legacy regarding the social importance of music and ritual. But Ndau histories, lives, and sounds have been as tangential to the academic record as to national policy. I follow the lead of the historians John Keith Rennie (1973) and Elizabeth MacGonagle (2007), who shaped the scholarly understanding of Ndau history but whose attention to Ndau ritual was understandably secondary to other concerns. Although other scholars of Ndau life, including the anthropologist Carin Vijfhuizen (2002), the development scholar Phillian Zamchiya (2011, 2013b), the historian Marshall Maposa (2012), the poet Tinashe Muchuri (2015), the religion scholars Tenson Muyambo and Richard Maposa (2013), and Godfrey Museka, Darmarris Kaguda, and Onia Matumbu (2016) address ritual only briefly, each recognizes its centrality to Ndau social life and political engagement.

The broader scholarship concerning Zimbabwe consistently recognizes the inextricable links between land and politics (Lan 1985; Alexander 2006; Moore 2005; Charumbira 2015; Fontein 2015b) and between music and political identity (Turino 2000; Chikowero 2015; Kyker 2016) in Shona Zimbabwe, but Ndau's historical differences and marginal existence lead to different dynamics between ritual, identity, and politics. In-depth studies of music usually emphasize either mbira music or urban popular music in Harare (Berliner 1993; Turino 2000; Eyre 2015; Kyker 2016). The country's Ndau-speaking communities live on the margins of its social life and political history and on the edges of Zimbabweanist scholarship.

Madhlozi spirits resemble other spiritual actors who help the living come to terms with colonial and postcolonial realities. Hauka practices in Niger (Stoller 1995), stambeli in Tunisia (Jankowsky 2010), brekete in Ghana (Friedson

2009), and diverse spirits in Madagascar all reveal the importance of outsider spirits on the continent and the dynamism of spirituality in contemporary Africa (Lambek 2002; Emoff 2002). The work by the anthropologists Paul Stoller and Michael Lambek and by ethnomusicologists Richard Jankowsky, Steven Friedson, and Ron Emoff provides models for understanding how madhlozi shape Ndau life and suggests provocative continental dynamics in which young spirits constructively harness postcolonial insecurity, conflict, and ambiguity.

Focused on the immediacy of ceremonial action, this book explores the historical, spiritual, and social roots and fruits of that action as ritual brings people together and shapes their collective approach to the future. In doing so, it can be summarized in three succinct ways. First, it is an ethnography of Ndau spiritual performance and the role that music plays in spirit possession ceremonies in the rural communities surrounding Chipinge, Zimbabwe. Second, it is an investigation of the immediacy of musical experience and the ways in which the ongoing present of ceremonial performance becomes emotional. Finally, it provides a model rooted in ethnography and the semiotic tools of C. S. Peirce to explain how music, meaning, affect, and experience intersect. I thus engage with three overlapping bodies of knowledge: Ndau spiritual life, semiotics, and studies of emotion and affect. I develop an ethnographically grounded model of emotion that takes the reader step by step from perception to physiologically and culturally informed response to expression. The goal is to provide a theoretical model for exploring emotional experience in ethnograph terms. Semiotic processes inform emotional experiences in important ways that illuminate the tight relationship between sound, meaning, experience, and emotion. Age-old practices remain vibrant and relevant in the twenty-first century.

As becomes obvious with sustained attention to performance in the madhlozi ceremony, experiences are driven by the historical, social, cosmological, and political meanings contained therein. Thus, the minutiae of musical practice connect to the formative moments of identity construction, social coherence, historical understanding, and emotional experience. More specifically, the habits and values that comprise the self inform people's response to performance signs with numerous effects. Because performance signs are understood to reflect local histories, local expectations, and collective purpose, they can become moving and transformative. Knowledge of the past and hopes for the future are involved throughout in a manner that is all about the present, experience in the moment. Therefore, I focus on the immediacy and importance of the here and now.

With this approach I develop and employ a sequential model of emotional experience that involves semiosis, physiology, evaluation, and expression. I treat affect as a ubiquitous element of experience. The valuation of signs along dimensions of value that implicate and potentially change aspects of the self is the core process in emotional life. In this way dimensions of value define emotions. Semiosis and emotion are shaped by agents, and in madhlozi ceremonies, the spirits are agents just as much as are the people who invite them. Each has desires and participates with purpose. In this model, as in Ndau life, spirits are parts of selves. In-the-moment relationships among the living and with the dead shape local realities. The now, as represented and felt during performance, can actualize the possible, bring the past into the present, and direct the affective dimensions of life productively toward an unknown future. Participants generate deeply meaningful experiences by engaging signs that intersect with the habits and values that shape their interpretation. These experiences only fully make sense within the broader social, spiritual, and historical contexts of early twenty-first-century southeastern Zimbabwe.

In the following chapters I introduce a lexicon drawn from C. S. Peirce and elsewhere as a set of robust and consistent tools with which to illuminate meaning in experience and explore how ritual *feels* without depending on tools developed for language or physiology. My theory suggests that music uniquely shapes experience, and the study of music as a semiotic domain is uniquely poised to shape a broader understanding of semiosis and phenomenology. Applying the work of Peirce to sound reveals the theoretical utility of semiotics and the practical utility of musicking in the productive phenomenology of ritual life.

In order to succinctly capture the continuity and relations of the theoretical keywords presented throughout this text, I offer the following:

Emotional experiences begin with **signs**, the gateway to histories, purposes, hopes, and dreams. The living and the dead demonstrate agency by making **interpretants** to these signs, which are the effects of **semiosis** that reveal the **objects** signified, whether via resemblance (**icons**), contiguity (**indices**), or stipulated generality (**symbols**). Through the mutually informed processes of biocultural evolution and socialization, people's potentially ever-changing **habits** guide these processes of experiential **interpretation,** but the ways in which different dimensions of **value** are brought to bear ensure that life, as semiosis, is never predictable. The **affective** dimension of interpretation ensures that the **self** is always implicated in these **intersubjective** moments of performance, spiritual engagement, and sociality. **Identities**, selves, and communities are made through **subjectivity** and intersubjectivity. **Musicking** in ritual is powerfully effective in ensuring **haecceity**, the narrow attention to the here and now, and becomes a means of shaping **affect**, **emotions**, and **feelings** through expressive **emotives** to increase the odds of reifying ceremonial ideals and expectations, transforming possibility, as icons and **rhemes**, into actuality, now indices and **dicents**.

I argue that physiology and culture are compatible, that emotion is meaningful and knowable, and that semiotic tools can help scholars avoid the pitfalls of linguocentric or neurocentric approaches by tracing the specific ways in which meaning is felt based on the histories and consequences of semiotic moments. Bringing the work of Peirce to affect offers useful tools for ethnographers exploring the ineffability of affective musical experience.

Gazaland and the Ndau

The town of Chipinge served as my home for almost two years and became my gateway to the rural communities beyond to the south and the east, where I conducted the bulk of my research.[2] These included Muzite, Chirinda, Jersey, Bangwe, Daisy Hill, Holland Farm, and Horus Farm.[3] Home to fewer than thirty thousand people, Chipinge is the commercial and political center of Ndau-speaking Zimbabwe. Chipinge District's varied landscape provides a wider contrast in terrain within a small district than one finds in many regions of Zimbabwe, which primarily rests on a large plateau (see figure 1.1). There are several chieftaincies that continue to exert influence in local politics. I spent my time in the jurisdictions of Chief Gwenzi, near Muzite, Chief Musikavanhu, to the west of Chief Gwenzi, Chief Mutema, northwest of town, and Chief Mapungwana, near Mt. Selinda.

In many ways, Ndau is further removed from the Shona orthodoxy than are other linguistic communities and chieftaincies that cohered into a loosely unified Shona identity during the nineteenth and twentieth centuries. Ndau has linguistic roots in Nguni-speaking communities to the south and political connections in the Mozambican ones to the east.

Historically speaking, drums and *makosho* gourd rattles have dominated Ndau musicking.[4] Perhaps more ubiquitous than the ceremonial practices that are my main subject, *muchongoyo* is the secular sound of Ndau identity and communal pride. Grounded in the drumming practices of Gaza Nguni soldiers who arrived from South Africa in the nineteenth century, muchongoyo is a presentational and competitive dance-drumming practice. The social *chokoto* dance has also been widespread, though perhaps it has moved from the center of local musical consciousness in recent years. In both, two drummers join

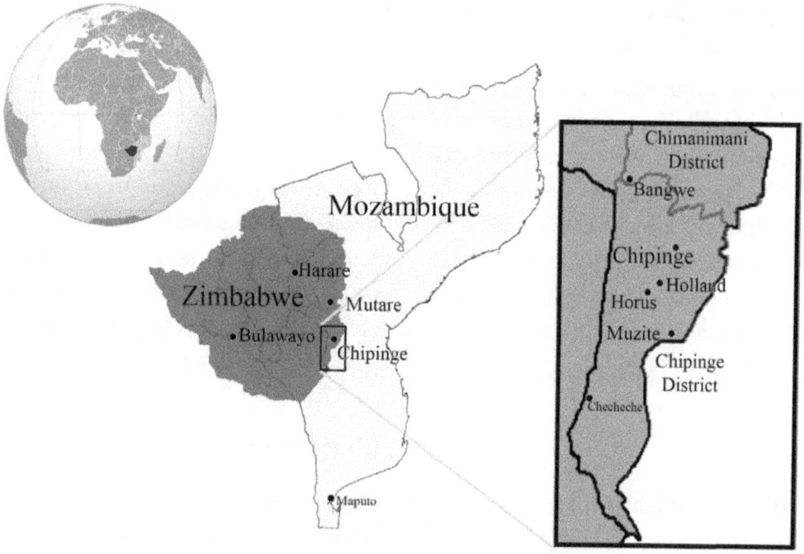

FIGURE 1.1. Map of Chipinge District

a row of singers to accompany a few dancers who present synchronized and acrobatic performances to onlookers.

The diverse genres of madhlozi drumming overlap with these secular styles and share certain performance values. Each category of spirit is invited by and associated with a different rhythmic motif on a different drum. This does not mean that there is a single rhythm used in every case, but the living and the dead alike are habituated to respond to certain rhythms in predictable ways. As the site of centuries of foreign intervention and migration, Ndau music reflects stylistic influences from multiple origins. Like muchongoyo, madzviti drumming descends from the Gaza Nguni practices of what is now South Africa. This drumming is explicitly duple and symmetrical. Zvipunha drumming, which followed the madzviti at Horus Farm, remains duple but is asymmetrical, using a signature rhythmic motif to communicate the purpose of the performance: zvipunha spirit possession. Mhongo spirits, the third to arrive at Horus Farm, dance to complex polyrhythms effectively represented in 12/8, with overlapping rhythms grounded in groups of two and threes. This polyrhythmic style is more common in other regions of Zimbabwe and Mozambique. Finally, zvaayungu drumming suggests the square rhythms of colonial influence, with clear downbeats and accents like the martial music of

British imperialism. All of these practices, sacred and secular alike, exemplify the inextricable link between music and dance.

It is not surprising that local music covers the gamut of purposes and contexts. Indigenous instruments that predate the onset of colonialism include a wide variety of drums, lamellaphones, musical bows, and a few simple wind instruments such as the *damba* (or *chigufe*) ocarina. Song and dance are virtually ubiquitous in these practices. While Zimbabwe is internationally famous for its mbira, the Ndau mbira is musically, socially, and organologically distinct.[5] It is primarily a solo instrument that relies on hexatonic scales and secular, individualized sung themes (Perman 2015). The plucked single-string *chipendani* and scraped single-string *chimazambi* have long been audible in Chipinge's eastern highlands, although their use has been fading in recent years. The soundscape of contemporary Chipinge is dominated by a diverse range of gospel genres, the guitar-driven pop of *sungura* (see Perman 2012), and, most recently, Zimdancehall.

Spirits in Chipinge

For Zimbabweans, the twenty-first century has been defined by struggle shaped by the ruling party's invasive efforts to remain in power, the economic collapse that brought tragically comic levels of inflation, and devastating levels of unemployment. Feeding one's family became a daily quest for many faced with shortages, inflation, mistrust, and distant political machinations that intruded on the day-to-day. The epidemic of HIV/AIDS was reaching the zenith of its devastating impact on the fabric of social life. That it coincided with a dramatic drop in the availability of reliable healthcare and medication, accompanied by increased food insecurity and international isolation, only made matters worse.

These challenges led, unsurprisingly, perhaps, to increased reliance on spiritual support. The struggles of everyday life were filtered by a broad understanding of spiritual power and the geopolitical forces that are simply beyond local control. When the rains were distressingly late during the rainy season in 2003, for instance, I heard two theories as to why, for bad luck simply wasn't an option. Either God was upset or white people with all the power were deliberately keeping the clouds away. Which was stronger, the divine or geopolitics?

Death is less of a barrier to social interaction in Chipinge than one might assume. As the Ndau musician from Mozambique C. Kamba Simango put it while working with the proto-ethnomusicologist Natalie Curtis in the early twentieth century, "The souls of the dead do not leave this world to go elsewhere, but remain here invisible" (1920, 15).[6] There is no equivalent to heaven where spirits reside; rather, they live in the hills, forests, pools, and caves of Chipinge's countryside, sharing the world with the living. Even within individual selves, the living and the dead coexist. A traditional healer working in the main market in the town of Chipinge named Jabulani Chinengawo Mulambo explained to me that "people are born with spirits."[7] They are an essential part of the self and are responsible for skills, talents, personality traits, and more.

Ndau residents of Chipinge have a reputation throughout the region for their relation to powerful spirits. Harare acquaintances would express concern for me when hearing of my trips to Chipinge and the purpose of my research. For outsiders, the Ndau are known as powerful and willing practitioners of witchcraft (*uroyi*) who employ spirits for nefarious ends. Yet when a close friend became ill in Harare, members of her family and I drove 450 kilometers to seek guidance from a *n'anga* (see the glossary in appendix A) near Chipinge and obtain local medication (*muti* or *mushonga*) without a second thought. The good and the bad both emerge from spirits. People travel from neighboring countries to visit the local n'anga, yet newspapers abound with stories of Chipinge's witches.[8] Credit for good harvests, long lives, or financial success is often attributed to the spirits, yet when a local woman did well with her auto parts store, almost everyone I knew attributed her success and accompanying selfishness to witches.

As a gesture of respect for the worldviews and realities of my Ndau informants, I resist the word *belief* (Perman 2011a). The only time it or its Ndau equivalent *kutendera* emerged in my fieldwork was when I uttered it. Differences of "belief" centered more on whether spirits are good than whether they are real. Pragmatic, anthropological, spirit-centered, and Christian approaches to truth can seem incompatible. The perspective of each leads to entirely different conclusions about what signs of performance and spirituality signify, producing quite different effects. There is a palpable undercurrent of antagonism between local Christians and adherents of indigenous spiritual practices. The reality of spirits is rarely questioned on either side of this divide, but evaluations of them are almost irreconcilable. What are known to be benign spirits for ritual adherents are taken as malevolent by local Christians. But both sides agree that spirits in Chipinge are real and powerful.

In line with the work of the anthropologist Eduardo Viveiros de Castro, I accept the possibility of multiple natures, multiple realities (2004).[9] Perspectivism, multinaturalism, Descola-inspired animism, and a renewed emphasis on ontology in anthropology have exposed the limits of cultural relativity. Who am I to privilege my own reality? The manner in which nature and culture are understood to intersect or overlap in local perspectives has a profound impact on how one's reality is understood and another's is accepted. In Chipinge, apostolic Christians and spirit mediums understand the world differently, but the disagreement centers on how reality should be evaluated and engaged more than on what reality itself is. Academics and missionaries from elsewhere are more likely to see a different nature altogether (Perman 2011a).[10]

Although there are malevolent spirits, they can be thwarted via positive relations with other spirits. The spirits invited during local ceremonial events are benign; they can be allies, friends, protectors, and bodyguards. Nonparticipants' focus on the negative tends to overpower the conviction among most participants that their spirits are not only helpful, but necessary,[11] and this is particularly true in an environment where Christians dominate the media and government. But spiritual power can change lives regardless of one's willingness to accept it.

One day, in Mt. Selinda, I met a man who was immediately open in talking about spirits in Chipinge and anxious to share his story. He grew up in Dangamvura (near Mutare) but was originally from Mt. Selinda in the Chipinge District. While living in Dangamvura and working at the Chibuku Brewery, he grew ill. Neither the local n'anga nor spirit mediums could help him, so they advised him to return to the Chipinge District. The n'anga there said that his father was telling him to come live in Chipinge so that the father could take care of his family. He quit his job and moved his family to Daisy Hill. Now his children are successful whereas his brother's are struggling.[12] His father spoke to him through two types of madhlozi spirits: mhongo and madzviti.[13]

Mweya means "spirit"; it also means "air or breath." Mweya connects the natural, the cultural, and the spiritual. Spirits are in the air, materialized in a tangible way, as more than just an idea (Engelke 2007, 203). Ndau spirits are almost always the spirits of living things that have died, usually people but also lions and baboons. *Mwari*,[14] or God, is so distant and inaccessible that he or she rarely comes up in conversation among non-Christians. The focal point of prayer, ritual, and daily attention is the spirits of the dead, both family members and outsiders. Every birth, death, drought, harvest, conflict, bit of good fortune, and misfortune is marked by ritual connection with the spirits. They are a visceral part of everyday life.

The key categories of spirit among the Ndau communities with which I worked include the ancestral *midzimu* spirits, outsider madhlozi spirits of social groups encountered in the past, and aggrieved *ngozi* spirits. The Ndau spiritual world is complex and multifaceted, with variety and disparity from one community to the next among both the spirits themselves and the words used to label them, so I make no attempt to provide a comprehensive study.

While the spiritual practices of the northern Korekore are quite different from Ndau practices, the anthropologist David Lan's (1985, 38) basic categorization of Korekore spirits works for Chipinge as well. In his terms, midzimu are benign spirits "inside the house," and madhlozi are benign spirits "outside the house." *House* refers to both the family lineage from which the spirits may emerge and the building within or without which the bulk of their ceremony takes place. There are other categories not included here that I discuss elsewhere (such as *nzuzu*) or that played no obvious role during my research (such as *marombo*).

Spirits can work with or against one another, but are all part of the same cosmology. As Mulambo told me, "That is what we were created for by God, us people of ancestral lineages, such that at different homesteads some have aggrieved spirits, others have outsider spirits, others have ancestral spirits" (Mulambo interview). Mpande Chikumbo, a former spirit medium, current apostolic minister, and civil servant working in the Chipinge municipal government who participated in my conversation with Mulambo, compared the local cosmology to a multilevel bureaucracy, a reflection of his own work experience. The living occupy the bottom rung. Family ancestors, the midzimu, are the most closely involved in those people's lives, but they need protection and a liaison to Mwari, who is otherwise a distant and inaccessible leader. The madhlozi fill that role, working under Mwari, protecting the midzimu, and helping the living.

MIDZIMU (*VADZIMU*)

After death a person becomes a spirit, but the kind of spirit that emerges, and its relation to the people left behind, depends on the circumstances of the death, the dynamics of their life, and the actions of their descendants. Life and death, the living and the dead, are connected in moral webs that shape both the spirit world and the lives that continue to be led.

The midzimu are the spirits of ancestors,[15] commoners and chiefs alike.[16] Ideally, when someone dies, their descendants ensure that a proper funeral takes place. A year later, they should hold a ceremony called *kurova guwa* or *kusemendera guwa* to welcome the spirit back into the family once again as a mudzimu (Kyker 2009; Muyambo and Maposa 2013).[17] Maintaining positive relations with one's midzimu can prevent misfortune and ensure protection.

Before undertaking a long journey, when I left their village to return home Davison Masiza and his wife Serena paused to clap for (*kuombera*) and thank their ancestors for watching over us. After meals, people clap to acknowledge the effort put forth by the women who cooked the meals and the ancestors that provided them with the means to do so, connecting the living to the dead by praising *dzinza* (family lineage), *mutupo* (totem), and spirits.

Midzimu are called on during ceremonies for advice, assistance, or appreciation. Ndau midzimu ceremonies tend to be quiet, familial events with little community involvement, public participation, or extensive music making, unlike those in many communities in Zimbabwe.[18] VaMasiza and his family would sing and clap for them but never used drums or invited others in the community.[19] According to VaMasiza, these ceremonies were usually quite brief. They were not secret but certainly were private. Midzimu are nonetheless central to Ndau cosmology, whereas the outsider madhlozi spirits are much more important to public ritual life. As Chikumbo pointed out, the midzimu need protection. Their bodyguards are the madhlozi.

MADHLOZI

The madhlozi are not ancestors, aggrieved spirits, or deities but, rather, the spirits of social encounters with outsiders who return to possess the bodies of local host spirit mediums to whom they are unrelated. They are the most important spirits in public ceremonial life because they work for the midzimu, the ancestors. All madhlozi come from outside the family lineages that drum for them.[20] There is no consensus about these spirits or the terms used to define them. There are multiple categories of madhlozi spirit reflecting different historical and geographic origins.

Mpande Chikumbo was one of the first people in Chipinge to help me understand Ndau spirituality and ceremonial life. He said, "Madhlozi is an umbrella term of everything that is not an ancestral spirit." But as I discovered during the course of my research, using the word *madhlozi* as a general term is a complex choice. None of the current literature about Ndau spirituality used it this way, nor did many of the people I interviewed. ChiNdau speakers rarely use a general term for these spirits.[21] Based on local use and the literature, there are four options: *madhlozi*, *mashayi*, *mhongo*, or nothing at all.

Given that madhlozi spirits emerge in similar ways, for similar reasons, with similar kinds of relations to the living with whom they interact, choosing nothing makes generalization and description difficult. The ChiShona language *does* have a general term, *mashave*, which is used widely in Shona regions of Zimbabwe (Gelfand 1962; Lan 1985). More and more people seem to use this term in Chipinge, although the spelling and pronunciation reflect the habits of ChiNdau rather than ChiShona, thus, *mashayi* or *mashavi*. Complicating matters, some people use *mashayi* to refer to a specific *kind* of madhlozi spirit. Rennie, for instance, defines the mashayi as spirits from "Mashonaland west of the Sabi" (1973, 100), a Shona word for a Shona spirit.

Rennie (1973, 99) prefers *mhongo* as a general term for spirits from foreign communities, as does Charles Blakney in his unpublished work.[22] For Rennie, mashayi are a kind of mhongo; for others, mhongo are a kind of mashayi. Given that everyone I spoke with during my research used *mhongo* in a narrower sense, I do not follow Rennie's usage. As a category, however, *mhongo* is much more diverse and complex than the other madhlozi I describe, which lends some credence to its use as a more general term.

Enos Simango, a spirit medium and master muchongoyo drummer, and others used *madhlozi* interchangeably with *madzviti* to identify warrior spirits from invading Gaza Nguni armies. *Madhlozi* has roots in Nguni languages, which makes it a logical synonym for *madzviti*.[23] For the sake of consistency, I use *madzviti* to refer exclusively to the spirits of those Nguni soldiers.

During my final substantive interview about Ndau cosmology and possession practices I spoke with Ambuya Mazveshe, a widely respected elder, musician, and spirit medium in Muzite. Everyone I spoke with in Muzite respected her authority with regard to spiritual matters and the integrity of her spiritual practices. She said simply, "We have madhlozi spirits of the madzviti, mhongo, zvipunha, and mashayi."[24] My use of *madhlozi* throughout this text relies on the expertise of both Mpande Chikumbo and Ambuya Mazveshe.

Madhlozi and midzimu are separate categories of spirit, but ancestry can be a factor for madhlozi mediums. A young medium from Muzite, Ngarife Matabuka, told me that one reason he was a medium for his particular dzviti spirit was that he descended from the Gaza Nguni invaders whose warriors became spirits.[25] His "possession" of his dzviti was one legacy of this descent.[26] "Outsider," "stranger," and "foreign" are all flawed translations in his case because there is continuity between the Ndau and their spirits, both midzimu and madhlozi. History, as experienced and retained through spiritual life, is embodied in spirits and their mediums, becoming an important part of Ndau selves.

Chikumbo explained how the madhlozi, which he called shavi, is related to the mudzimu.

> The situation whereby, for example, you had a *sekuru* [grandfather] who had a shavi, and that sekuru says that if my son John has a son I will come

> to his first-born son and he will start doing my works. Usually when he comes together with that shavi he was using he will come with that shavi. So immediately when he appears the shavi works alongside him. But the shavi will only come at the invitation of the ancestral spirit. They have to be invited. Mudzimu claims the whole person and says this is mine, but shavi cannot make a claim.

The madhlozi work for the midzimu.

Each category of madhlozi reflects a specific origin and historical moment. They are the bodyguards of the ancestors. Even in conversations in ChiShona or ChiNdau, the modified English word was used: *mabodyguard*.[27] People rely on their ancestors to help with all aspects of life. Chance plays no role in the course of local events, and coincidence is nothing more than the balancing of spiritual debts and credits, so to speak. In order to ensure that one's ancestors can help and are satisfied, people placate the madhlozi, their ancestors' bodyguards. Chikumbo extended his bureaucracy metaphor and explained:

> That army of other spirits which are not directly linked to me genetically, they are called *mavhimi* (hunters). And these mavhimi are now mhongo. The mhongo is a messenger of a mermaid spirit. The messenger, the soldier of vadzimu. This mudzimu here is the commander at a home. In order for him to manage the home he has got an army. This is exactly what the structure is. They've got an army, the mudzimu. . . . His direct advisor is the njuzu. He appears to be superior to the njuzu but I'm telling you the *njuzu* is superior to him. He is superior because he says this is my home. The president, his life is in the hands of the bodyguards. But he is superior because we voted for him. The bodyguards exist because he is there. This structure comes into operation because there is a mudzimu who has been accepted at a home. The njuzu now finds a place to go, and he is the one who trains the mudzimu [in] survival techniques and how to coordinate these other, smaller spirits. So it's actually structured, there are CIDs [Criminal Investigation Department agents]. Take for example the mudzimu, this person has a mudzimu who has got an enemy on the other side. They want to fight. He sends an army of his zvipunha, girl spirits.

Here, multiple madhlozi spirits work together to protect the ancestors and their descendants.

There are several other categories of *madhlozi* spirits that possess people during ceremonies. Based on my conversations and the wide disparity in the literature, it seems clear that the pantheon of spirits varies from one community to the next and shifts over time. For instance, the zvaayungu, who first emerged after independence in 1980, have become vitally important for some communities and are absent from others. Similarly, other spirits may have faded from importance as historical trajectories and values shift. Like the living communities they visit, the community of the dead is fluid. Nothing is fixed.[28] They led unresolved lives that continue after unresolved deaths.

NGOZI

Not all deaths take place in the ideal circumstances mentioned above; not all spirits are benign. If someone dies without children, if a person is murdered, if he or she was a witch (*muroyi*) in life,[29] or was aggrieved in some way, that person might follow a different path than that reserved for the midzimu.[30] In the worst cases, as with murder, the person becomes a ngozi, an angry, aggrieved, and vengeful spirit. Ngozi can be terrifying and wreak havoc (Bourdillon 1987, 133). On death, a person can only become one spirit. As Mulambo put it above, "some [households] have aggrieved spirits, others have outsider spirits, others have ancestral spirits."

While I was living in Muzite, my hosts Moses Zharikira and Tendai Chitopo delayed classes at the primary school where they both taught in order to call a colleague's relatives in Johannesburg.[31] Apparently, this teacher had begun beating his mother and causing problems. Everyone suspected a ngozi and informed his relatives so they could start dealing with it. Appeasing an angry ngozi is possible, but difficult, requiring the intervention of a n'anga and long, likely expensive, ritual processes of appeasement and compensation.

The n'anga Mudiwa jokingly told me, "They say a mother's wrath cannot be paid off because the mother remembers that for nine months you were in here [the womb] and then you cross me, ah. . . . But if you are good to each other it's good but if you conflict it does not come out well."[32] Relations among the living and between the living and the dead can have long-lasting repercussions. Ngozi can hold a grudge against a family for decades. Thus, ceremonial life takes on additional importance in assuring public acknowledgment of spirits and their value. Living morally and respectfully, and inviting spirits to ceremonies, ensures happy spirits and flourishing lives.

Doro (Madhlozi Ceremonies)

Everyone who lived nearby was invited to the Horus Farm ceremony—referred to as *doro*, after the word for beer—which serves as the primary site of the analysis and ethnography to follow. The immediate goals were spirit possession and communal participation in order to demonstrate respect and appreciation for the spirits and ensure the continued protection of the living and their ancestors by those spirits. Ceremonies such as this are the primary communal expressions of collective spirituality. Ceremonies are also held for more specific reasons ranging from illness to tragedy, from drought to financial success. If the spirits are happy and feel respected, the community should do well.

A young woman named Patience told me that her father, a newly resettled farmer, loves madhlozi ceremonies.[33] Patience hated them, not because she was Christian or had unrealized aspirations of modernity, but because it was simply too much work.[34] As a woman of the house she was responsible for helping feed everyone, clean everything, and ensure that they, as hosts, were doing right by their guests and community, living and dead. Hosting a ceremony can be quite expensive since the hosts must ensure that mediums and musicians are present, that enough beer has been brewed (not only to honor the spirits but also to engender overnight participation), and that there is enough to feed all the people, who attend multiple meals. Sometimes, more than one hundred people will participate.

During the twenty-four hours that I was at Horus Farm, everyone participated in a series of ritual moments as one category of spirits after another came and went. In each stage, three to six people played drums and rattles, six to twenty mediums became possessed, and dozens of the rest of us sang and clapped. Like other madhlozi ceremonies, it was sequential and participatory, and it lasted all night. Spirits entered their host mediums, danced, and departed. When one group of spirits left, a new group quickly replaced them. Musicking, dancing, drinking, joking, sleeping, eating, and possessing were everywhere, keeping the pace of activities high for more than eighteen hours.

Every ceremony is unique. Communities aren't required to invite every spirit to every ceremony or conform to some kind of script. At Horus Farm the madzviti came during the late afternoon, zvipunha in the evening, mhongo overnight, and zvaayungu the following morning. This is a common sequence that felt like four short ceremonies back-to-back. Each spirit brought their own energy, engagement, and expectations. As figure I.2 shows, each category of spirit has its own songs, rhythmic patterns, drums, and language.

The intensity peaked repeatedly as each category of spirit came and went, as shown in figure I.3.[35] The pinnacle of the event was just after dawn. Nearly a dozen mediums danced themselves to a frenzy as one mhongo after another awoke within them. Masiza played the mateza furiously as the packed outdoor space filled with energetic singing, clapping, makosho playing, and dancing. Only when the mhongo danced through sunrise did the attendees dance along in great numbers. By then, everyone was exhausted but euphoric. VaMasiza

Time of day	Chapter	Spirits	Description	Era of origin	Drum and rhythm	Language
Late afternoon	3	Madzviti	Nguni warriors	19th-century Gaza occupation	Makandira 	Swazi or Zulu
Evening	4	Zvipunha	Young girls	c. 18th century; early Ndau	Chigubhu or deza 	Chingotoro
Overnight	5	Mhongo	Danda from Mozambique	19th-century Gaza ocupation	Mateza 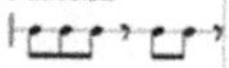	ChiDanda
Morning	6	Zvaayungu	Chimurenga soldiers	1970s; Second Chimurenga	Usually chigubhu 	Chilapalapa

FIGURE 1.2. Ceremonial sequence at Horus Farm

took it upon himself to poke fun at those who had neglected to join in or had made a mistake, while constantly urging the women to bring more beer. He wore a chingunda wig as intensity gave way to joy and whimsy, the markers of a truly successful ceremony.

The household was large but typical. It included a main house, where the important guests would be ushered to eat or catch some sleep during the long overnight ceremony. Nearby, a smaller house served as the kitchen, and across the courtyard was a large roundhouse that was the central space for the ceremony. Multiple fires were burning so people could gather, warm up, and escape the frenzy of the ceremony. The household was surrounded on all sides by dormant maize fields.

The roundhouse was impressively large; its mud-and-dung walls were painted with ochre for a two-tone finish. The thatched roof, gray with age, had a shallow slope owing to the size of the house. Because there was neither electricity nor running water, the pacing of the ceremony was dictated by the sun and by the dozens of women working tirelessly in the background to keep everyone fed. In each phase the spirits awoke inside the roundhouse before exiting to dance in the yard, hence their status as "outside the house" (Lan 1985, 38). Attendees ranged in age from infants carried on their mothers' backs to the elderly seated leisurely in the center of groups of men and women. Many of the men who were present paid only passive attention to the events and gathered instead around a fire sharing beer and telling stories. Some men, like Masiza, participated actively as musicians, but much of the musical labor was done by the women.

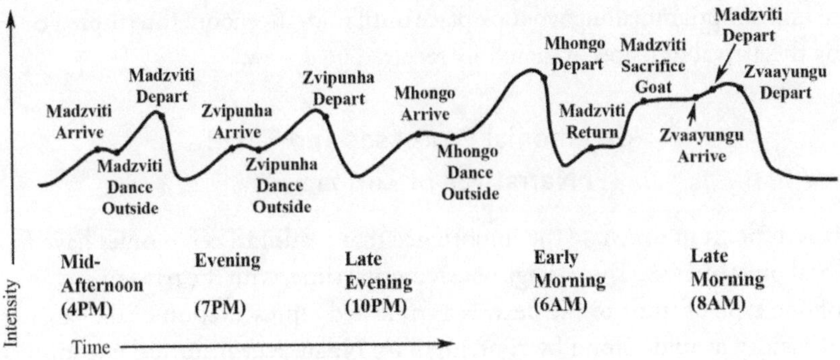

FIGURE 1.3. Shifts in ceremonial intensity at Horus Farm

We took a break each time one group of spirits departed. VaMasiza and I either joined the men by the fire or retired to a sitting room to eat as privileged guests. When each phase began, we stooped beneath the classic Ndau veranda shading a bench that ran around the circumference of the house to enter a low doorway cut from the overhanging thatch. We navigated the sea of seated attendees in near darkness and took our seats along the bench reserved for elder men and privileged guests.

It always took at least an hour for the spirits to awaken in their mediums, but their arrival was never really in doubt. Possession unfolded similarly in each case. Mediums took snuff (with the exception of those for the zvaayungu, who prefer cigarettes) and donned apparel and accessories appropriate to the spirits' role in life as soldiers, healers, or caretakers. People played drums and makosho rattles, sang, and clapped. The music was casual at first, giving novice drummers like me a chance, before experts like Masiza took control. Each time the spirits arrived, we'd file out into the yard to continue playing, singing, and watching the spirits dance.

The Horus Farm event was unusual because the anticipated sequence of events was disrupted when the madzviti returned uninvited after dawn, compelled to dance again. They were so pleased after dancing again that they authoritatively urged our hosts to bring them a goat to sacrifice for the shared meal to follow. The chastened zvaayungu arrived quietly around the corner as experienced attendees gracefully kept the two groups of proud warriors apart. When the satisfied madzviti left a second time and the zvaayungu had danced for an hour or so, Masiza urged me to turn off my recorder. It was time to relax. Everyone was exhausted but so pleased with the proceedings that hours of impromptu muchongoyo took place until mid-afternoon, interrupted only by the arrival of plates of gratefully received goat stew.

Ceremonial Processes and Time: Narratives of Zimbabwe

It is difficult to overstate the importance that madhlozi ceremonies have for local practitioners. The passage of ceremonial time, with the passing presence of one type of spirit to the next, is a truncated representation of the passing of history as understood by contemporary Ndau. Key historical encounters produced the spirits who now grace the ceremonial space. As people progress though the course of a ceremony they essentially revisit their own history. But neither the history represented, the spirits who represent it, nor the practices used to engage with them are static or fixed in time like recordings or history textbooks.

Multiple histories shape the encounters that brought madhlozi spirits, beginning with Bantu migration and moving through the rise and fall of the Monomutapa and Rozvi kingdoms; the emergence of important Ndau chieftaincies; the nineteenth-century arrival and authority of the Gaza Nguni; the appearance of Cecil Rhodes with the Pioneer Column and the sudden dominance of British colonialism; Zimbabwean nationalism and the resulting Chimurenga war, with its accompanying ZANLA, ZIPRA, Rhodesian, FRELIMO, and RENAMO military forces;[36] Zimbabwean independence and the emergence of Zanu-Ndonga as an opposition party; the Movement for Democratic Change (MDC), fast-track land reform during the so-called Third Chimurenga, and the ultimate end of President Mugabe's thirty-seven-year rule in 2017; and even visiting academics; *a luta continua*.

SOCIAL ENCOUNTERS IN THE HISTORY OF NDAU SPIRITUALITY

The perspective afforded from my seat on a hill on land resettled during fast-track land reform in the early twenty-first century looking across a courtyard filled with the spirits of nineteenth-century soldiers provides an important alternative to the normative narratives of Zimbabwe's history. The most salient episodes in the recent history of the country, events thoroughly documented in Zimbabweanist historiography, are often most easily remembered via binary oppositions that exclude Ndau perspectives and experiences.[37] The gravitational pull of the three "Chimurengas" on Zimbabwean historiography can inadvertently shape an understanding of local historical processes as rooted in a series of Shona-centric binaries. The story of Zimbabwe's first active and collective resistance against the colonial ambitions of the British South Africa company during the First Chimurenga in 1896 typically recounts the antagonism and cooperation between Zimbabwe's Shona and Ndebele communities, famously embodied in the prophetic martyrdom of the spirit medium Ambuya Nehanda (Charumbira 2015). The Second Chimurenga, which ended colonialism by armed conflict in the 1970s, is presented via a similar binary, with Robert Mugabe, his Shona base, his party, ZANU, and their armed wing, ZANLA, on one side and Joshua Nkomo, his Ndebele base, ZAPU, and their armed wing, ZIPRA, on the other. More recently, when land reform initiated the Third Chimurenga, twenty-first-century politics was defined by President Mugabe and ZANU-PF facing the opposition of Morgan Tsvangirai and the urban base of his Movement for Democratic Change. In each of these transformative moments, Ndau perspectives have been absent. The Ndau communities of Chipinge have always lived in the shadow of these dominant narratives. Their stories provide alternative narratives to the orthodox stories of Zimbabwe's political history.

These are national and nationalist histories that inevitably prioritize the "winners" of Zimbabwe's historical battles and the communities coincidentally located near the country's urban centers. National histories can seem foreign, because people in rural Chipinge don't always feel like a part of the nation.

Madhlozi are spirits of encounter. They are the spiritual embodiment of encounter itself and all the trauma, chaos, and violence that define it. Their emergence in ceremonial life is the continual emergence of history, ever unresolved and living in the spirits of the dead. In his groundbreaking work Rennie highlights a series of changes around which he organizes local history (1973). Although this sort of linear sequencing of history can mask and simplify the complexity and chaos of actual events, there is a certain coherence between Rennie's list and the performed sequences of the madhlozi ceremony. This sequence, whether as text, as a chart (as in figure 1.4), or as a danced sequence of possession, performs history and makes it knowable.

Rennie highlights four changes that shape Ndau life, history, political organization, and spirituality. I add a fifth that reflects events since Rennie's dissertation was published in 1973 and prefer "transformation" to "change."[38] Change is incessant and inevitable, but the episodes and encounters highlighted here profoundly transformed local life.

Because they contributed to the conditions that brought madhlozi spirits, I focus on moments of transformation that resulted from political change and the traumatic encounters that shaped local spiritual life.

1st Transformation	Mutema becomes chief in Chisanga and his chieftaincy operates as a Rozvi client state.	Late 17th century	People begin to coalesce into the "Ndau"
2nd Transformation	Mutema gains independence and develops ties with other chiefs such as Musikavanhu.	Mid-18th century	Monomutapa and Rozvi influence ends. Chieftaincies become locus of identity.
3rd Transformation	Gaza Nguni enter the region under Soshangane after the rise of Shaka in South Africa.	19th century	Ndau are subjugated by Gaza Nguni.
4th Transformation	Arrival of British as well as other colonizers and missionaries	20th century	Ndau under British rule. Ndau identity placed within Shona framework.
5th Transformation	End of colonialism. Zimbabwe becomes independent under Prime Minister Robert Mugabe.	1980–present	Postcolonial conflict within Zimbabwe emerges.

FIGURE 1.4. Historical transformations in local governance (based on Rennie 1973)

FIRST TRANSFORMATION: THE ROZVI STATE AND EARLY NDAU CHIEFTAINCIES

There is evidence of human presence in the Chipinge area prior to the Bantu migrations from Mbire in the fifteenth and sixteenth centuries. The former Muzite headman Vhukani Muzite called these early people Manyakadzivuta (see also Rennie 1973, 55). Beyond myths of their strangeness and primitiveness, they have had little acknowledged influence on contemporary Ndau society, which only began solidifying as a coherent habitat of identity when the early chiefs came to power in the seventeenth century.[39]

Before the latter seventeenth century, the Karanga loosely ruled parts of the Chipinge area through the powerful Monomutapa state,[40] one of the most influential early kingdoms in southern Africa. Monomutapa was an important locus for early identity formation throughout Shona-speaking Zimbabwe. After the Rozvi state rose to power in Murehwa and Mutoko under Changamire, they swept south toward Chipinge.[41] Mutema was installed as the chief in Chisanga near present-day Ngaone in the 1680s (Rennie 1978, 264). Mutema's chieftaincy operated as a client state of the Rozvi but also established the political and ceremonial traditions that eventually served as the foundation of collective Ndau identity (Rennie 1985, 168).

Elder Ndau men whom I interviewed, as well as those cited in written histories of Ndau society, still trace their lineage to the Rozvi communities in the Mbire region near Hwedza and Mutoko.[42] The political authority of the Mutema chieftaincy is in part justified by this Rozvi heritage, regarding the Rozvi as the first in a series of outside conquerors. As Vhukani Muzite explained to me, "Legend says that the first people here were called Manyakadzivuta. They were defeated. Then other people came from out there (Mbire). They came from where they ran away. Maybe others joined up with them to make an army of the conqueror and all that. They (Manyakadzivuta) just disappeared from here. Those who remained are the VaNdau."[43]

Enos Simango is from the Bangwe community under the jurisdiction of Chief Mutema in the dry lowlands along the Save River. He told me, "Chief Mutema is Rozvi. The Rozvi come from Mbire. Mbire at Hwedza."[44] Conversely, the authority of the Musikavanhu lineage rests largely in rainmaking abilities originally stolen from the Rozvi (Meredith 1925). The widespread origin myths centered on this theft eventually united the chieftaincies of Musikavanhu and Mutema, laying the foundation for a coherent Ndau identity.

SECOND TRANSFORMATION: ROZVI DECLINE, MUTEMA INDEPENDENCE, AND DANDA

The breakdown of the Mutapa Empire at the end of the sixteenth century had long-lasting repercussions that informed contemporary Ndau identities and helped shape the communities who now emerge as mhongo spirits. As the Mutapa Empire faded, several secondary states were supposedly formed by sons of the Mutapa in what is now Mozambique when Portuguese pressure splintered the hinterlands of the Monomutapa Empire (Rennie 1985, 167). Teve, Danda, Sanga (Chisanga, Quissanga), and Shanga connected nascent Ndau communities with the authority of the Monomutapa state (Beach 1980, 162; Rennie 1985).[45] The first and largest of these was Teve in the early sixteenth century. As mentioned above, Mutema was installed as the chief at Chisanga and became the dominant chieftaincy through much of Chipinge's subsequent history (Rennie 1973). Crucially, Mutema achieved independence from the Rozvi and allied with the Musikavanhu chieftaincy to the east (Rennie 1978, 266). This political shift coincided with legitimacy emerging from spirit possession rather than the possession of rain charms.

Danda first achieved independence in 1590 under the rule of Sedanda, the son of Nyamunda, who ruled Teve at that time (Rennie 1985, 167). It lies roughly halfway between the Zimbabwe-Mozambique border and the Indian Ocean in present-day Mozambique, directly on the path taken by Soshangane during his migration with the Gaza Nguni north into Zimbabwe. It was thus heavily influenced by this period of local history. Most people I spoke with agreed that mhongo spirits originated in Danda; hence many of the spirits are called VaDanda.[46] Mhongo spirits link coastal nzuzu, the emergence of Ndau and Danda identities, and the impact of the Gaza State.

THIRD TRANSFORMATION: THE GAZA STATE

Perhaps the most explicit connection between key historical encounters and contemporary spiritual communities is that between madzviti spirits and the Gaza Nguni soldiers whom they were in life. After Shaka came to power in the early nineteenth century in what is now South Africa, waves of Gaza Nguni armies moved north into Mozambique and Zimbabwe under the leadership of Soshangane. The Gaza State eventually moved its capital to the center of Zimbabwe's Ndau community near Mt. Selinda, ending Mutema's independence. The resistance of local chiefs helped unify the secular and sacred aspects of a chief's authority as Ndau communities and Gaza Nguni invaders intermingled for almost a century (Rennie 1978, 271). Rennie suggests that the word *Ndau* as an identity label originated when Gaza soldiers referred to subjects of the Mutema chieftaincy, which is often identified as the heartland of the Ndau region (Rennie 1973).

The Gaza ruled from the 1820s until pressure from the competing interests of ambitious British and Portuguese colonial figures pushed them aside. By the time Soshangane's grandson Ngungunyane left his capital on the Mzilizwi River in the Chipinge highlands to return south in 1889 (MacGonagle 2008, 36), competing negotiations between Portuguese and British ambitions over these territories led to his capture and eventual exile in the Azores (Wheeler 1968, 600). The soldiers who lived and died in Chipinge now return as madzviti spirits.

FOURTH TRANSFORMATION: SETTLERS, COLONIALISM, AND WAR

The end of the Gaza State came quickly when the Portuguese to the east and Cecil Rhodes and the Pioneer Column from the south arrived and established colonial authority. In addition, American Methodists founded a mission at Mt. Selinda in 1896. By this time, locals were fighting British intrusions into their lives during what is now called the First Chimurenga, and life was never the same (Charumbira 2015).

Once Rhodes crossed the Limpopo in 1890 colonial dominance came in a hurry, even in remote Chipinge. Wary of Portuguese interests, Rhodes encouraged settlers from South Africa to move to the Chipinge area and allocate land for themselves (Moyana 1984, 110). Moyana writes, "The Moodie trek set off for Gazaland with 104 families early in 1892. . . . The Trekkers proceeded to Gazaland and found themselves on the Tanganda Drift which they named New Year's Gift on New Year's Day. . . . The trek ended at a place called Chipinge where the trekkers started a settlement" (110). Settlers took the best land for themselves and created "Native Reserves" in the arid lowlands of the Save River Valley. By 1900, only eight years after the settlers arrived, the average area per person in the Reserves (on arid, untenable land) was thirty acres; the average area among Europeans (on land in the highlands with ample rainfall) was six thousand acres (Moyana 1984, 113).[47]

But this was not enough, and a commission was established to further entrench segregationist land policies. In the 1920s Chief Musikavanhu testified before the commission, saying, "All we want is some land where we can live with our people, we would be very pleased if land could be set aside where we could live with our people" (Moyana 1984, 115). Chief Gwenzi simply acknowledged that he had no land for his people.

Instead of listening to these pleas, the Southern Rhodesian colonial government catered to settlers' fears and passed the Land Apportionment Act of 1930, institutionalizing land segregation and entrenching the racist policies that redefined local life. With alarming speed locals traded subservience to Ngungunyane and the Gaza Nguni for virtual homelessness at the mercy of the British South Africa Company and the Crown. The choices for Ndau residents were few. They could remain on land now defined as European and work for the right to stay (with no wages), they could move to reserves and purchase areas and try to make it on their own (on arid land in a time of drought), or they could look for work in South African mines, leaving behind wives and families for extended periods abroad. In all cases, rents and taxes, usually beyond one's means, had to be paid.[48] Reflecting on a ceremonial madhlozi performance on land at Horus Farm retaken from this era of land segregation in the twenty-first century gives Moyana's description of this period renewed poignancy. Inevitably, patience was strained, colonial authority was resisted, and rebellion was prepared.

The decades that followed led to a series of robust and brave independence movements tied to growing ideas of nationalism and of Zimbabwe. Given the racist foundation of Southern Rhodesia's success and the growing moves for decolonization throughout Africa and the British Empire following World War II, there was never a time when questions of racial inequality and access to land, education, and opportunity were settled. Rhodes's initial claim of "equal rights for all civilized men" was always a false promise (Turino 2000, 121).

After a series of nationalist movements came and went in the 1950s and 1960s,[49] the eventual ruling party, ZANU, was formed when it split from ZAPU on August 8, 1963 (Tavuyanago 2013, 28). By then, as the Ian Smith regime proved determined to retain power and the support for the efforts of ZANU and ZAPU to undermine it grew, conflict seemed inevitable. Once ZANLA directly engaged the regime at the Battle of Sinoia (now Chinoyi) on April 28, 1966, the war for independence, the Second Chimurenga, had begun (Martin and Johnson 1981, 9).

The first president of ZANU was an Ndau politician, Reverend Ndabaningi Sithole. He is remembered among Chipinge's elderly population with admiration, even reverence. For many, he is a local hero. But after years of internal power struggles, Robert Mugabe assumed control of ZANU in 1974 while Sithole was in prison (Sithole 1999). Sithole never recovered his position in ZANU, and his supporters in Chipinge never forgave Mugabe for his supposed betrayal. Sithole eventually founded his own political party, Zanu-Ndonga, which never had strong support nationally but was influential in Chipinge politics until his death in 2000.[50]

Because Chipinge sits along the Mozambique border, several armies constantly moved through the area. Shona soldiers fighting in ZANU's armed wing, ZANLA, were based in nearby Mozambique, and Rhodesian soldiers fighting for Ian Smith and Chipinge's sizeable white community moved through in search of those ZANLA fighters. Following Mozambique's independence from Portugal in 1975, FRELIMO and RENAMO soldiers there continued fighting for control during their civil war. With the exception of the predominantly Ndau ranks of RENAMO (Vines 1996), each army consisted of foreigners, but even RENAMO's funding came from groups determined to destabilize local independence movements, beginning with the Rhodesian state and then shifting to the patronage of apartheid South Africa (Hall 1990, 39). It was a time of constant aggression and upheaval.

According to Vhukani Muzite, the whole region was a "no man's area" filled with fighting. During the war, nobody lived between Muzite Township and the border because of land mines and roving soldiers. Rhodesian soldiers killed spirit mediums if they were suspected of helping the rebels. The tension between ZANLA and Rhodesian forces was compounded by the arrival of RENAMO, whose Ndau power structure helped push Zimbabwe's Ndau communities into the heart of the conflict on both sides of the border. Vhukani stated,

> They were in Mozambique there but because the soldiers here did not like RENAMO, they used to go and try to quiet down RENAMO, taking

> cattle from Mozambique and coming with them here. So RENAMO was now retaliating coming here and they once burned buses at the township here. Some people were even hurt. They would leave and write here saying, "Do not come to Mozambique. . . . If you come there and do silly things you will all die here."

There are still paths along Muzite's Mozambique border that children are taught to avoid because old land mines may remain. Younger men remember being hidden by their parents to prevent them from being forcibly recruited by the trespassing armies. Mugabe's ZANLA and Samora Machel's FRELIMO are remembered with particular venom for exploiting the goodwill of the local communities. Several soldiers who died in the Chipinge area during the fighting in the 1970s return as the zvaayungu, although their complexity resists such a straightforward explanation. Their arrival after the successful fight for independence and the creation of an independent Zimbabwe in 1980 suggests that the end of colonial rule did not end the struggle.

FIFTH TRANSFORMATION: INDEPENDENCE AND LAND REFORM

Despite achieving independence, Prime Minister Mugabe and the ruling ZANU party never won the backing of Chipinge's Ndau population. There was too much mistrust. But the decade of the 1980s was a period of undeniable optimism. Zimbabwe's schools and hospitals were the envy of the region. The economic challenges facing the general population and unresolved questions about land were deferred in the face of freedom, independence, and self-governance. Sithole's Zanu-Ndonga party won parliamentary seats in both Chipinge voting districts multiple times after independence. Though it remained marginalized, Chipinge had hopes of a future fulfilled.

Yet the end of the twentieth century brought economic ruin and increased authoritarianism.[51] Socialism faded, economic neoliberalism dominated, and Mugabe's rampant spending on social services grew untenable (Raftopoulos 2003). Giving in to external pressure and unforgiving budget realities, Mugabe welcomed the World Bank's Economic Structural Adjustment Program in 1990 and ended his supposed socialist experiment. As Zimbabwean life grew worse, resistance and opposition increased. In order to appease growing frustration among local war veterans, Mugabe gave each Z$50,000, crippling the local dollar and causing rampant hyperinflation.[52] By the end of the decade the Movement for Democratic Change was founded under the leadership of Morgan Tsvangirai. Zanu-Ndonga faded after Sithole's death, opening the door for ZANU-PF and MDC influence. An ever-worsening drought and mounting corruption that managed to sustain a dual exchange rate for foreign currency increased the pressure on Mugabe and ZANU-PF.

Having avoided reconciling the land issue for twenty years, Mugabe was now determined to right those historical wrongs as quickly as possible in an effort to retain power and local favor. After suffering his first electoral defeat since independence when his new constitution was rejected, he blamed the local white minority and "the West," entrenched repression of dissent and opposition, and cooperated with war veterans as they began invading local farms (Raftopoulos 2003). Emboldened by the chaotic form that land reacquisition took, Mugabe also spearheaded a campaign to wipe out informal markets and settlements, long urban hotbeds of support for the opposition. During Operation Murambatsvina, which began in 2003, the police and army bulldozed houses, shops, and entire neighborhoods in order to weaken the MDC's urban base. Several n'anga were forced to move their market stalls after the police bulldozed the central Chipinge market. Homes and markets built illegally along the A9 road entering Chipinge were destroyed. Insecurity increased.

But land reform had undoubted positives as well, as evidenced by the joyous events at Horus Farm. Old settler farms like Holland, Horus, and Daisy Hill have been resettled and are now home to vibrant communities farming for themselves. Families like Masiza's can now drum and sing for their spirits on their own land. Many of the histories I have just described are performed implicitly and explicitly in the madhlozi ceremony. From Masiza's perspective, the madhlozi bodyguards of their ancestors must be looking out for them. The contexts in which communities engage their spirits, resonating through histories of subjugation, struggle, and survival, make every ceremonial interaction one of potential joy, relief, or anguish, full of the possibility of unrealized ideals and expectations of better days.

TWENTY-FIRST-CENTURY CHIPINGE

Land reform reconfigured life in Zimbabwe, changing livelihoods, altering the environment itself, and making life decidedly more complicated (Manzungu 2004, 54). The impermanence of currency in the hyperinflationary climate of the country made the daily search for it paramount. Young men and women looked anywhere they could to make money, whether by crossing the Limpopo into South Africa, braving security forces to illegally mine for diamonds, or seeking riskier avenues abroad. Others, like many of the people who generously contributed to my research, remain, patiently keeping their families together, working the land, and waiting for better days. Because of political and economic pressure, the threats to lives and livelihoods caused by AIDS, and the risks of speaking out against any of these dynamics, hope was deferred (Orner and Holmes 2010).

But hope is emerging from the shadows once again. After thirty-seven years President Robert Mugabe's rule came to a sudden, peaceful, and widely celebrated end in November 2017. As in many places in Zimbabwe, in Chipinge people rejoiced. Of course, with the succession of President Emmerson Mnangagwa, the old guard of the ruling ZANU-PF party remained firmly in control, despite Mugabe's death in 2019. Most residents of Chipinge never felt fully a part of Mugabe's idea of Zimbabwe, and his rule was merely the latest in a series of governing power dynamics in which the local population lived under the authority of an outside power. Despite decades of feeling neglected, many in Chipinge feel a rekindled sense of the possibility of resurgence and renewal in the face of much struggle.

A tragic irony of Zimbabwe's recent misfortunes has been that the more people feel compelled to brew beer for their spirits and bring their communities together, the more expensive it becomes. Feeding a hundred people and brewing enough beer to keep them going and show respect for the spirits becomes a Herculean task in the face of shortages and rising prices. Ceremonial activity inevitably thinned as a result, potentially compounding what spiritual labor could otherwise alleviate. But these challenges are not inherently new; they are only the newest. People still sing, dance, and music in ceremonies for their spirits.

THE LOGIC AND DYNAMISM OF SPIRITS

As I hope these histories make clear, the spirit realm is no more fixed or static than that of the living. Madhlozi reveal the fallacy of purity, stasis, or resolution. Not only is the spirit world a dynamic space, it is a product of dynamism. Madhlozi are incomplete, unresolved, and in-between. Madzviti are neither Gaza nor Ndau, zvipunha neither mother nor child, mhongo neither mermaid nor VaDanda, zvaayungu neither black nor white. More than "outsiders," they are the spirits of instability and traumatic social encounter. When the vagaries of history, conflict, and trauma interrupt lives, madhlozi emerge. Lives rendered incomplete and unresolved by the historical episodes described above carry on beyond the grave. Mothers without children and soldiers without territory become bodyguards of the ancestors, essential to local people's desires to survive and thrive. They combine living and dead, ancestor and outsider, even past and future. It is their liminal existence between disparate realities that connect them, providing the continuities that make life manageable despite trauma and insecurity. Thus they are not strangers, nor are they selves. Their between-ness connects seemingly disparate realms of local life, encouraging new experiences of continuity.

But it is up to the living to capitalize on their protection and preserve their ways of life. Mediums make continuities possible, becoming the focal point of ritual practices in which musicking becomes spiritually, politically, and emotionally meaningful. The logic of spirits and mediumship emerges from these episodes of historical transformation and instability. Musicking productively facilitates the local relationships that matter most, emotionally forming ideas of self, spirit, and society. On that July day on resettled land, mediums and their spirits brought centuries of imperialism, land theft and reform, and political insecurity to bear as people came together to prepare for the days and years ahead.

The spirits often recognize how different things are now than when they were alive. As Chikumbo explained,

> The mhongo now adapts. . . . You see, long ago we used to do it this way but now I agree that we may transform slightly. . . . He agrees to shift boundaries for your better because you say, I cannot get anywhere an elephant's hide for a blanket, what if I get a blanket with a picture of an elephant? He says, well, you can. Because he knows you will be arrested for poaching in the game reserve trying to kill an elephant and get a blanket made of the elephant skin. And he would tell him he understands. But the mhongo will not accept anything else in place of his spear.

Spirits are not all-powerful; they must accept things that are beyond their control. Whereas before they might demand real gold, something shiny might now suffice, something iconic to the quality that indexes intent. They adapt.

For instance, the zvipunha are older than the spirit medium Ambuya Nehanda, but they have learned to appreciate her importance to the community. After Ambuya Nehanda inspired people in Zimbabwe at the time of the First Chimurenga, the spirits who visited Enos Simango's mother began to allow songs about her as well. Enos Simango explained,

> Those are the zvipunha now. . . . Others are now used to the songs that we have modernized. . . . Around 18-something (19th century), we used to sing Mbuya Nehanda here. So, there are also some modernizations that they did in the way they sing the song of Mbuya Nehanda. . . . The drums will be played like this: *ketindike, ketindike, ketindike, ketindike,*

> *dhi ndeki ndeki ndeki ndeki* . . . and they would be dancing. "Mbuya Nehanda ehe Mbuya Nehanda heya Mbuya Nehanda oiyere." My mother used to get possessed with these, she had this chipunha. We were raised being carried by a chipunha.

In demonstrating the song for me, beating its rhythms, and reminiscing about his childhood, Simango also demonstrated the agency of spirits. They not only reflect the histories from which they emerged, but they also shape the histories yet to come.

CHAPTER 2

Moving Signs

The Experience of Affective Semiosis

Seated in the dark ceremonial roundhouse in the depths of night, hours after the ceremony began, with hours yet to go before it concludes, I watched Davison Masiza play the drum as he watched a young woman become possessed by her chipunha, the spirit of a young girl: three people embodying different kinds of experience. Beyond us the house was crowded with men surrounding me and Masiza and women beyond the woman dancing in front of us. It was dark but loud. Beyond Masiza's single drum, there were people clapping, playing makosho rattles, whistling, singing, shouting encouragement, and moving their bodies. The air was thick with effort and attention. Collectively, we were all working toward the same goals, but our experiences diverge.

First, the young woman: She was entranced, moving with the abandon of someone lacking control over her body. At times, she was mere inches from VaMasiza's drum. Her head thrashed about, her muscles were tense, and she uttered occasional grunts and yells as she physically struggled with the imminent emergence of her spirit. At this moment she was still herself, a young woman deeply involved in the experiences at hand but with no awareness of her own involvement; she was essentially missing out on the experience of her own experience. Second, the drummer: Masiza was fully engaged and focused on the woman in front of him as he played aggressively, consistently on top of the beat. He played with purpose, acutely aware of what he was doing, but concentrating solely on the sounds he was producing and the woman reacting to them. It is difficult to know with certainty, but it is quite likely that the rest of us in the room were absent from his attention, part of the background context of his focused experience. It was just him and the dancing woman. Third, the ethnomusicologist: I was watching closely, holding my recorder in my hand and absorbing what was going on. I tried to pay attention to the rhythms that Masiza was playing and the other sounds in the room, including makosho, singers, and hand clapping. I was also attending to the woman shaking in front of us, wondering if her spirit would emerge and if spirits would possess the other mediums nearby, and the man to my right, who was helpfully trying to explain everything that was going on, for he'd seen it all before. I was taking it all in, trying to process it as quickly as possible and hoping my recorder was working since it was so dark I couldn't quite see the buttons.

Values reinforced in habits contribute powerfully to stable senses of identity and community. During each of these ongoing presents, signs were interpreted. We each responded according to values and habits acquired through lifetimes of semiosis, the heredity of evolution, and the relationships formed with friends, family, and spirits. The dimension of experience informed by the way these signs relate to those values as interpreted through our habits is affective. A ubiquitous element of agentic interpretation, the affect of our experience flows like water, varying in intensity, informing the coming moments in our ongoing engagement and potentially changing our understanding of ourselves and the world in which we live. Affect makes experience meaningful. Three people having three *kinds* of meaningful, affective experience: first, a woman (the medium) attends to nothing; second, a man (the musician) attends to one thing and one thing only; third, a man (the researcher) attends to and is thinking about as much as possible.

Phenomenology and Semiotics: Firstness, Secondness, and Thirdness

My analysis and interpretation of these events are grounded in the theories of C. S. Peirce. Just as music studies offer insight into the nature of meaning and affect that other communicative studies don't, Peirce's pragmatic philosophy, rooted in his unique brand of phenomenology and manifest in his semiotic theory of signs, provides useful tools for understanding the meaningful experiences that define local ceremonial life. I hope that ethnomusicologists find tools for identifying the specificity of meaning in sound, anthropologists learn the necessity of acknowledging sonic meaning in the understanding of ritual and interpersonal relationships, and affect theorists recognize ways to bridge the disciplinary gaps between critical, humanist, and scientific approaches to emotion.

As with the triplet-driven rhythms of *mhongo* drumming, in order to engage with Peirce's tools one simply needs to be able to count to three. Firstness, secondness, and thirdness are, for Peirce, the "Universal Categories."[1] Initially abstract, they open up mechanisms for clarifying the complexity of reality as it is experienced and understood. Firstness is "that which is such as it is . . . regardless of anything else" (Peirce 1998, 267). It is the phenomenon; it is reality (Turino 2014, 190). From the perspective of perception and experience, Peirce describes firstness as qualia, as quality of feeling. One classical example is redness. The idea of redness exists, but you can't really encounter it or perceive it until it is manifest in a second (Turino 2014, 190). Via struggle, brute force, cause and effect, or contiguity, secondness is "that which is such as it is as being Second to some First, regardless of anything else" (Peirce 1998, 160). Once the redness is observed, for example, in the fabric tied around a spirit medium's waist, the quality of redness is brought into relation to that fabric. Until then, it was possibility. If firstness is possibility, secondness is actuality; if firstness is qualia, secondness is relations. Thirdness is representation; it is "that whose being consists in it bringing about a secondness" (Peirce 1998, 267). Thirdness brings a first in relation to a second; it mediates (Peirce 1992, 248). Signs are thirds.

These categories apply to one another and subdivide endlessly (Short 2007, 89), so one can always go deeper. But the basic ideas are quite simple: phenomena in and of themselves (first), two phenomena in relation to one another (second), and a third that mediates between two phenomena (third). Each can be considered a fundamental element of reality, but it is in their utility in exploring experience, semiosis, and meaning that they become invaluable. These basic categories are the key to Peirce's theory of signs, the key to his phenomenology, and the key to reality.

Heeding Turino's call to bring Peircean thought to the core of ethnomusicology, I use these categories to observe, distinguish, and generalize experience.[2] As I watched VaMasiza drum for the medium dancing before us, three kinds of experiences aligned with Peirce's categories. The medium was experiencing firstness, in this case, trance. Not all firstness is trance, but in trance no distinctions are made, and the experience is only recognized after the fact. Like most spirit mediums, this woman had no memory of these events once the spirit departed.

VaMasiza, while focused on his drum, was in a state of secondness, which can range from a distraction-free mode of focused concentration during musical performance to a slap in the face. As optimal experience, flow is defined by Csikszentmihalyi as a heightened sense of concentration during which one is focused solely on the task at hand, whether writing, driving, knitting, cooking, or musicking for an entranced spirit medium (Csikszentmihalyi 1990; Turino 2008). VaMasiza was not in trance. He was aware of his experience, although he could only reflect on it via memory after the fact. He perceived signs and responded to them, but partially and narrowly (Turino 2014, 212). Flow is essential to creativity, participatory performance, and ceremonial efficacy.[3]

Finally, there is thirdness. Peirce (1998, 160) defines thirdness as representation; semiosis is thirdness. This productively distinguishes Peirce's own semiotic from Saussure's (1966) semiology, in which signs are essentially seconds: signifier plus signified. For Saussure, signifiers relate to signifieds, what Peirce calls objects. For Peirce, these relations are not signs yet but, rather, seconds in need of a third, an interpretant. The interpretant is that which a sign determines in its interpreter (Peirce 1998, 409). It is an effect. Thought is the ongoing reflective engagement with the world: thirdness. While observing Masiza and the medium, I was in a heightened state of thirdness, thinking about what was happening around me, reflecting on the signs I perceived. By definition, I was not nearing a flow state or trance. I was not engaging in heightened concentration. My detached reflection was hardly ideal during events such as this. Each of our respective experiences was fundamentally and ontologically different.

Serving its own purposes of collective security, respect for ancestors and for God, and social joy, collaboration, and coherence, spirit possession is the fulcrum. It is the motivating purpose for hosting ceremonies, inviting mediums, learning to drum and sing, and inviting friends, family, and neighbors. Following the helpful distinctions of the ethnomusicologist Gilbert Rouget (1985), spirit possession is not a form of trance, or firstness. It could be, if experienced via trance, but as we will see, some mediums are aware of their possession and have a conscious relationship with their spirits. Trance is firstness, a category of experience without distinctions. Possession is secondness, a relation of spirit and medium. It emerges through struggle. Flow (and other secondness experiences) and thought (and other thirdness experiences) are different from trance (and other firstness experiences) in that they are semiotic experiences. They involve interpretation done with purpose. These experiences are rooted in signs, habits, and values.

SIGNS

Every moment in a madhlozi ceremony is complex, with multiple roots and fruits extending and informing the shifting ground of experience in the here and now. In the brief instance described above, there were more components than any single book could possibly address, even if the written word were capable of capturing every aspect of experience. In that moment, there was the sound of VaMasiza's drum, the sharpness of his stick striking the head, the sight of his elbow pressing the drumhead and changing its pitch and timbre; there were the darkness, the press of people all around us, the scent of smoke and beer, the cold, unforgiving cement bench; there were the singing voices joining VaMasiza, accompanied by shakers, clapping hands, and stomping feet; there were the speaking voices inadvertently working against him, the monologue of the man to my right, explaining things for me; there was the red light of my recorder, the quickening of my own heart, heightening my alertness to the sheer energy in the room; there was the shout of the woman in front of us; and there were dancers moving all around, half-seen in the darkness.

Beyond this immediacy, in the background, were people's memories of past events like this, VaMasiza's purpose in awakening the spirits, others' purposes in attending, the preparations that our hosts made cooking food and brewing beer, the woman's acceptance of the spirit within her who demanded to dance; there is the long history of encounter among southern African communities and European arrivals that eventually led to this spirit's arriving in this woman at this time; there is land reform, which undermined the Zimbabwean economy and caused anger and rebuke among the international community but also gave the family hosting our event the land on which these events took place; there are the well-trained, practiced norms of rhythmic patterns, song lyrics, and tonal organization; there is awareness of the consequences that these sounds have had before, the spirits who have already come and gone; there is the familiarity of friendship and family relationships, the anticipation of some, the resignation of others; there is God, looming in the distance; there are the ancestors.

Even the future is involved. Purposes will be realized if the spirit eventually arrives, the community might joyously respond with dance, people will pause from physical effort to eat, drink, and socialize. Hopes could be fulfilled; there will be inevitable exhaustion, drunkenness, possibly relief, preferably joy. Conversations will ensue, as will more dancing, my own increased understanding, rooted in these moments, that will inform the next comparable experience I have; this book, the result of hundreds of moments like this, full of abstract ideas, physical exertion, rote responses, and surprise. Tears, boredom, laughter, shouts, clarity, confusion, social bonding, death, bereavement, absurdity, spiritual awakening, and anger at neighbors all play a role.

The interpretive actions that process all of this, understanding what they can and making connections that string pasts and futures together through complex presents, are semiotic. Semiosis balances habits, expectations, and values with surprises, hopes, fears, and desires in physiological, imaginative, perceptive, or affective ways. Life is semiotic and the world is perceived through signs. Semiotics, the study of signs, provides a theory of perception, meaning, and experience.

Peirce (1992, 478) defines the *sign* as "anything which is determined by something else, called its Object, and so determines an effect upon a person, which effect I call its Interpretant, that the latter is mediately determined by the former." Semiosis is thirdness, bringing the signs that are sensed and imagined in relation to histories, purposes, ideologies, and ontologies that are represented via perception, imagination, and interpretation. Despite its complexity, at its center semiotics has three basic components: sign, object, and interpretant, with a necessary fourth component—an agent to interpret (see figure 2.1). Every sign is part of a triadic relationship, and every triadic relationship is meaningful (Peirce 1931–58, 1:345). Each component is necessary and of equal importance. If one is missing, there is only potential. The phenomenon, as a whole, is first; visceral confrontations with it—a blast of cold air, a bump to the shoulder, a scream—are second; and interpretation, appraisal, thought, and judgment are third.

Objects determine signs; signs determine interpretants; interpretants bring the sign and object together in the mind of the perceiver. Signs include the sensory material through which we experience that which is outside ourselves and receive the world around us, but they are understood to emerge from the objects they represent (Peirce 1998, 487). In order for a sign to have an effect or interpretant it must represent something else.

Peirce's definition of the sign includes the essential, but often overlooked, component of a person. A full understanding of musical meaning necessitates ethnography (Turino 2014, 188). Short pushes back against this somewhat, arguing that interpretability is enough (2007, 160). Yet without learning the internal contexts of people during instances that matter, one can only be speculative, partial, or autobiographical. The person is not a *part* of the sign (hence the dotted line in figure 2.1), but there is no sign to understand without the agent to interpret it. Thus four elements shape experience: object, sign, interpretant, and agent. Each of the four chapters of Part II explores ceremonial experience from the perspective of these basic elements.

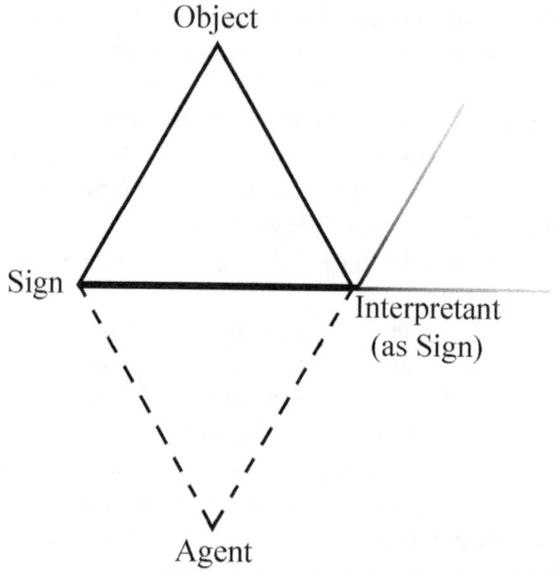

FIGURE 2.1. Sign (image inspired by those of anthropologist Paul Kockelman [2011, 174])

In waking life, excepting unusual circumstances like trance, semiosis is unceasing. What Turino (2014, 203) calls "semiotic chaining" is the continuous perception of signs defined by "interpretant-making" (Tomlinson 2016, 159), the ongoing processes of mediating one's relationship with the world through signs (Turino 2014, 203). Interpretants are signs, and thus the recognition of one sign immediately produces another. The fading lines moving to the right in figure 2.1 represent the next link in this chain, when the interpretant operates as a new sign. The interpretants of signs are not always predictable, which renders interpretant-making in semiosis a potentially creative and poietic dimension of life, a poiesis that "unveils the truth inherent in things" (Lambek 2002, 16). As ceremonies unfold, no one knows if the anticipated spirits will arrive, if something unexpected will happen, or if people will end up content, moved, bored, or filled with regret. These feelings reveal the reality to which they respond.

Peirce's complete theory of semiotics, as embedded within his pragmatic phenomenology, is complex and daunting. Although most of the elements that he theorized have utility, it is unnecessary, even impossible, to absorb everything at once. The foundation consists of firstness, secondness, and thirdness. He has trichotomies of signs, sign-object relations, the relations of these to

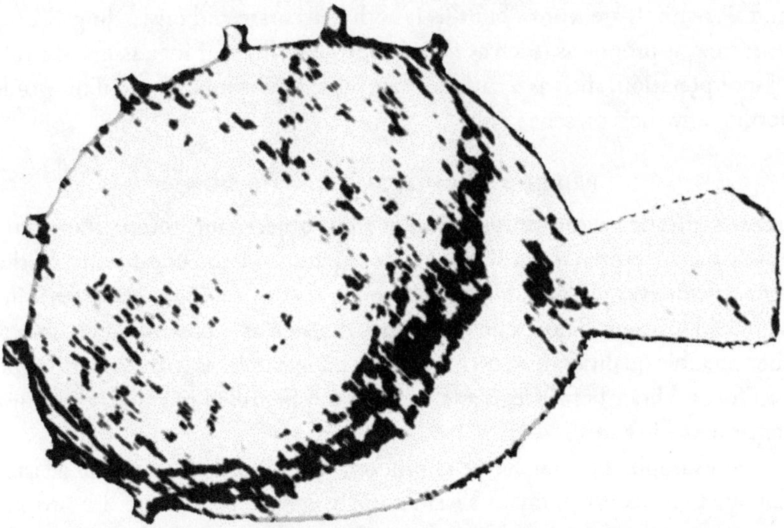

FIGURE 2.2. This ↑ is a *deza* drum.

interpretants, kinds of objects, kinds of interpretants, kinds of reasoning, and so forth. Within philosophy, anthropology, and musicology the most widely understood and employed trichotomy describes that of the sign and the manner of its relation to an object. This is Peirce's Second Trichotomy. Because it includes the most widely known of Peirce's technical terms, I introduce it here; it includes icon, index, and symbol.

Icon, a first, is a sign of resemblance. It can't be authentic, it can't be true; its characters resemble those of the signified object. The drawing shown in figure 2.2 is an icon of a deza drum used in mhongo ceremonies. At least, it is for me; you likely thought of something else, even if it was something similar. *Index*, a second, is a sign of contiguity. It is connected to its object through co-occurrence or cause and effect. In the caption for figure 2.2, the ↑ is an index of that drawing. In the phrase "this deza," the demonstrative pronoun is an index of the word *deza* and the drum to which it draws the reader's attention. *Symbol*, a third, is a sign of stipulation. It represents its object through a law of interpretation (Short 2007, 221). *Deza* is a symbol in ChiNdau for a drum used in mhongo ceremonies. Every instance in this paragraph is a replica of that general sign. Once you know what it means, you should respond appropriately. The word *drum* is a symbol in English, a general sign for a general class of objects. It can often appear as if all words are symbols and all symbols are words, but this is both inaccurate and misleading. Words operating as pronouns (such as *that* above) are indices. Things assigned a rule of interpretation, such as a national flag, operate as symbols even if no words accompany their presence.

PEIRCE'S TRICHOTOMY OF THE SIGN

These semiotic relationships between sign, object, and interpretant only emerge as interpreted via signs. Peirce expands on the complexity of the signs themselves with his First Trichotomy, that of the sign: qualisign, sinsign, and legisign. Before one can interpret a sign as representing an object, interpretable qualities must be manifest in an instance, as with redness in the medium's fabric. Before legisigns or types can be called to mind, one must perceive the instance.

For example, on that July 2 afternoon, when I arrived with the Masiza family at Horus Farm, my ears were initially greeted by a sound. I heard the drummer strike the frame of the drum. The qualities of this sound—sharpness of attack, rapidity of decay, and flatness of tone—were what Peirce called qualisigns. They were only potential signs until manifest in an instance, a sinsign, which is what greeted my ears at that moment. The combination of those qualities suggested that I was hearing a drum. It resembled drums I'd heard in the past; I was hearing an icon of a drum. As I listened, I recognized that each instance was followed by others in a discernible pattern of twos and fours. Again, experience suggested that what I was hearing was an instance, a sinsign, of a madzviti pattern. It was a token of that type, madzviti drumming, which can only be attended to as it is replicated in a sign; the instance matters. Even symbols become valueless without an index connecting them through instances to something specific. The sound of the drum, as the sign, leads to the recognition of form and type as an interpretant when it connects to the madzviti pattern as its object.

I also knew from experience that every time I had heard this pattern, madzviti spirits had been present in the bodies of their host mediums. So after identifying the pattern, I interpreted the pattern as an index of the spirit because the two were always co-occurrent; they were contiguous. I found myself looking around for spirits. I knew what to look for because helpful interlocutors had combined indices like pointing and pronouns with words like *madzviti*, *spirits*, and *Gaza soldiers* to define them for me. *Madzviti*, in referring to the people wandering around with spears, operated as a symbol for this complex spiritual category. Masiza and others had stipulated this sign's object for me to ensure that I knew what it meant.

This instance of semiosis relates the sign-interpretant relation to the sign-object relation. The sign represents the relation between these two relations (Kockelman 2011). Put another way, the interpretive process *creates* the relation between a sign and an object (Deacon 2012a, 12). Meaning emerges from the interpretation of these relations. One sign means that the drumming has started. Another means that I recognize the pattern. Another means that others join the musical texture. Yet another means that the spirits are desired. Drumming is the means to that purposeful end, the telos that shapes everyone's experience. Because each of these effects is different, based on the representation of different objects, the signs are different.[4] Further subdivisions of these basic elements emerge later in this book, but all rely on Peirce's basic terms: sign, object, and interpretant.

MUSICKING AND THE SENSES

Most commonly, spirits are "awoken" with performance. Using the signs and processes of music, dance, speech, and gesture in conjunction with beer, food, snuff, camaraderie, and general participation, Ndau communities invite, arouse, and engage with their spirits. While anthropologists can often be accused of privileging language and musicologists charged with overvaluing music or sound, ceremonial environments such as the one I witnessed at the Horus Farm homestead are deliberately and delightfully multisensory. No single mode of semiotic representation can fully shape the experience everyone desires. Beer brings the crowd, food keeps them going, spirits are more comfortable with the paraphernalia of their lives. Musicking is the most public and perhaps the most obvious modality of possession, but is not the most important factor in ceremonial success. The Muzita-based medium Ngarife Matabuka explained to me that the only absolutely essential element for possession was snuff, or *forya*. He said, "Without songs, without beer, without anything. . . . The spirits only need tobacco snuff."

Although musicking and dancing provide the central signs of ceremonial activity before, during, and after spirit possession, they are rendered ineffective without the other important sources of sensory stimulation; musical sound, in isolation, is meaningless. Forya, drums, song, clothing, spiritual objects, beer, food, and forms of greeting and communication all enhance the ability of music and dance to generate powerful collective experiences. As a participatory event, music draws people in, and dance ensures the smoothest possession experiences for spirits and mediums alike.

Music can take a long time to induce possession or inspire dance. But people play and sing until it works, until the energy level is high enough. After an hour of performance, sounds become different signs than they were in the initial moments. When the signs are right, mediums dance. At first, they dance in the style of the spirit being called by imitating them and inviting them to wake up. As the spirit awakens, they take over the medium's body and dance alone. The dance steps are no longer imitative icons of others but, rather, indices of authentic spiritual embodiment.

Every category of spirit has preferences for time of day, repertoire of songs, the drum used, and a signature rhythm. Rhythmic motifs frame ceremonial proceedings and indicate to the living and the dead whose turn it is (see figure 1.2). Each rhythmic signature is a powerful spiritual index that uniquely frames other performance parameters. The relation between musical sound, mediums, and possessing spirits is visceral in its intimacy. Madhlozi are so closely tied to the sounds of their songs that literally beating the rhythms on the heads of mediums is sometimes required to induce possession, as Mapfumo explained to me. Both rhythms and spirits are rooted in the specific histories from which they emerge.

It is striking how rarely the living engage in conversation with visiting spirits beyond polite greetings and goodbyes. Symbols seem trivial. The spirits come to dance and to be remembered. Sharing this experience is usually enough. What matters is dancing, doing. The way the living and the dead experience one another's presence and performance shapes the purpose and consequence of their ceremonial interactions. As people come together to employ a range of sensory expressions they can be moved, comforted, placated, censured, and cajoled depending on the objects signified. Beyond the text of the songs being sung, often in languages that few understand, words recede in importance. The resonance and emotional weight of these experiences is driven by nonlinguistic semiotic modes and can be more powerful for that reason. Participants' experiences are shaped by embodied interpretants of complex semiotic expressions, by musicking.

HABITS

Seated in a comfortable sitting room in suburban Harare, far from the hills of Chipinge, Enos Simango is telling me his story. A highly respected muchongoyo performer from Chipinge who has lived and danced in Harare for decades, Simango shaped the form of muchongoyo used in the National Dance Company and its subsequent spin-offs almost single-handedly.[5] We met because of this legacy. But he is also a spirit medium. As we sipped tea with our host, Julia Chigamba, we talked about muchongoyo, Chipinge, and the Ndau language.

Eventually I asked him about the mhongo. He had long been a healer and medium for a mhongo spirit, so I was excited to hear his perspective. "Mhongo live in the water," Simango responded. He paused before continuing, "They are . . . amm, I struggle to talk about them. You know I have those spirits." He laughed nervously and was visibly reluctant to continue for fear of awakening his spirits. At first I thought I had insensitively asked questions that were too private and that he felt uncomfortable sharing this information with me. But he explained that he had such a close relationship with his mhongo, the source of his healing skills, that he worried that our simple conversation could initiate possession. Bringing them to mind, without drums, songs, or snuff, was enough to make him tense. Becoming possessed would be awkward and inappropriate in our mutual friend's living room, regardless of her hospitality.

Signs have histories grounded in prior relations to objects. Repetition, predictability, and purpose shape habits of interpretation that profoundly inform the ways in which signs are interpreted. Experience and the accompanying interpretation of signs are shaped by the habitus, defined by the French sociologist Pierre Bourdieu as "the durably installed generative principle of regulated improvisations" (1977, 78). Following Turino (2014) and Mahmood (2005), I emphasize Bourdieu's extension of phenomenology rather than his engagement with structuralism.

Habits are not simply reflexive or rote repetitions but are tendencies. People tend to respond to circumstances and stimuli on the basis of similar circumstances or stimuli experienced in the past (Turino 2008, 95). Simango's habits of mediumship clearly imposed on the circumstances of our conversation. Defining *habit* as a "tendency" both recalls and departs from Bourdieu's more rigid explanation of the habitus as structured principles that structure practice (Bourdieu 1977, 72); it determines how people act but is open to change and improvisation.

These tendencies inform semiotic interpretation and help people act with agency. Habitus accommodates habits that are deeply rooted and ostensibly unchangeable as well as the transient, ever-evolving habits that help us relate to the world at every waking moment. Habits as principles and tendencies of response exist within the complex, polysemic, multisensory context that is everyday life. It is possible to predict people's responses to specific stimuli to a certain extent, but no stimulus exists in a vacuum. Even as Simango's habits as an instructor and interviewee were privileged, the stimuli of my probing questions initiated responses that Simango struggled to control. The habits that generate one's thoughts and actions from moment to moment allow the chaos of practice to be a bit more manageable.[6]

Peirce (1992, 129) observed that habits are the essence of belief, a pragmatic approach to truth that seems appropriate for ethnomusicological inquiry. It is sufficiently "content-free" that the perspectives of the people and practices being investigated can speak for themselves. Competing orthodoxies can be true for each orthodoxy's own practitioners. As learned and grounded in experiences with signs, habits frame our interpretation of signs and lead to our responses. Some habits, but by no means all, are explicitly cultivated. Habits reveal aspects of truth and belief without subscribing to any particular version of the truth. Following the anthropologist Martin Holbraad and others, this orthodoxy concerning truth is an ontological one; it is about the world more than about a worldview. Spirits in Chipinge are not ideas in which people believe but beings with presence, values, agency, and habits of their own (Holbraad 2009; Viveiros de Castro 2004). Simango's fear and the spirit he wanted to keep at bay were real.

Habits are inherited via genetics and evolution or acquired via socialization and experience. Biocultural evolution unites the biological with the sociocultural. Tomlinson (2015) stresses the need to address both biology and culture and the ways each informs the other so as to develop in tandem. In the Ndau communities where I worked, habits can also be acquired via spirits, as with Simango. Within the spiritual contexts described in the following chapters, biological determinism must be balanced with a spiritual and cosmological flexibility. For participants in ceremonies, spirits are parts of selves; skills, personality traits, and unique talents are credited to the spirits within. Thus habits can emerge genetically, culturally, spiritually, and socially, to say nothing of each person's idiosyncrasies. Each of these dimensions is shaped by experience.

DIMENSIONS OF VALUE

Semiotics shows, productively and irrefutably, that experience is meaningful. Beyond symbolic generality or systematicity, meaning brings affect to the center of life. Every discernment of self from other carries potential meaning. A phenomenological account shows that affect is irrefutably meaningful. Affect itself, however defined, is rooted in value, with evaluation a core aspect of interpretation as signs are attended to, perceived, and appraised with purpose.

Dimensions of value refers to the open axes of interpretation along which a sign's relation to the purpose with which it is engaged and evaluated is understood; value is the foundation of evaluation. In semiosis, value is intrinsic to life (Kohn 2013, 133). Short includes a long list of evaluative dimensions in his explanation of Peirce's theory of signs, including "success/failure, better/worse, good/bad, correct/mistaken, justified/unjustified, real/unreal, true/

false" (2007, 154). These dimensions address significance and purpose, which are essential in pushing understandings of semiosis and emotion beyond mechanistic sequences. Mechanical processes don't allow for valuation (153; see also Deacon 2012b). Signs can satisfy or deny that which is desired; they can reify the undesirable, thwart the anticipated, and confirm the improbable. Dimensions of value shape emotions, which emerge when interpretants resolve, generate, or sustain tension in specific dimensions of value. The more signs represent objects that matter, the more value is at play, and the more potentially intense an emotional response can be. Emotions are "judgments about important things" (Nussbaum 2001, 19).

My conversation with Simango signified valued spirits in complex ways. He valued his spirit but not its arrival. At that moment it contradicted other values tied to being a guest, an expert, and a stranger to me. In the following chapters, clarifying the ways in which signs signify value and intersect with habits of interpretation opens up a path to understanding meaning as emotional.

I am especially interested in how ideals intersect with expectations, a relationship ripe with emotional potential. Simango's expectation that our conversation could awaken his spirit intersected in challenging ways with his preference to remain lucid and in control. Success, truth, justification, desirability, and reality become emotionally salient as they are (or are not) realized in performance. Interaction with others would be impossible if we did not assume that others act with purpose and use our interpretants to impose objects on others' signs (Kockelman 2016, 44). Possibility is a first, as is probability, as is desirability. Interpretants of signs, such as sweat, a quickening heartbeat, clarity of thought, or *affect*, place these firsts in relation to a second, the ideal in relation to the actual, the probable in relation to the desirable, the improbable in relation to the probable. Simango's decision to shut down conversation after evaluating the likelihood that his spirit would emerge reduced the possibility of that possession. Semiosis places dimensions of value in relation to one another in such a way that basic aspects of the self are implicated, and thus this valuation is emotional. *The valuation and evaluation of signs along dimensions of value that implicate and potentially change aspects of the self is the core process of emotional life.*

Self, Subjectivity, Identity

Both the living and dead are agents, interpretant makers, and actors with selves grounded in meaningful experience. Dimensions of value rooted in habits shape the ways those agents interpret signs of experience in order to participate in processes that determine who they are and how they relate to the world around them. A trichotomy of self-subjectivity-identity allows ethnographic grounding to account for what can otherwise appear ambiguous and elusive. Although each of these terms is productively employed in anthropology, ethnomusicology, and other social fields, I define self, subjectivity, and identity in distinct, nested ways rooted in Peirce's fundamental categories. Self (a first) includes one's physical body and all of one's habits of thinking, doing, feeling, and being; subjectivity (a second) is the partial and immediate selection of habits and physical capacities engaged in the here and now; identity (a third) is a representation.[7]

Self, subjectivity, and identity are never fixed but are perpetually in formation as people interact with one another and the world around them. The self is more stable than subjectivity or the context-specific and partly self-directed aspects of identity, but this should not suggest fixity or stasis. It is constantly in formation throughout one's life. Subjectivity and identity are partial aspects of the self. As phenomenologists and others argue, the self is not necessarily an isolated, discrete individual. It emerges through a perpetual relationship with the world and others.

Although each of one's particular habits is potentially common to others, collectively they are unique only to one individual. No two individuals have the same collection of experiences that shape these habits. When the self is understood as a composite of habits (physical, mental, emotional) and the physical mind-body that realizes and enacts them, the partial and variable nature of subjectivity and identity, as well as the elusiveness of spiritual experience such as spirit possession, become clearer. Habits are tendencies of response; they indexically connect behavior and the environmental stimuli that inform them.

SELF

The self includes everything: habits, body, genetics, even spirits, and it develops via one's ceaseless interaction with one's surroundings (Turino 2008, 95). The habitus is a formative component of the self just like one's body and its capacities. These habits and capacities are not things that someone has but "something that one is" (Bourdieu 1990, 73). The self is an ever-evolving assemblage as process. In his neuroscientific account, Damasio argues that the self, as process, is ever-present during moments of consciousness with varied "intensities" (2010, 9). Although it is surely a coincidence, this resonates with Brian Massumi's (1987) emphasis on affect itself as intensity, implying that affect is the intense "self-making" component of experience.

For Ndau mediums and participants in madhlozi ceremonies, the process of self is also spiritual. Relationships with spirits contribute to people's senses of who they are. As Mulambo said, people are born with spirits. The moral sensibility that one acquires, in part, through these relationships with spirits is captured in the word *unhu,* which the ethnomusicologist Jennifer Kyker translates as "a moral sense of personhood" (2016, 17). *Munhu*, meaning "person," is defined by unhu. The relationship between a medium and his or her spirit is an aspect of the self just as the body is. Simango was the man he was on that day in Harare because of the spirit within him and the spirits that helped raise him. But that is only a partial accounting. I could never hope to know Simango's self. Habits and the selves they shape emerge from a life of semiosis. Each experience in a person's life contributes to an ongoing process of perceiving and responding to a never-ending complex of signs. This sequence of signs shapes habits that are constantly being formed by generating these tendencies and principles of response. Habits become a sense of self in solution.

SUBJECTIVITY

Subjectivity employs the habits of the self that are called upon in the ongoing present, whether or not they are foregrounded, explicit, or taken as representative. They are experienced in the moment but may not be actively presented as important or foregrounded as identity. Neither self nor identity fully encapsulates the specificity of habits that matter in the moment because they are not about the here and now. Subjectivity is a second, filling the space between self and identity. Self and identity are both *general* senses that inform my moment-to-moment engagement with the world. Subjectivity is not general but, rather, immediate, specific, and transient. Subjectivity is one's relationship to others in the ongoing present. These habits often operate as what Bourdieu (1977) called doxa and may be low in one's focal awareness, such as vocal timbre or posture.

As I spoke with Simango and Chigamba certain habits came to the fore, but less of what took place was habitual because we had little shared experience together. We were formal, less open. He used English more than usual, I used Shona as I could. My local habits were still ill-formed, so they required a kind of concentration that was different from the others.' The very fact that I had to think about how to be, in the moment, shaped the kind of experience I was able to have. Race, gender, age, experience, and education all likely informed the way we interacted in subtle ways.

IDENTITY

Some of Simango's anxiety was tied to identity. He represented himself as a muchongoyo instructor, an expert in Ndau music. I represented myself as a foreign researcher and a student. We both identified as guests in another's home, mandating a different kind of self-representation. Identity is a representation of the self; it is a partial selection of habits that we employ to represent ourselves to the world around us (Turino 2008, 102). Identity is more mediated than is subjectivity, but it is also partial. Habits of identity become significant only when they are taken to another level of signification as being especially meaningful. My vocal timbre, posture, and general comportment may change when I talk to my parents, my students, a police officer, or a close friend, reflecting my shifting subjectivity within each of these unique contexts, but these signs only become habits of identity if recognized by me or others as essential to who I am and indexically connected to important aspects of self. Simango's admission that he was a mhongo spirit medium changed the way I understood him, adding a layer of identity. In this regard, one's positionality lends itself to an active agency as one responds to the surrounding world via the experience of subjectivity.

IDENTITY AND NDAU

Most residents of the Chipinge and Chimanimani Districts and of neighboring districts in Mozambique identify as Ndau.[8] The term cannot be reduced to an ethnicity, a language, or a political formation, but it can usefully index each of these. Like all signs of identity, it is used to represent people in specific ways. Ndau is generally categorized as one of several subgroups of Zimbabwe's Shona majority in the literature. Linguistically, spiritually, politically, and historically speaking there is much that Ndau communities have in common with others in Zimbabwe, but there is much to distinguish them as well. There is also a long and lingering history of political tension between rural Ndau communities and their more politically powerful Shona neighbors. Consequently, most rural Ndau are loath to identify themselves as Shona; they claim Ndau identity as distinct and far removed from the Shona majority.[9] Younger people I spoke with in Chipinge, however, often identified as Shona.

Each of the dialects of Shona (Zezuru, Karanga, Korekore, Manyika, Ndau, and so on) has its own linguistic, social, and political history, but Ndau is perhaps the furthest removed from the official norm of standard Shona.[10] It has been influenced and modified by contact with neighboring Mozambican communities and the invading Gaza Nguni armies of the nineteenth century.

Ndau is centrally important for some and less important for others. Like identity frameworks everywhere, Ndau is nested in such a way that the socially constructed and the natural become intertwined; nature and culture are destabilized as reliable categories of analysis (Ahmed 2004; Descola 2013). Most of the identity variables in Chipinge are influenced by multiple forces; kinship, politics, the natural world, and the spiritual realm are interconnected.

At the lowest level is family identity: *mhuri* (family). In patrilineal Ndau communities, this intimate identity is nested within the patrilineal lineage, or *dzinza*, including generations of patrilineal relatives, ancestors, and midzimu (Vijfhuizen 2002, 18). The dzinza is nested within a *mutupo*, a totem inherited through the father. A mutupo is broader than a dzinza, but narrower than ethnicity. A mutupo is usually an animal that reflects common ancestry and is accompanied by a series of restrictions and expectations pertinent to that animal. This is a cultural-natural category of kinship rooted in spiritual understanding and political history. Paraphrasing the anthropologist Phillipe Descola (2013, 144), mutupo is an ontology. Ndau surnames (Sithole, Mhlanga, Simango, Muyambo, and so on) typically reflect totems.[11]

Ndau could be next in this nested hierarchy, but mutupo identities cut across ethnolinguistic labels such as this. Nested identity frameworks overlap as well, so few people will identify with the same sets of groups. While I resist the term *ethnicity* given its imprecision and occasional implications of immutable membership and primordial origins, many locals with whom I spoke casually define *Ndau* as an ethnicity, an ethnic group, or a tribe.

Before *Ndau* became a collective term, group identity was defined by political authority and residence within a chieftaincy. *Ndau* as an identity term separate from chieftaincy emerged during the reign of the Gaza Nguni and became entrenched during the colonial period.[12] Regardless of one's interpretation of ethnicity in theoretical terms, it exists within the habitus of locals as a discursive category that shapes actions and attitudes and has become fixed to a specific region (Moore 2005), the Chipinge and Chimanimani Districts. But it is only one variable among many. Depending on class, education, location, or aspirations to modernity, a Chipinge resident could define their ethnicity as Ndau, Shona, or even African. These frameworks intersect with national projects through which people embrace, resist, or accept their status as Zimbabwean or Mozambican. The spirits invited during ceremonies contribute to these processes of identification.

INTERSUBJECTIVITY

I define *intersubjectivity* as the moments when one's subjectivity is informed by lived engagement with others in real time, shaping future relationships and their accompanying habits. Relationships have a formative role in one's ever-emerging self; the self is social. Socialization begins at birth or earlier, and basic habits of the self form collectively.[13] Understanding this demands consideration of the intersubjective foundation of selfhood. Intersubjectivity also shapes the variable senses of identity and subjectivity that emerge from one context to another, hence the importance of ethnography and social analysis in understanding any one person, let alone collectivities rooted in intersubjectivity. It helps explain why one's habits as a son or a father, a sister or a wife, differ. I suggest that part of the reason for the anxiety that Simango felt during our interview was that the lifelong habits he'd built up with his mhongo spirit were different from the shallower habits he'd built up as a dance expert for outside interviews. Our interaction was grounded on habits shaped by similar interactions with other musicians or with American researchers rather than with each other specifically. The conflicting sets of intersubjective habits put Simango in a challenging position because his spiritual relationship was deeper and more valuable.

Intersubjectivity between people and spirits is especially important for understanding Ndau cosmology. Ndau relationships with spirits are central to who they are. The identity of spirits resident in mediums can lead to specific food taboos, the need to wear particular clothes, or the need to avoid certain colors and can have a profound impact on one's personality. These relationships connect the living and the dead at a deep and essential level. One acquaintance of mine, known for his hot temper, was often excused because he had a particularly volatile spirit. The woman mentioned at the beginning of this chapter was likely not yet engaging in any intersubjective habits because she was entranced entirely within herself. As her spirit awakened, however, the habits of intersubjectivity between the two of them were likely to drown out all other stimuli. VaMasiza, the drummer, was ensconced in a narrow selection of intersubjective habits, focused almost solely on the woman dancing in front of him and less focused on others contributing to the sound of the event with song, clapping hands, and rattles. During the ceremony I was in a more complex state, relating to others but less reliant on the habits of doing so because we had yet to know one another intimately.

Madhlozi ceremonies focus on these intersubjective habits and the relationships that reinforce these very communities as they are reiterated and renewed.

Ceremonial performance reinforces intersubjective habits between the living and the dead and entrenches them as essential aspects of self and identity.

Like subjectivity, intersubjectivity is secondness, with little of the reflection of thought that characterizes the thirdness of identity. This recalls Victor Turner's concept of spontaneous communitas, a direct, immediate, and total confrontation of human identities, a deep rather than intense style of personal interaction (1974, 79; see also Turner 1969, 134–40).[14] With their productive opposition to structure, moments of spontaneous communitas elicited by performance not only bring individuals together and highlight what members of these communities have in common but also demonstrate how these commonalities are essential to who participants are and will become (Turner 1974, 79–80). Communitas is a specific and ideal form of intersubjectivity in which social differences and hierarchy are minimized.

Although Turner restricts communitas to certain kinds of ritual activity, I find it useful to think of it as a collective form of flow (see also Turino 2014). Flow, as "heightened concentration," is an optimal mode of experience, a state of secondness; communitas is an optimal mode of *shared* experience, also a state of secondness. Ceremonies are moving because they emphasize intersubjective habits that can reinforce communities during moments in which social habits are formed and reinforced. For the philosopher Kathleen Marie Higgins, musical experience can generate comfort and make explicit our shared connection with others (2012, 144). When participants at a ceremony work together, concentrate on the task at hand, focus on awakening the spirits and keeping them happy, and participate with joy, the communitas that results not only helps ensure possession but feels good because it alleviates conflict between the possible (the ideal) and the actual.

Communitas emerges from participation combined with flow. Forms of interaction during performance can signify relationships, interaction, and community, generating interpretants of affirmation and reinforcement. When one of the objects of collective action is community itself, those ideas can be manifest in the signs of performance. When drumming patterns synchronize with the makosho, hand clapping, vocal, and dance patterns, they can be interpreted as signs that are causally connected to social relationships and community, signifying relationships and solidifying habits. Sign and object are experienced simultaneously, bringing individuals together in spontaneous communitas and demonstrating how commonalities are important to selves and identities (Turner 1974, 79–80). Intersubjective habits connect people with one another and with their spirits. They are the building blocks of communities and selves and can be deeply moving. Those habits are essential aspects of Ndau spirit possession.

Spirit Possession (*Kumukirwa*)

Anomukirwa; *anobudirwa*; *anosvikirwa* (he or she becomes possessed by a spirit). Each of these sentences can be used in ChiNdau to refer to the process whereby a spirit assumes control of the body of a host medium. This is the central activity of madhlozi and midzimu ceremonies. Mediums thus play an important role in the ongoing dynamics between the living and the dead that are crucial to a community's flourishing. The verbs in each ChiNdau sentence above are approximate synonyms for the English phrase spirit possession: *kumukirwa*, *kubudirwa*, and *kusvikirwa*.

The most commonly used form in Chipinge is *kumukirwa*, a reflexive verb I translate as "to be awoken within."[15] In Shona the preferred term is *kusvikirwa*, "to be arrived upon," which recalls possession relationships in which musicking calls a spirit from elsewhere to reside on or in the medium.[16] This term is also heard, albeit infrequently, in the Chipinge area because Shona is spreading through the school system. More common is *kubudirwa*, "to be emerged from within," which resonates with *kumukirwa* since, in each of these discursive reflections, the spirit doesn't arrive from elsewhere but is already present and must be awoken by ceremonial technologies—music, dance, snuff—in order to emerge. The difference between a spirit arriving from elsewhere (kusvikira) and a spirit emerging from within (kumukira or kubudira) reveals a profound distinction between the ontology of spirits in Ndau communities and in Shona Zimbabwe; Ndau spirits are inherent aspects of selves. Each verb implies a relationship between a medium and a spirit. The reflexive form (ending in *-wa*) focuses on what is happening to the medium, and the nonreflexive form (ending in *-ira*) addresses what the spirit does.

People here are born with spirits. As Mulambo told me, they can be ancestors, outsiders, or aggrieved spirits (midzimu, madhlozi, or ngozi). The relationship between a person and the spirit within is a part of who a person is, an aspect of self, whether or not the spirit eventually manifests itself via possession. The past, which is inherent within spirits who are inherent within selves, becomes part of the self (see Fontein 2015b, 15). For mediums, spirit possession is a form of intersubjectivity reflecting a lived relationship that has been a part of the medium since birth.[17] Madhlozi, for example, are responsible for one's unique skills, personality traits, or talents. The self is shaped by this intersubjectivity. Considered in conjunction with the complex of habits acquired via evolution and socialization, spiritual influences are part of one's inheritance at birth.

In some cases the spirit wants more and pushes the person it inhabits to become a medium (Berliner 1993; Lan 1985; Bourdillon 1987; Kyker 2009). The person in question has little say in the matter. If they resist, they will likely suffer misfortune, which spirits use to communicate with their prospective medium. Once diagnosed by a n'anga, the person who is suffering should undergo a ceremony in order to awaken the spirit and initiate possession, which often leads to a life of service. One word for "spirit medium" is *homwe* (pocket).

Mediums can have several spirits, but spirits choose only a single medium. Matabuka explained it to me as follows:

TONY PERMAN: So a single person can have two madzviti?
NGARIFE MATABUKA: They can have two or three.
TP: At one time—
NM: One time. The father comes out, it comes out through you, the child comes out, it comes out through you. They come out through the spirit medium, the children, the father and the children together. The father starts within five minutes. . . . If you have given us a short time . . .
TP: So now . . . it is changing?
NM: Yes, he goes and changes and takes the father's clothes.
TP: The father comes out.
NM: He comes out and dresses in the father's clothes and dances, after they give each other time and say, The child is coming so I am going, and he goes. When the child comes, he takes [the clothes] of the child . . .
TP: Of the whole family.
NM: You will see that there are a lot of women there; it is such that this woman holds the clothes of the father, this other woman takes the clothes of the first child . . . so when the father goes, the woman with the father's clothes leaves them, the second woman stands by the child. As the child awakens . . . the woman would know that this cloth is of the child and she will have water to drink and runs with it.

Though all have resident spirits, not everyone becomes a medium. Both medium and spirit have agency, although they rarely act simultaneously. There is mutual reliance because the spirit needs the medium in order to become embodied and dance, and the medium needs the spirit to protect the ancestors and help ensure a safe present and future.

The medium's relationship with the spirit can be understood as a habit, part of the habitus (Fontein 2015b). Possession, then, is a process by which the medium learns to focus on this habit and his or her relationship with the spirit as an aspect of self, thus allowing the spirit's agency to come through via possession. Mediums are subject to the power of the spirits and their history but acquire their own sense of agency as well (Lambek 2002, 25). This relationship is one that can be cultivated and perfected as mediums learn to focus on it (Kramer 1993; Friedson 1996, 2009; Becker 2004; Fontein 2015b; Perman 2011a). The differences between the medium and the spirit must be stripped away to such an extent that the spirit can take control of the medium's body. The medium loses awareness of their own presence, loses control of their experience, and relinquishes control of their consciousness.

In Chipinge co-consciousness is incredibly rare. Mediums usually have no memory of events, no experience of the experience. Matabuka was occasionally aware of the dzviti spirit inhabiting him and could remember being possessed, but he was never in control or fully lucid. Even this minimal copresence spirit and medium was unusual. If consciousness requires a sense of self-consciousness (Damasio 2010, 10–11), then the process of focusing on the spirit leads the medium away from consciousness.

Ceremonial performance practices emphasize spiritual relationships by enabling people to focus on habits that bring the other partner in the relationship, the spirit, to the fore. By so doing, mediums allow their spirits to embody them and assume consciousness. Communities use music or dance to awaken spirits in their mediums and encourage them to dance. The living depend on madhlozi spirits for protection, guidance, and security in the face of constant personal, familial, and communal challenges. Being disembodied, however, these spirits rely on the living for occasional and temporary corporeal existence. Musicking is not necessary for this to happen, but it certainly makes it easier.

Models for Experience: Affect, Emotion, Feeling, Emotive

Emotions, affects, or feelings seem to provide the key to understanding humanity itself. Though dependent on the habits and values of self, they form the foundation of people's daily quests, choices, struggles, and understanding of the world around them. Emotions connect the physiological and the ideological as "embodied thoughts" (Rosaldo 1984, 143), synthesizing the ontological and the epistemological. They make manifest the evolutionary responses of a neurophysiological organism to the world, ensuring survival (Damasio 2003, 39) and thrive (Nussbaum 2001, 31). Affects comprise the process by which boundaries of self and other are made, thus shaping human sociality (Ahmed 2004, 10). Feelings inform subjective experience, connect lives through social relations, structure society, and "solve" social experiences (Williams 1977, 133); "affects are becomings" (Deleuze and Guattari 1987, 256). Emotional experiences make us feel alive (Fosha 2000, 14). Interest in consciousness, creativity, culture, society, trauma, or attachment necessarily involves questions about emotion. Nationalism, national sentiment, political agency, and resistance are affective practices. It is unsurprising that emotion and affect have moved nearer the center of many disciplinary endeavors, from critical theory to anthropology to neuroscience.

However, the range of disparate and often diametrically opposed disciplinary approaches presents a challenge when developing a comprehensive approach to emotion, affect, or feeling. As with the terms *music*, *meaning*, and *experience*, if I mean one thing when I write *emotion* or *affect* and you mean another when you read it, communication is unlikely. Emotion is perhaps even more riddled with inconsistent multivalence than are the terms discussed in the prologue. One person's *affect* is another's *emotion* is another's *feeling*; each might refer to either a specific and knowable kind of experience or a ubiquitous element that infuses everything we do. Affect or emotion is the dark matter of humanity: everywhere at once, yet understood from so many partial and discrete perspectives that it remains just beyond the horizon of understanding.

Emotions are irreducibly semiotic and physiological, but never static. Unless affects are immaterial they travel in signs, circulate via semiosis, and are interpreted according to the purposes with which agents express and interpret those signs. Affect becomes a characteristic of purposeful, agentic semiosis. Even if moments of emotional experiences can be isolated, experience is never fixed. Emotion is "the very embodiment of the intrinsic incompleteness of subjective experience that constitutes its perpetual becoming" (Deacon 2012b, 512); affects are becomings. Ultimately, a comprehensive approach to emotion should allow for emotional processes as a potential human universal while also accounting for the ways in which formative social, personal, experiential, and semiotic differences rooted in cultural specificity make emotion such an inherently anthropological object of study. I remain convinced that a rapprochement of affect theory, neuroscience, and ethnographic fields such as anthropology is achievable.

Different theoretical paradigms approach the act of definition in different ways. Perhaps like many semioticians (and unlike many affect theorists), I need specificity. The lack of consensus among neuroscientists, affect theorists, philosophers, anthropologists, and ethnomusicologists makes transparency more essential for effective communication than agreement. Most words are symbols (in Peirce's sense), which only work as such if their meaning, in the sense of the object represented and the anticipated recognition of such, is agreed on.

In anthropology there is a legacy of privileging discourse and cognition in the shaping of cultural life.[18] Such pioneering anthropologists as Michelle Rosaldo, Catherine Lutz, and Lila Abu-Lughod treat emotion as a sociocultural construct, arguing that accepting emotion as discourse is a prerequisite for study (Abu-Lughod and Lutz 1990, 13). Their dedication to an ethical sense of cultural relativity and acceptance of diversity shifted attention from structures and functions to embodied experiences, despite privileging the symbolic properties of language and discourse in limiting ways. In methodological terms, language provides all of their privileged evidence, leaving physiology and nonsymbolic modes of expression unaddressed. For years my favorite definition of *emotion* has been Rosaldo's "embodied thoughts" (Rosaldo 1984, 143): short, succinct, and balanced. She integrated the physiological and the cognitive before it was cool. Many of the discursive approaches that she inspired in anthropology seemed to lose sight of the fact that emotions are felt in our minds and hearts as much as in our stomachs and skin (143).

Conversely, physiologists, biologists, and neuroscientists grounded in the heritage of Descartes, Darwin, and William James (Ahmed 2004, 5) prioritize the physiological and treat emotion as innate and universal; emotion is "wired-in" (Fosha 2000, 13). The neuroscientist Antonio Damasio (2010, 116) says that emotions are a product of evolution. These basic claims have become contentious in debates about science and the humanities. Nonetheless, neuroscience and a humanistic perspective are compatible (Becker 2004). Damasio provides a lucid model for exploring emotional experience that seems open to the role of culture, relativity, social relations, and diversity advocated by anthropologists (Damasio 2004; Perman 2010). Much of one's response to potentially emotional signs is rooted in habits of the self. That these habits can either be inherited, as Damasio suggests with his emphasis on evolution, or acquired, as anthropologists have long suggested, should actually facilitate a rapprochement between these potentially disparate paradigms, hence the musicologist Gary Tomlinson's emphasis on the feedback of biocultural evolution (2015).

Affect theorists have worked to fill the spaces exposed by this supposed opposition between language and the body by returning the body to the humanities and circumventing language. The history of affect theory is beyond the scope of this book, but if one thinks rhizomatically, it has multiple roots.

Grounded in part in Deleuze and Guattari (1987) and in the interpretive translations and extensions by Massumi (1987, 1995) and others, affect is often characterized in the literature by intensity and a focus on the body.

Neuroscience and affect theory both depend on physiology that somehow precedes the messiness of culture, consciousness, and cognition (Leys 2011); affect becomes "prepersonal (Massumi 1987, xvii), "presubjective" (Hofman 2015, 47), and "precognitive" (Martin 2013, 154). The affective has emerged as an intellectual rebuke to semiotic modes of interpretation since it is understood as "irreducibly bodily and autonomic" (Massumi 1995, 89). Whether framed as parallel to or autonomous from social signification (O'Sullivan 2001, 126; Massumi 1995), affects are heralded as a key to the code of human experience but work through their potential rather than their meaning (Stewart 2007, 3). The affective turn emerged, in part, to refute meaning-centric approaches and the "pernicious reign of signification" (Hemmings 2005, 554).

Affect is highly significant but carefully framed not to signify. It simply corresponds to movements from one bodily state to another (Massumi 1987, xvii). Deleuze (1978) goes so far as to define *affect* precisely as those thoughts that are *not* representations, a distinction that has been continually reiterated by Massumi (1995), Stewart (2007), and others. In these approaches affect becomes indexically associated with a series of descriptive terms, often culled from musical language, such as "intensity" (Massumi), "attunement" (Kockelman 2016, 52), and "resonance" (see Robin James's discussion of Jean-Luc Nancy in R. James 2012).[19]

Emotion and meaning are inextricably linked, as has been suggested by scholars from widely divergent disciplinary perspectives.[20] Based on years of research on musical practice and the role of meaning in such practice as an ethnomusicologist, I resist affect theory's disdain for and dismissal of meaning. Efforts to detach affect from a reliance on symbols, language, and discourse conflate meaning and discourse and separate affect from meaning itself, doubling down on the previously implicit binary between language and the body.

Affect became autonomous, somehow outside the social and the significant, as in the title of Massumi's famous piece "The Autonomy of Affect" (1995).[21] As Tomlinson (2016, 151) makes clear, Massumi's approach not only limits signification to the linguistic but also seems to eliminate agency as well, dissociating affect from consciousness. Biological determinism and the turn to neuroscience also leave little space for agency, purpose, culture, or meaning. Deacon (2012b) argues that scientific theories rooted in empiricism only grant heuristic importance to purpose, meaning, and value, privileging elements of experience that have physical correlates. He describes phenomena that relate to a telos or to something absent and immeasurable via physical evidence as *ententional* (27). More than one hundred years earlier, in 1903, Peirce (1998, 158) argued that "all nature abounds in proofs of other influences than merely mechanical action even in the physical world." Consciousness and emotion are thus rendered incomplete in scientific accounts. As with a neurophysiological focus on the body as the product of evolution, when meaning is enclosed as systemic and linguistic, vast realms of meaningful human experience are ignored and disappear.

As an ethnographer, I accept that ethnography comes with its own methodological blind spots, specifically with regard to the internal physiological components of emotional life. Attempts to measure something in the body of mediums, musicians, and other participants in a ceremony are overwhelmed not only by practical challenges but ethical ones, as well. Even if I could measure heart rates, hormone levels, or brain waves, not only am I unqualified to understand them fully but doing so would disrupt the experiences informing those physiological measures and complicate the already complex power dynamics that shape the relationship of ethnographer and informant.

But acknowledging the embodied dimension of emotional experience down to the molecular level does not necessitate quantitative physical data, especially if the contributions of neuroscience can be productively accommodated by the humanities, and vice versa. I want to retrieve the contributions of affect theory while returning meaning to the core of experience and follow the examples of Damasio, Becker, and others who integrate explanations of emotion that rely on both the physiological and the cognitive. Emotion involves everything that makes us human, including homeostasis, genetics, cultural habits, spirituality, parenting, and personal idiosyncrasies, far more than any one approach (including this one) can competently address. As the ontological turn shapes anthropological inquiry, nature and culture as oppositional categories are increasingly unstable (Descola 2013). Anthropologist Viveiros de Castro's (2004) multinaturalism extends the cultural relativist contributions of Lutz, Abu-Lughod, Rosaldo, and other anthropologists to destabilize the very categories with which neuroscience is concerned. He suggests that divisions between nature and culture should not be used as a basis of analysis without rigorous ethnographic interrogation (Viveiros de Castro 2005, 1). Rather than undermine the findings of neuroscience, this should open up scientific inquiry to the needs of ethnographic understanding. The organism that experiences emotion must be understood quite differently if the spirit of a long-dead warrior resides in its body.

My Model: The Sequence of Emotional Experience

I define emotions as processes of response to and appraisal of signs that signify objects of value and thus effect changes in the body and habits of the self. They are semiotic processes in which the affective dimension of semiosis is manifest in physiological change. In emotions, the self changes, even if temporarily. While grappling with performance during my fieldwork in Zimbabwe, I observed a four-step sequence in emotional experience that is grounded in the self and its place in the world: affect, emotion-appraisal, feeling, and emotive. Each step is a judgment, one perceptual, one physiological, one cultural, and one public. Each points to specific, definable moments of experience. As I use these terms, (1) *affect* is the emergent aspect of all experience that engages and initiates these processes. It is a ubiquitous feature of semiosis engaged with agency. (2) *Emotion-appraisal*, drawn from Damasio, is the specific embodied moment when stimuli (read: signs) are physiologically evaluated relative to purposes of thriving and surviving (Damasio 2003). (3) A *feeling* is one's awareness of these bodily appraisals. (4) An *emotive* is one's expression of the emotions that are felt (see figure 2.3). The sequence I outline here is grounded primarily in the neuroscientific theory of emotions and feelings offered by Damasio as seen through the lens of semiotic ethnography.

From the moment I asked Simango about mhongo spirits to the moment he disrupted the flow of that conversation, he went through a complex emotional experience of which I was only marginally aware. The emotive tip of expression was the only evidence of the iceberg of appraisal beneath the surface. Moving backwards through the sequence described above, saying "You know I have those spirits" was an emotive (step 4), a public expression of his feeling. In this case, I argue that it resolved the tension between ideal and expectation via acknowledgment. The feelings he expressed seemed to be those of anxiety, fear, and a cultural awareness of spiritual agency (step 3), caused by a physiological emotion-appraisal as the spirit within suggested imminent awakening (step 2). As he perceived my question and the complex personal and spiritual histories involved, his affect shaped the entire complex but fleeting moment (step 1). That affect remains ambiguous, difficult to put into words for me and for Simango. The emotion-appraisal, as a physiological response to that affect, is equally veiled to the strengths of ethnography; perhaps his heart rate quickened, maybe he sweat. But the feeling was apparent to him, and his emotive changed the habits of the self in that moment from anxiety to calm. Our conversation could continue.

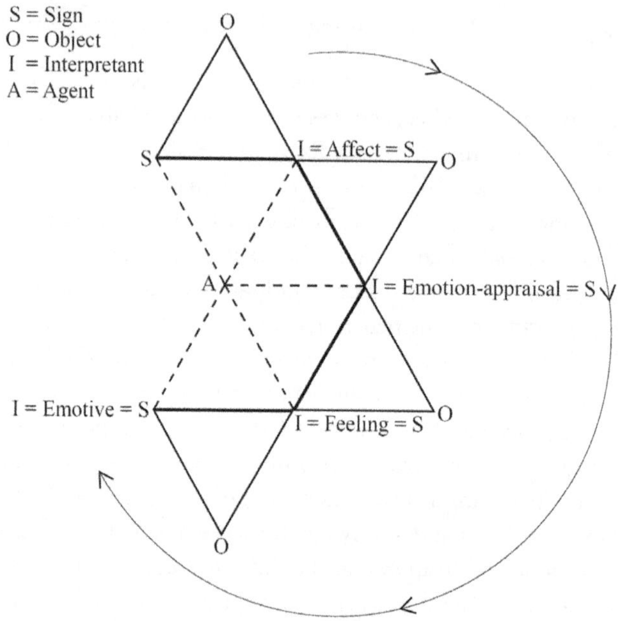

FIGURE 2.3. Four-step sequence of emotional experience

The roots of this approach extend to multiple practitioners of American Pragmatism: C. S. Peirce, William James, and John Dewey, whose conflict theory of emotion has faded from memory (Dewey 1894, 1895). Though constrained by the minimal knowledge of the brain at the time, Dewey's work remains productively compatible with Peircean semiotics, most contemporary anthropological theories of emotion, and recent neuroscientific explorations. Emotion, for Dewey, is intellectual, physiological, and purposeful; it is rooted in habits and values (1895, 15). He foreshadows the tension between dimensions of value that are central to emotional experience when he defines emotion as the tension of habit and ideal and the physiological changes that occur as this tension is resolved (30). Simango's struggle fits Dewey's definition perfectly. The pragmatic focus on what works, the intersection of habits and values, and an appreciation for the thoughtfulness of physiological processes can assign specificity to affect theory, linking attention to signs, habits, and values to the intensities of ubiquitous affect.

As with all semiotic processes, and Simango's, emotional experiences are sequential. Each step in this sequence is an interpretant of the previous step as a sign, and a sign of the next step as interpretant.[22] The key semiotic tool for opening affect to meaning and revealing the centrality of perception to emotion is the interpretant, the effect of a sign that binds that sign to its object.

A sign is perceived. If mind and body are rejoined in a post-Cartesian unity, this perception can happen in a number of affective ways: touching a hot stove, hearing an anticipated drum rhythm, feeling the snuff as it enters the sinuses, or listening to an ethnographer's question.[23] The body appraises the perceived sign-object connection and responds on the basis of habits of expectation and value rooted deep in the habitus of self. Tears may follow, perhaps adrenalin. This interpretant is emotion, or emotion-appraisal. As a sign, this emotion can be *felt* consciously. After feeling this emotion, the agent in question may feel moved to express it, to publicly reveal the emotion being felt, the emotive. I argue that Simango was a different person after he publicized his struggle; doing so calmed his anxiety and kept his spirit in a comfortable slumber.

No sequence need continue through all four steps. People don't always express their feelings, need not feel all of their emotions, or even have emotional appraisals of all affect. But if the intensity is there, if the self is affected and habits have changed, emotion seems inevitable.

STEP 1: AFFECT

The first step is affect,[24] a symbol I employ to characterize a ubiquitous element of all experience, of all semiosis. It identifies the initial moment of interpretation that potentially triggers all emotional life. *Affect,* from the Latin *affectus,* means "to act upon or be acted upon." Within semiosis, within the ongoing poietic response to signs via interpretants (effects), acting and being acted upon are ubiquitous. There are always variable degrees of intensity to one's encounter with the world. Indeed, this intensity can be what marks the boundaries of the self and the world or the other.

Affect is necessarily a physiological process, but it is also an act of perception, an act that brings us into relation with a sign whether we like it or not. Feelings, as perceived, remembered, or imagined, forcefully elbow out competitors (Short 2007, 77). In neuroscience, emotions are physiological processes that emerge from the ongoing regulation of life (Damasio 2003, 30–32). They are part of every experience (Deacon 2012b, 512). In certain schools of clinical psychology affect is pervasive, infusing everything we do (Fosha 2000, 4). These observations can be productively incorporated into a social theory of emotion by marking affect as a ubiquitous dimension of experience.

Affect theorists treat affect as intensity. For Stewart, "rogue intensities roam the streets of the ordinary" (2007, 44). As I argue, semiosis, experience, and emotions are all processes. Bodies and thoughts are implicated in every agent's act of sign making and interpretant making. Affect is a ubiquitous aspect of this process. To be human (or beyond, as Kohn urges) is to engage in semiosis affectively. Treating affect as ubiquitous frees the language of affect from its overlap with emotions and feelings, allowing each to helpfully signify a different aspect of emotional experience. If experiences are accepted as processual, then structures, states (Massumi 1987; Hemmings 2005), and "orders of representation" (Stewart 2007) are misleading. If affect is ubiquitous, with ever-present shifts in intensity, "bodily states" no longer exist;[25] they are an illusion.

By employing affect to identify that characteristic of semiotic consciousness in which "I" am involved in confronting the signs of the world and of others with varying degrees of intensity, Massumi's understanding of affects as intensities regains relevance. When awake, when interpreting signs, agents are always acting and being acted upon. Nothing stands still long enough to be fully structured. Deleuze and Guattari's definition of affects as becomings thus emphasizes the processual nature of experience, recalling Raymond Williams's (1977, 129) lesson that reducing the social to fixed forms is wrong. Semiosis is affective. It is an ongoing process undertaken by interpreters as agents who are constantly implicated in the signs being interpreted, and, as organisms in the world, respond with varying degrees of intensity, from dormancy to ecstasy. Semiotics and the Peircean phenomenology within which it should be understood open up the definition of meaning in such a way that agency returns to affect and clarifies the ways in which the physiological is made meaningful. Within purposeful, poietic processes of semiosis, emotion and meaning are linked.

Affect is the interpretant of a sign. Interpretants within the minds and bodies of beings with agency, including people, spirits, and many other organisms, *always* have an element of affect.[26] Every interpretant is affective. Signs do not require deliberation in order to elicit response, but interpretants do modify consciousness (Peirce 1998, 412). One could argue that this is precisely the role that emotional experience plays in life. Perception is not a choice, and it can elicit responses of wide-ranging intensity. Affect, itself meaningful, distinguishes semiotic thirdness from other forms of ontological thirdness such as thermodynamics or chemical reactions. If intense enough, affect becomes the sign of an emotion.

STEP 2: EMOTION-APPRAISAL

My understanding of emotion-appraisal as a step in the sequence of emotional experience is based on Damasio (2003, 2004, 2010). He, however, simply uses *emotion* (Damasio 2010, 116). I use *emotion-appraisal* solely to distinguish the specificity of this narrow understanding from the colloquial use of *emotion* that variably covers affect, emotion, or feeling. His work is based on that of William James, who famously said that the bodily change that follows from perception is emotion itself (1884, 189–190).[27]

Damasio distinguishes between emotions and feelings as processes within the same sequence of experience. For him emotions are unlearned, automated, physiological responses to stimuli rooted in evolution and genetics (Damasio 2010); they form the most complex piece (aside from feelings) in what Damasio (2003, 31) calls the "homeostasis machine." They regulate life. Multinaturalist anthropologists might question some of the assumptions concerning the uniformity of nature that inform these basic claims, and evolutionary theorists might argue that evolutionary habits like emotion are learned over the generations in processes of biocultural evolution. Yet Damasio's emphasis on emotions as the physiological responses to signs that involve the self and its regulation seems compatible with ethnographic approaches to emotional experience.[28]

Apart from the science behind it, which I am unqualified to critique, there are three reasons why Damasio's approach is useful. First, it emphasizes the body and physiology without excluding cultural and personal influences on these processes. As explained above, after years of humanistic research on the emotions that privileged language and discourse, this is significant. Although culture could be more explicitly accommodated, there is room in his theory for cultural, perspectival, or neuro-diversity.

Second, although Damasio does not rely on semiotics or comparable theories of signs or meaning, his explanation of emotions seems to be built on similar principles. He approaches emotions as responses to stimuli as they are processed in the brain (Damasio 2010, 117–18), suggesting that emotional experience is sequential: a stimulus (or a sign) impacts habits and values of the self, whether based on evolution, culture, or otherwise, and triggers a physiological response.[29] The body *appraises* the sign.[30] The stimuli that trigger emotions can be effectively renamed as signs representing objects perceived in interpretants. Dimensions of value allow agents to evaluate how the objects signified by signs impact survival and flourishing. These pre-conscious and autonomic physiological processes are rooted in homeostasis and flourishing. Martha Nussbaum embraces the concept of flourishing to define emotions as "appraisals or value judgments of signs that have varying levels of importance to one's own flourishing" (2001, 4). Values shape emotions; emotions shape the self and its capacity to thrive.

Third, I value Damasio's approach because it affords a means to study emotion without expecting it to explain everything. Ethnographers have little to say about the role of the amygdala but a great deal to offer about the ways in which emotional life is understood and experienced. This is where feelings enter.

STEP 3: FEELING

The act of feeling emotions more directly reflects cultural, personal, and social influence on these seemingly autonomic processes. Damasio identifies feelings as the private awareness of emotion-appraisals. As he so succinctly put it, fruit flies have emotions, but they don't feel them (2003, 42). Feelings, for him, are tied to a perception of one's bodily state and cognitive change based on the triggering objects (2010, 124). In other words, feelings are interpretants of the sign-object relationships signified in emotions.

Agents *feel* the tension between habit's expectations and the ideal, the conflict between the possible or the actual, or another dimension of value. While seemingly instinctive (James 1884), importance and its valuation are based on habits (Dewey 1895, 19–20). For Dewey, value is the projection of emotional importance (19). Importance generates emotional appraisal and experience for Dewey, James, Nussbaum, Damasio, and myself. While evolution might "concoct" the specific physiological dynamics of emotion-appraisal, we learn what to value through experience, socialization, and practice.

The Ndau word for feeling, *kuzwa*, can also mean "to understand."[31] Within it, there is a clarity of awareness that feeling reflects a certain understanding of the state of the world and one's place in it. Feelings contribute to the "changes in the body and habits of the self" that are central to my definition of emotion.

STEP 4: EMOTIVE

The final step is the emotive. The term was coined by the anthropological historian of emotion William Reddy (2001). It is one possible interpretant to the feeling as a sign. For Reddy, emotives are exploratory and self-altering (128). Emotives extend J. L. Austin's definition of performatives as speech acts that describe something, change the world, and alter the self (Reddy 2001, 128).[32] While Reddy continues Austin's emphasis by privileging linguistic expressions, Richard Wolf (2001, 413) has rightly pointed out that nonlinguistic expressions such as music and dance can and do alter the self during emotional experiences.

Language is not always ideally equipped to help people experience their emotions, express them, or deal with them afterward. Even tears can become thoughtful and emotive. For the ethnomusicologist Steven Feld (1990), Kaluli displays of ritual wailing in Papua New Guinea are "wept thoughts." Musicking has long been understood as tightly bound to emotional experience.[33] Whether music imitates, expresses, arouses, or induces, to use the four modes of connection outlined by Higgins (2012), musicking is deeply integrated into learned modes of emoting in socially, culturally, personally, and biologically appropriate and sustainable ways. Within musicking, emotions become the objects represented in sound (as Higgins's imitations or expressions) but also the interpretants of musical signs (as Higgins's arousals and inducements). There is no singular relationship between them.

This model is a tool. It provides a way to acknowledge and integrate multiple disciplinary approaches to the problems posed by emotional experience and ground them in multiple methodologies. I rely on ethnography, but the openness of the model should accommodate other approaches as well. Signs initiate complex processes of perception, interpretation, and experience that both distinguish self from other and integrate self with other. Emotion-appraisals bring the sensory material of the world in touch with habits and values of the self grounded in evolution, community, and culture. People feel these emotions as learned and may choose to express them. Emotive expressions, whether in language, music, dance, or otherwise, are the effects of emotional experience; they are the interpretants to feelings of emotions. They then become signs themselves in new semiotic chains, meaningfully connecting these emotions to whatever happens next, purposefully and often collectively. In events such as the madhlozi ceremony of rural Chipinge, emotives are public ways to engage with the emotional experience of life and the circumstances that shape the signs triggering those emotions in the first place. Histories of social encounter and spiritual activity intersect with the struggles of community and purposeful life to shape the affective dimension of experience.

PART II

Ceremony at Horus Farm

CHAPTER 3

Late Afternoon

Madzviti *and the Foundation of Interpretation*

Ndasvika . . . ndasvika pano ngenyaya yeZulu.
I have arrived . . . I have arrived because of the Zulu.
—Ndau translation of a song for the madzviti spirits

He [the dzviti] takes the spear and says, No, you are silly. You want one thing, death.
—Mpande Chikumbo

The Madzviti at Horus Farm

On July 2, 2005, I arrived at the home of Davison Masiza Muyambo at about 2:30 in the afternoon. Born in 1946, VaMasiza was a poor farmer living on resettled land claimed from Holland Farm (about twenty kilometers south of Chipinge) during the chaos of fast-track land reform a few years earlier. Like his neighbors, he did a little bit of everything on the farm, primarily growing maize but also raising cattle, goats, and chickens and tending a sizable garden cared for by his wife Serena, or Mai Masiza. He was a sought-after, skilled, and energetic ceremonial drummer and an entertaining, hard-drinking mbira player.[1]

VaMasiza's presence was always welcome when people gathered to drink as he productively traded mbira songs for *sope* moonshine. Born near Muzite in Mozambique, Masiza moved to colonial Southern Rhodesia as a young man and led a life typical of many Ndau men his age. In a common Ndau rite of passage, he moved to South Africa seven times between 1959 and 1967 to work as a foreman in a mine. While there, he became an accomplished mbira player. For decades, Ndau men's gravitational pull has been south to Johannesburg for its work opportunities in ways that Harare and the urban centers of Rhodesia and Zimbabwe rarely have been. As he aged and shifted his energies from mining to farming Masiza settled in Zimbabwe, raised eleven children with Serena (he also had four from a previous marriage), and put his musical skills to work during madhlozi ceremonies (in particular, zvipunha and mhongo drumming). Although I was first introduced to him because of his expertise on the mbira, his insight into ceremonies and his skill as a drummer, so central to local people's relationships with spirits, became a formative influence on my research.

On this day he'd invited me to accompany his family to a ceremony hosted by a distant neighbor and longtime acquaintance on another newly resettled farm to the west. He did this for several reasons. Mainly, he was a kind and generous man who had become a friend and guided my research. He also embraced his unexpected new identity as my mbira teacher and enjoyed the responsibility of directing my education in local musical life. The notoriety that bringing his student, a muyungu, would generate was fun for him as well, as evidenced by his request that I bring with me not the familiar Ndau mbira that I studied with him but the Shona mbira, the *mbira dzavadzimu*, which was almost as foreign to these rural Ndau-speaking communities (who only heard it on the radio) as it was to my own students in Iowa (though not quite).

He had also invited me in order to appease the local headman, a ZANU-PF appointee who had heard the rumors of my presence. Zimbabwe was nearing a political and economic nadir at this time. The greater Chipinge district, in which Masiza lived and which had resisted President Robert Mugabe's authority since before the country achieved independence, was the latest site of engagement in expanding ZANU-PF's control. Earlier in the year, Masiza had been summoned and scolded by the headman because of rumors that he'd been spending time with a muyungu and, more important, because he hadn't introduced me.[2] Masiza rightly felt that he should bring me in order to prove that it wasn't a secret, to prove that I really was interested in music, and to alleviate any suspicion that Masiza himself was up to something inappropriate from the perspective of the local ZANU-PF authorities. It also didn't hurt that I had a car. The four-kilometer journey was far more relaxing in the passenger seat of my comically small Toyota Starlet than it would be on foot, even if it wasn't much faster.

So VaMasiza, Mai Masiza, and I set off into the hills of Chipinge in my made-for-city-streets hatchback. There were no real roads. For many resettlement schemes, land was all there was. Social services were rare, with no infrastructure for access to clean water or healthcare (Maposa, Hlongwana, and Gamira 2010, 197). So we inched along cow paths and trails, crawling over long-dried furrows containing the brittle remains of harvested maize at a walking pace before parking next to some loitering cattle in the field at our host's homestead. The welcome we received was warm, familiar, and instantaneous. Almost one hundred people were divided loosely into groups of adult men, adult women, younger men, young women, and children in perpetual motion. Men gathered around one fire across the central space from the ceremonial house, while women were gathered around another fire near the kitchen. The madhlozi ceremony's purpose—one part religious ritual, one part block party, and one part reunion—reliably generated a festive, joyous mood.

Our departure had been delayed and our bumpy ride had been slow, so it was almost 4 o'clock in the afternoon when we arrived to the sounds of *makandira* frame drums, makosho gourd rattles, hand clapping, and voices. The sun was starting its descent to the west and the ceremony had already begun. Based on past experience, I understood the sounds as those of the madzviti. Several men and one woman, dressed in cowtail skirts and red fabric and carrying spears, were wandering about, punctuating the dusk with screams: the madzviti.

We quickly lost Mai Masiza in the sea of women working tirelessly to keep the ceremony running. After being scolded for distracting people with mbira music, Masiza ushered me into the central ceremonial roundhouse where people were working hard to bring the remaining madzviti. The women who scolded us here understood that semiosis is related to attention. Interpretants can be considered as a change in one's attention (Kockelman 2015). Agency as a form of intentional interpretant making requires attention, and they were right to admonish us for pulling people's attention from the tasks at hand.

The dark space we entered was organized casually but carefully along axes of age and gender, shared habits of organization so embedded within people's learned tendencies and expectations that no one really thought about it. Peirce characterizes this kind of habit as a law, a legisign that is general and conventional (Peirce 1998, 314). I was one of several men, most much older than I, seated along the bench against the wall. Younger men sat on the floor in front of us, legs outstretched. The few boys in the room took whatever space they could find, constantly shuttling from one spot to the next as men with seniority claimed the space for themselves. The women sat along the opposite side of the room on reed mats and blankets on the floor.

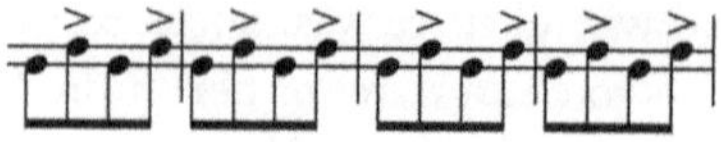

FIGURE 3.1. Basic madzviti rhythm

Madzviti performance ideally includes multiple makandira frame drums, several makosho players, hand clapping (*maoko*), and singing (*kuimba*). Multiple people, usually women, play rhythms specific to the madzviti on makandira of different sizes. Each ceremony includes multiple pieces called *ngoma*, with some lasting twenty minutes or more and others lasting just over a minute. In the roundhouse six women stood to the side holding makandira in their left hands. The layered texture of duple rhythms provides the familiar sounds that these spirits brought with them from the south in the nineteenth century (see figure 3.1). Other women accompanied the drumming with duple patterns on the makosho rattles and dense call-and-response vocal patterns sung to the invited spirits.

In the center were several male and female mediums dressed as madzviti. Given our late arrival, it wasn't long before the remaining madzviti arrived in their host mediums, who were dancing in the center of the room. Each medium shouted in a pent-up grunt (*kugaudza*) and danced with renewed fervor as the spirit awakened. The exact moment when consciousness shifted from medium to spirit was difficult to determine, a threshold crossed with obvious struggle accompanied by apparent inevitability. The madzviti did everything with aggression and purpose. They greeted each other like aggressive old friends, shaking hands with arms extended straight, thrusting their combined fists above their heads with one grunt and down toward their knees with another. Once they'd all arrived, everyone followed the drums and spirits out to the yard so the madzviti could dance.

Objects: Semiosis and Experience

Rituals such as this rely on and reinforce habits that form the core conventions of a spiritual and musical habitus. Good habits develop from good ritual practice. In many ways, the spirits we encountered during the ceremony had arrived more than one hundred years ago. This interaction was the latest in a series of encounters that have profoundly shaped local life and experience. Their meaning depends on the histories, encounters, expectations, and desires that shaped the spirits' emergence and are shaped by their presence. The multiple sign-object relations grounded in experience and habit triggered the events that followed in a chain reaction of semiosis. Musicking facilitates the relations between the living and the dead as much as it does those between the present and the past. Meaning resides in the relationships that musicking establishes where it takes place (Small 1998, 13).

OBJECTS OF SIGNS

When I first heard a definition of tradition that actually made me think about what tradition might be, positively or negatively, Ed Bruner was standing on a seminar table at the University of Illinois. If memory serves, he defined *tradition* as "the memory of how people did something the last time." Ceremonial practice often hinges on this type of tradition. Each iteration is an effort to resemble past iterations. As habits form, regularity generates consistency. At Horus Farms, one person would often ask another how they did it last time. Much of what has already happened is resignified in the present, literally re-presented. In this sense, signs are the interpretants of earlier signs of similar objects. Spirits are imbued with the histories of their own lives as they hear their invitation and possess their mediums, possessed by history and possessed by purpose.

The ceremonial signs of madzviti spirits depend on the histories that led to their arrival and the goals, purposes, and desires that inform people's involvement and participation. A semiotic object is that which is represented by a sign. Objects lead to signs, but signs are the gateway to the represented, just as the words in this paragraph reach you before the objects they represent do. Smoke wouldn't indicate fire if the fire hadn't been there to generate the smoke. Smoke doesn't cause fire; fire causes smoke and is interpreted as such. A medium can't resemble a spirit, unless the object of the sign, the idea of the spirit, already exists in the mind of the perceiver. In order for a sign to have an effect and generate an interpretant, it must represent something else. Conversely, in order for a sign to represent something else it must have an effect, and the sign must also represent that something else to someone in some way. Objects need signs, interpretants, and agents that connect to them in order to operate as such. Objects determine signs; signs determine interpretants; interpretants bind the sign to its object. Something perceived (sign) represents something else (the object), which has an effect (the interpretant) to someone (an agent).

The way a sign relates to its object is related to the way a sign relates to its effect (Kockelman 2005). Objects precede signs in the world, but signs precede objects in the mind; a sign can only represent a specific object as it is interpreted. The effect of a sign reveals its connection to an object. Each semiotic component—sign, object, and interpretant—is of equal importance and necessity. For Peirce, "the triadic relation is *genuine*, that is[,] its three members are bound together by it in a way that does not consist in any complexus of dyadic relations" (1955, 100). Reality, from the point of view of the Ndau practitioners of the ceremony described here, is not the post-structural manifestation of semiotic play but, rather, the cause and ground of representation.

Peirce distinguishes between the immediate object and the dynamic object in order to help with the slippery sequence between sign and object. Immediate objects come from signs; signs come from dynamic objects. Immediate objects are the objects only as they are represented by signs, usually incompletely (Short 2007, 196). The dynamic object is the "real object" (Peirce 1998, 409), or the mediate object (480), to make its distinction from the immediate more explicit. A grunt by a medium is heard by most people as an index of an awakening spirit, but it represents this awakening in a limited capacity. All that is known from the sign, all that is represented by that solitary grunt, is the effort of awakening. The immediate object is that effort of the awakening spirit, shaped by experiences with spirits. Later, after other signs cue the awakening spirit in other limited capacities, attendees will recognize the specific dzviti spirit that was awakened as real. The first object, the immediate object, is contained within the sign. The second, the dynamic object, is outside the sign, and acquaintance with it comes from experience (480). That initial grunt hints at the eventual recognition of the spirit. The sign will be interpreted as successfully representing the spirit hinted at by the grunt over time, as the immediate and dynamic objects are understood to be one and the same. The spirit is the real object.

Because of the associations that people have with their spirits, the fear that these associations can induce, and the evidence of the spirits' strength and short tempers, encounters with the madzviti can be emotional. But one has to see them, hear them, and feel them in order for that to happen. Affect always emerges via signs within a context of what is already known, including past perceptions, expectations, and motivations. Each sign is perceived along a chain of semiosis. In this case, through the sights and sounds of the madzviti performance, locals encounter multiple pasts that are ceremonial, social, personal, and historical. This is the ground of semiosis and of the experiences to unfold. The makandira drums at Horus sounded similar to the drums heard at previous events. They also sound similar to the drums used by soldiers in the Gaza State. Two histories are represented, one of ceremonial practice and one of Gaza Nguni authority. Similarly, the skirt I saw on the spirits as I arrived looked like those worn by madzviti spirits at previous ceremonies, as well as by the soldiers these spirits were when they were alive. Past relationships between signs and objects inform the interpretation to follow. But the object signified is not necessarily general, fixed, arbitrary, or predictable. Things change, meanings shift, and the unexpected is always a possibility.

When things go well, spirits suddenly share the same space and time with the living participants. Actors from more than a century ago are present, acting of their own accord, alive. Locals from the twenty-first century share the here and now with locals from the nineteenth century. What was, in one moment, a historical object mediated through partial representations is now an interpreting agent. In madzviti possession, the past comes to life.

CEREMONIAL OBJECTS: SIGNS OF HISTORY, SIGNS OF PURPOSE

Among the numerous possible objects in play, I focus on two general categories tied to the dead and the living: the historical and the purposeful (or teleological).[3] Historical objects are represented in speech, stories, books, artifacts, names, social and political organization, and so on but are also directly embodied in the spirits themselves and emerge from their original lives. Madzviti spirits lived as Gaza Nguni soldiers when the Gaza State ruled Ndau territories. This history is central to the transformation of the madzviti from soldier to spirit, from living to dead. Lambek argues that spirits such as this carry the weight of the past with them (Lambek 2002). The arrival of spirits is a historical act and an interpretation of past moments that intersects with historically weighted responses of other interpreting participants (Lambek 2016, 318). The past joins the present (Chakrabarty 2000). Spirits and mediums possess and are possessed by history.

Whether this history is exactly what happened or not, these are the objects that are understood and represented in the signs of performance. Spirits are signs of their past lives (Alonso 1988). A tension emerges between events as they are understood to exist outside of representation (the dynamic objects) and their ever-evolving representation (as immediate objects), which can modify the history that is represented. By encountering and engaging with agents from distant times through the interactions of the madhlozi ceremony, locals may redefine how those objects of history, as represented in the spirits of today, are understood and *felt*.

But ceremonies do not exist primarily to be living history lessons. That is not their purpose, and interpretation presupposes purpose (Short 2007, 189).

Purpose, motivation, and desire are the dynamic objects that compel Ndau communities to engage with madzviti spirits and compel spirits to return the favor. The ceremonial signs are initiated, uttered, and performed with purpose that defines the manner in which they are eventually interpreted. People play, dance, take snuff (forya), wear regalia, talk with n'anga, and brew beer with purpose. They are the means that locals select in order to satisfy certain ends. People want to invite their spirits and communicate that invitation musically.

Likewise, spirits want to be invited; they need their mediums' bodies in order to dance. Both communities are motivated to act. The affect of this motivation can vary considerably depending on the circumstances. It can be celebratory, fearful, or obligatory. Ceremonies are a means to these compatible ends, but ceremonial experience is also an end in itself. Both the meaning and the emotional experience of ceremonial performance are defined by desire and purpose and the ways in which these are realized through ceremonial action.

INTERPRETATION AND CONTEXT

Kohn presents context as an effect of the symbolic (2013, 38). The primary context in which semiosis takes place is one of purposefulness (Short 2007, 158). Chikumbo says, "The madzviti want to dance." These disparate assertions may seem irreconcilable within spirit possession ceremonies, when so much that matters remains unsaid (Masquelier 2001, 5). It is likely impossible to know who the madzviti are without employing the generality of language in conversation. The systems within which language functions as such provide essential contexts in which interpretation occurs. But nonsymbolic semiotic processes also shape the contexts of semiotic encounters. Context is not *solely* the effect of the symbolic. I join other ethnomusicologists in arguing that one of the strengths of music rests in its ability to engage people with one another, with the dead, and with their history (Emoff 2002; Friedson 2009; Jankowsky 2010). Musicking shapes the moment-to-moment reality of experience in real ways that can coalesce with external social and spiritual contexts, even before language and the symbolic.[4]

The interpreting agent is essential to semiosis and its analysis. Signs only operate when a mind perceives them as such. In semiotic terms, a mind is capable of making an interpretant with purpose. Not all interpretants are made with purpose, but the capacity is there. In this way, I hope to deny agency to rocks, lawnmowers, and bacteria while opening it up to spirits and animals. A mind is capable of semiosis. In the madhlozi ceremony there are two categories of perceiver: people and spirits. They engage with one another in projects of mutual interest and compatibility to ensure the success of the ceremonies, but their means and ends, though connected, can be quite different. Desires and motivations, so central to the processes of semiotic engagement at the heart of ceremonial life, emerge from distinct subject positions. Agents act with purpose in the making of interpretants. At Horus Farm, the signs perceived (heard, seen, smelled, tasted, felt, and imagined) are themselves the effects (the interpretants) of historical events and recollections of past ceremonies, as well as social and personal semiotic encounters, habits, and expectations. Key ceremonial moments are rooted in these habits, histories, and purposes.

History and Madzviti

Sometime around 1817, Chief Zwide kaLanga and his Ndwandwe army captured and killed Chief Dingiswayo of the powerful Mthethwa Kingdom just south of present-day Eswatini (Eldredge 2015, 183). From one perspective, this aggression initiated a chain of events that led to my watching madzviti dance on resettled land in rural Zimbabwe almost two hundred years later. From another perspective, it might be more important that when Zwide's army attacked the Zulu Kingdom in 1821,[5] the young Zulu king Shaka kaSenzangakhona outsmarted and defeated Zwide (Liesegang 1983, 179), consolidating his control over the region now known as KwaZulu-Natal (Eldredge 2015, 183). Perhaps the arrival of the Portuguese, the British, the Afrikaners, and the Griqua, with their demands for slaves horrifically disrupting the balance of power in southeastern Africa, is the key (Harries 1983; Cobbing 1988). In the midst of these power struggles the Ndwandwe army split into multiple factions; three generals, Zwangendaba, Nxaba, and Soshangane, each took armies into Mozambique to establish their own fortunes and kingdoms (Etherington 2013). Whether focusing on Europeans, Shaka, or the Ndwandwe, isolating an origin or an explanation can say as much about the purpose for which history is being told as it does the events described.[6]

As a native English speaker trained in the United States, this framing of past events as a history that shapes the present makes perfect sense, but within Ndau epistemologies it is less simplistic. There is no perfect translation for the word *history*; the closest ones are *nyaya* (story) and *nhoroondo* (narrative). Tendai Chitopo and Moses Zharikira, teachers from the local primary school who helped me with translation, always requested *nhoroondo* when I interviewed Muzite elders about local history. But nhoroondo needn't be detailed or particularly significant. It benefits from a lack of discursive and epistemological weight, which can be advantageous when trying to avoid the teleological pitfalls of historicism (Comaroff and Comaroff 1992).

The times and places that madzviti spirits embody are not mere remnants of an earlier age; they are not anachronisms lingering in the present because of custom (Chakrabarty 2000). Rather, these legacies and long-dead actors are vibrant contributors to the present. In the Ndau cosmos, every represented era is relevant for both present and future. Historical imagining, an understanding of the present in relation to multiple pasts, is understood and developed largely through performance. In the context of rural Ndau communities, one bereft of texts, the most powerful connection the living have with their predecessors and the events concerning their ancestors is through ceremonial performances. The ethnomusicology of history offers a useful perspective on the making of history by showing how performances like this *are* history for the practitioners involved; the past is always present. Despite the lives they led in distant moments, spirits remain active and constitutive forces in the present.

History books about the nineteenth century in southern Africa were largely shaped by Europeans and their students. Treating the past as a series of momentous events tends to frame the present as an organic and coherent entity that can be explained by the events that preceded it (Chakrabarty 2000, 23). This kind of history is a product of the discourse of modernity (Chakrabarty 2000; Scott 1999). For people operating from a modernist perspective, history's teleological and progressive march requires a configuring of the past in a way that bolsters the present.[7]

GAZA NGUNI AND THE NDAU

The arrival of the Gaza Nguni was pivotal in shaping a distinct Ndau identity in Zimbabwe and Mozambique and paved the way for the madzviti's important spiritual role. The rise of the Zulu Kingdom to the south drove Soshangane and his Gaza Nguni soldiers north into Mozambique and Zimbabwe. Local Ndau chiefs wrestled for authority with the Gaza Nguni invaders as the two communities intermingled for almost a century. The soldiers who lived and died in Chipinge and who now return as madzviti via possession are descendants of the political instability to the south at the beginning of the nineteenth century.

Soshangane's Gaza was not the first Nguni army to arrive in eastern Zimbabwe, but it was certainly the most influential.[8] He kept the capital of the Gaza Nguni Kingdom on the Mzilizwi River near Mt. Selinda from 1836 until 1839 (Rennie 1978, 258; MacGonagle 2007, 95), before returning to the Limpopo River near present-day Manjacaze in Mozambique (Liesegang 1983, 181).[9] After Soshangane's death in 1858 a civil war broke out between his two sons Mawewe and Mzila (Liesegang 1983, 180). When Mawewe retired to Swaziland, Mzila became Soshangane's successor and returned the capital to the Ndau heartland from 1862 until 1889.[10] Mzila's son Ngungunyane (also spelled Ngungunyana or Gungunyane) took over in 1885, but the Scramble for Africa had already started by the time Ngungunyane came to power, and the Gaza State faced increasing pressure from the Portuguese to the east (Ndlovu-Gatsheni 2016, 7).[11] He moved the capital one last time back to its southern location near the Limpopo River in 1889 (Liesegang 1983, 179–81) before competing negotiations between Portuguese and British ambitions led to his capture and eventual exile in the Azores (Wheeler 1968, 600). Gaza authority was quickly replaced by the overt colonial rule of the Portuguese on one side and the British on the other of the newly drawn boundary,[12] but their legacy obviously continues in multiple ways.

The migration of the Gaza Nguni into southeastern Zimbabwe, their political domination over area residents, and their eventual integration within these nascent Ndau communities helped distinguish the Ndau from their Shona-speaking neighbors. Soshangane's move to the Chipinge highlands in 1836 and the increasing influence of the Portuguese in Mozambique combined to undermine the authority of the Monomutapa State, paving the way for Gaza Nguni dominance in Ndau-speaking Zimbabwe during most of the nineteenth century (Rennie 1978, 271). From 1828 to 1889 the Swazi and Zulu soldiers in the Gaza Nguni army resided in what is now Chipinge and permanently shaped Ndau language, identity, political organization, performative modes of expression, and cosmology.

Although MacGonagle (2007, 91–105) makes the cruelty of the Gaza Nguni clear and ably demonstrates locals' fear of their rule, Ndau responses and levels of cooperation were also somewhat strategic, self-determined, and varied; some men became Nguni soldiers, whereas others remained independent (Rennie 1985). Local men began piercing their ears after the Nguni came to power. The meaning of this piercing shifted from being an index of subjugation and assimilation into Nguni society to being an index of Ndau distinction and difference from other communities, such as those west of the Save River, who had never been under Nguni authority (see MacGonagle 2007, 102). Vhukani Muzite, the former Muzite headman, referred to it as a sign of being conquered. During our conversation he grabbed his earlobe and said, "This was an identity card," acknowledging acquiescence to Nguni rule and assimilation into Nguni society, although it ended long before he was born. Men like Hlatywayo Matakura and Matabuka discussed this period with undisguised pride in the Ndau history of interaction with the Gaza Nguni. The historian David Beach (1984, 56) goes so far as to suggest that the opportunities offered by the Gaza Nguni were attractive to young Ndau men eager to join their ranks.

Ndau identity, particularly in the highlands, where the Gaza capital was frequently based, is defined by this experience. However traumatic the Gaza occupation may have been (see MacGonagle 2007, 2008), it contributed a sense of distinction to Ndau communities that otherwise feel detached from Zimbabwe's Shona majority.

The word *Ndau* itself was a Gaza Nguni nickname (MacGonagle 2008, 37) for subjects of the Mutema chieftaincy in the heartland of the Ndau region (Rennie 1978).[13] Local surnames reflect the totems that accompanied the Gaza. Muchongoyo, the most common Ndau dance used to perform pride in one's community at the local and national levels, is modeled explicitly on Gaza military dancing. MacGonagle (2008, 46) argues that assimilation to the Gaza State is what made Ndau men feel Ndau.[14]

MADZVITI SPIRITS (THE DEAD)

Pileni Dube, shown in figure 3.2, was possessed by his dzviti spirit at a ceremony at Samson Mapfumo's house in Muzite, within sight of the Mozambique border. This image captures a poignant moment for me in that it was the first time a dzviti greeted me directly. They were typically uninterested in, perhaps even unaware of, my presence. I can't include a photo like this from Horus Farm because those madzviti spirits ignored me completely. These spirits tie the broader Ndau community to the histories of encounter that led to this moment, when a twenty-first-century community invited spirits from an occupying military force willingly and joyfully.

Enos Simango explained that "Shaka the Zulu's soldiers were called dzviti. They were big soldiers, generals. Some of those soldiers died in war in the wilderness. Their spirits would rise in the wild and we call those spirits dzviti." Terminology is confusing because people often use *Zulu* to refer to Gaza, something MacGonagle (2008, 40) noticed as well. Nineteenth-century identity terms are often replaced with their twentieth-century counterparts, and so *Ndwandwe* becomes *Swazi*, *Sotho*, or *Ndebele*, and *Gaza* becomes *Zulu*.

Soshangane incorporated people into his lineage as he consolidated power (Etherington 2013, 117). Because the Gaza Nguni army included soldiers from multiple backgrounds who joined (under coercion or not) at different points along the way, there are various types of madzviti spirit. Chikumbo named three main categories: *zanzi* (high Zulu, the elites of the Gaza army), *endhla* (Swazi and Sotho soldiers recruited along Soshangane's northward route), and

FIGURE 3.2. Pileni Dube's dzviti spirit

hole (indigenous Ndau soldiers recruited or coerced into the army). He also mentioned a group called *ngwaningwani* that "originate from the Ngwane tribe from Swaziland." Similarly, Matabuka said, "The ones on top are Zulu, followed by Swazi, and then Ndebele." These categories are hierarchical, with distance from a Zulu center determining one's position. Zulu spirits are the most powerful, followed by the endhla spirits, the Ndebele (in Matabuka's list), and hole indigenous recruits.

These distinctions don't always seem to matter. Pileni Dube claimed that "MaSwazi ne MaZulu, the same, neMandebele, the same." When interviewed in Chikore, Freddy Sithole agreed, saying, "Shangani, Zulu, and Ndebele are one and the same thing" (quoted in MacGonagle 2008, 40). Matabuka even said, "The Zulu spirit speaks Ndebele." In my conversation with Dube and Matabuka, the names *Zulu*, *Swazi*, and *Ndebele* were used almost interchangeably. *Gaza*, as a label, was never used.[15]

Matabuka and Dube identified madzviti and Gaza soldiers with Swazi.[16] Hlatywayo said, "Those madzviti were Swazi."[17] Chief Rodwell Muzite agreed, saying, "The spirits come from Swaziland [Eswatini]. . . . So they say, We come from Swaziland, they say, We are Swazi."[18] Given the fluidity of nineteenth-century political allegiances and corresponding identity frameworks, this is not surprising. Many of the identity terms heard in contemporary South Africa,

Eswatini, Mozambique, and Zimbabwe emerged from the volatility of the nineteenth century (including "ethnic" labels such as Shona, Ndau, Danda, Tsonga, and Shangaan).

Though they are dead, the madzviti are dangerous, and murders among the living are often attributed to angry and meddlesome madzviti spirits. Enos Simango told me, "'The Dzviti' means 'the destroyers,' the likes of Soshangane's people." Chikumbo said bluntly, "He kills; he has no time to waste. . . . They've got some people who have been arrested several times when his dzviti, when he is possessed by his dzviti, they kill." The police might come to arrest someone for murder who is told, in Chikumbo's words, "Yes, you see that person who is covered by the red blanket? It is you, when your dzviti came he struck him dead for being a witch or for being a prostitute." Not even dreams are free of their influence, Chikumbo continued: "The dzviti will be coming persistently with spear in hand in your dream to kill you and you won't even remember that he is lying to you because his spirit can no longer hold a spear, but he is coming intimidating and threatening and you think, Really he is coming to kill me, and you find yourself at the in-laws and say, No, I have come to pay lobola."[19] In these ways the madzviti use the threat of violence to encourage moral behavior.

Mudiwa, a n'anga from Buffelsdrift, said "They're crazy" even as he hung their makandira drums in his home to buttress his healing practice. Another n'anga from Chipinge, Joseph Mutwanha, told me, "What is called dzviti now is a soldier, a real soldier. These soldiers are the madzviti because that is what we call a killer." Chikumbo said,

> *Dzviti* means someone who takes over things which do not belong to him. . . . The madzviti were saying, "This is our territory but we want to take over cattle, we want to take over wives, we want to take over land." This is what the dzvitis were doing. So they [have] a more hostile approach. . . . A dzviti will say he has no time to negotiate with you. . . . The madzviti, eh, if you look at them, their attitude is just military; they don't have to say, Come here, sit down, I want to ask you questions. He takes the spear and says, No, you are silly. You want one thing, death [chuckles]. They don't have to talk to you. I want to give you what you deserve.

Chikumbo's description resonates with stories about Gaza activity.[20] Etherington (2013, 120) quotes a local source who explained that after every military victory Nxaba would steal the cattle of the conquered people and kidnap young men and girls. Eldredge (2015, 210) suggests that Shaka's Zulu warriors would kill women and children from Zwide's defeated Ndwandwe and seize their cattle. Madzviti attitudes reflect an occupying army's reputation for brutality. More pertinent to the ceremonial dynamics of madzviti possession, the spirits are not interested in conversation—"They don't have to talk to you." That is not why they return to possess their mediums; language and conversation are secondary.

Despite the danger, people spend time, money, and effort to awaken them inside the bodies of their mediums. Ambuya Mazveshe said, "Here, one who heals has a dzviti."[21] Like all madhlozi, they are bodyguards of the ancestors. Soldiers in life, they remain soldiers in death, using the threat of violence to protect their charges—the ancestors. The madzviti are typically the first spirits to arrive during Ndau madhlozi ceremonies, as they were at Horus Farm.

There is nothing benign in the madzviti's power, and they continue to instill fear and awe in the wider community. Local Christians identify madzviti spirits with the devil, calling them *mademoni*, or "demons." They avoid them at all costs. My close Christian friends would refuse to attend functions in certain rural areas for fear of possession by mademoni. With the proper respect and concern they can be powerful protectors and allies, but their power can be unleashed in less-than-desirable ways.

Madzviti spirit mediums dress like the Gaza Nguni soldiers that their spirits were in life to facilitate possession and placate the spirits once possessed by making them feel more comfortable. As a way to mark this identity they wear skirts made of strips of cow hair called *chigejo* and headgear reminiscent of that which Nguni soldiers wore and always carry spears called *makondo*. As Enos Simango explained to me, they sometimes carry a short spear for stabbing called a *chiqibo,* a small battle-axe, or a shield called a *chihawo* or *chihlangu*.[22] Other participants often put a corn cob over the point of the spear to protect everyone in attendance from potential aggression. Madzviti also carry small containers of water called either a *katende kemvura* or a *chipfuko* as a way to keep cool by either drinking water or sprinkling it over themselves throughout the ceremony. Like other madhlozi spirits, the madzviti always wear red-and-black cloth. As I watched video of a Muzite ceremony with Pileni Dube, I mentioned that his spirit didn't seem to be wearing any red. He scoured the video seriously until we could both see the red detail obscured by his green shirt. It is a necessity.

In many ways, Ndau respect and honor for these "bodyguards of the ancestors" is insurance for their own protection once they pass away and become ancestral spirits in need of protection themselves. The spirit world is a volatile place; the role of the madzviti as the ancestors' bodyguards is highly valued. Chikumbo told me that madzviti have to "fight through a realm of spirits" to reach their mediums. The relationship between the madzviti spirits and the living is volatile, and the living still fear their destructive power, but ceremonies offer the living an opportunity to express their respect for the madzviti, appease their demands for snuff, and grant them opportunities to dance. Despite the power of the madzviti and the inherent danger lurking beneath the surface, as long as they are shown the proper respect, the living can retain control of the relationship and determine when the spirits arrive, how long they dance, and when they leave. Satiated spirits protect the living and their ancestors.

Madzviti Return

Early in the morning at Horus Farm, after the zvipunha and mhongo spirits had come and gone, the madzviti spirits unexpectedly returned. This was unusual; madzviti spirits predictably arrive in the late afternoon, dance, and depart before other spirits are called. But on this occasion they returned to aid their living hosts in the ceremony and show their appreciation. They also complained that they had not danced enough earlier and wanted to dance again before the ceremony finally came to a close. So the zvaayungu spirits, usually the last to arrive, were forced to wait for their more privileged spiritual elders to dance again.

These madzviti possessed their mediums at about eight o'clock in the morning as drummers and singers shifted their expectations about the zvaayungu and hurried to provide the appropriate sounds. The spirits greeted one another once again with flamboyant handshakes accompanied by welcoming shouts, indexing the strength and power everyone associated with them. Once the spirits had arrived, greeted one another, and knelt to snap in welcome and thanks to the elders among their living hosts, indexing the respect and appreciation their hosts expected, they danced with renewed vigor, anxious to finish what they had started hours earlier.

The madzviti requested that a goat be sacrificed to feed everyone who had attended and worked to make the ceremony a success as a gesture of appreciation. The spirits gathered together to discuss the goat with palpable authority. The children were excited to watch but hid behind their mothers' skirts at the slightest hint of attention, thankfully rare, from the spirits. We gave them a wide berth and watched as they circled the doomed goat, dancing and singing. Although only one song was used throughout, the spirits stopped people twice to complain about the sound before starting up again. The spirits led the singing the entire time. Suddenly, after almost fifteen minutes of singing and circling, one dzviti leapt forward and drove his spear into the goat before collapsing to the ground. Women ululated and everyone cheered. The singing stopped because of all the distraction, but the drummers carried on without interruption.

After each dzviti had danced to his satisfaction, the women began singing the required departure songs. Each dzviti would brandish his spear, roam the dance space, pour water on his head, and occasionally feign aggression toward members of the crowd. Some snapped a respectful goodbye to the elders once again. After a few false starts, the spirits left one at a time. Some ran full speed from the ceremonial space, while others walked with slow dignity. Their attitude depended on the personality of the spirit in question, a personality well known to the drummers, singers, and other community members. Their purpose fulfilled, the spirits left quickly and everyone moved on to the next phase, defined by a different purpose.

Desire and Purpose

Kuda means "to want." *Madzviti anoda kutamba* (madzviti spirits want to dance). *Kuda* can also mean "to need," "to like," and "to love," a multivalence that gives it more depth and complexity than any of its pale English translations. *Anoda kubuda* (the spirits want to emerge [within their mediums]); *unoda kuenda* (the spirit wants to leave [the medium's body]); *vanhu vanoda kurapwa* (people want [need] to be healed); *munoda kuti uuye kumusha* (you want it, so the spirit comes to the home). These uses, these contexts, all speak to desire. People and spirits want certain things; they have desires that inform much of what happens during ceremonial practice. Desire is real. More specific than hope (Crapanzano 2004, 100), it is an object intentionally signified, expressed in words at times, as Enos Simango, Matabuka (twice), Mulambo, and Ambuya Mazveshe did above, but the *authenticity* of these desires is often represented and communicated directly with signs more obviously connected to the here and now than with words. Illness, drumming, snuff-taking, singing, and dancing become signs of an object of desire. The expression of desire gives these semiotic acts purpose. The values that shape these desires also makes the events to follow potentially emotional as desires are fulfilled, unexpectedly or not, or remain unrealized.

Desire drives purpose, but the two are not the same thing. For Short (2007), purpose is an outcome toward which agents act (110). Desire becomes specific with purpose; the spirit wants to dance right now; the drummers want to get mediums dancing on this particular floor at this specific time. Even if that setting is sometime in the future, the wanting of it is already there. The purpose for which to realize these desires is more general. It is not yet actual (92), has yet to be attained, and so is not quite specific (Deacon 2012b, 29).

Purpose may be immaterial and general, but it drives semiosis and interpretation during madhlozi ceremonies (and in much of life). Purpose causes performances. Success or failure to realize purpose can terminate semiosis as well, ending the perpetual process of interpretation *toward an end* as attention shifts to other sign- and interpretant-making processes, just as the sacrifice of the goat above quickly led to the madzviti's departure and turned everyone's attention to the zvaayungu.

TELOS

Purpose defines the ends toward which the means of performance are selected. People play drums, take snuff, brew beer, and gather to bring their spirits out, to wake them up. Spirits make people sick or cause misfortune to draw attention to neglect or to facilitate the process of possession, which they need in order to dance. Deacon (2012b), following a long line of thinkers traced to Aristotle, calls this study of purposive phenomena *teleology.* The actions of participants are meaningful largely because they have been employed as the means toward these purposeful ends, hence Kohn's reimagining of the word *meaning* as "mean-ing" (2013, 72). The telos here, the ends toward which people act, is shaped by purpose.

It is problematic to interpret history teleologically, as having unfolded *toward* the current state of affairs or some unknown but anticipated future to which history is *progressing* (Chakrabarty 2000; Comaroff and Comaroff 1992). But telos matters to semiosis, and it is important to distinguish between the lack of historical telos and the centrality of semiotic telos in the interpretation of agents, dead or alive. Purpose drives interpretation and action during ceremonial life toward its own fulfillment. Desire, though distinct from purpose, becomes an object of semiosis, the connection to which informs interpretation and experience, making the most routine of gestures potentially moving. When people are dancing during the madzviti ceremony, music *feels* good when its purpose is realized.

The distinction between Peirce's immediate and dynamic objects helps clarify these processes. Purpose, as a signified object, can be both, but interpreters initially only perceive the immediate object. Success is determined by how the immediate and dynamic objects align. When the women at Horus struck the makandira, this act was eventually interpreted as multiple signs representing multiple objects, but one purpose was to signal the desire to invite spirits to come. They intended the drumming to be interpreted as a sign by the spirits, and specifically, as a signal of that purpose. When coincident with the other attributes of ceremonial performance, striking the drum indexes purpose.

In this way ceremonies are always in part about the future. The purpose is always yet to be realized in the moment, connected to an ideal outcome imagined by all parties. This predictive component is an important aspect of indexicality (Kohn 2013, 37). At different moments ceremonial drumming either indexes the spirits or the purpose to invite them and consequently predicts their arrival. The connection is understood as real, so if the spirits don't actually arrive, something must have gone wrong; the mistake serves as an index of something else, likely unknown at that moment. The spirit can respond as the drummers expect and hope by possessing the medium, can recognize the intent but choose not to come for reasons that would have to be determined later, recognize the intent but question its legitimacy because the signal itself is inadequate, or misinterpret the sign.[23] Thus telos is causal (37). This is one way in which the past and future are brought to bear on the present. Ritual thus shapes habitus, ideally reiterating valued habits.

Spirits and people might have slightly different purposes, but there is no serendipity in Chipinge. Everything has purpose and cause. I attended one ceremony in which the musicians played in earnest, the mediums danced with obvious effort, and the spirits never arrived. Rather than interpreting this to mean that the musicians played poorly, the mediums didn't try hard enough, or that they simply had bad luck, participants moved quickly to concern about offended spirits; the living must have done something wrong.

The Dead and the Living

Madzviti spirits want to dance, and they need the living in order to do it. It is that simple. It is a spirit's favorite thing to do. This desire is one key to relationships of reciprocal dependence that the dead have with their living interlocutors. At the risk of being tautological, dance is embodied so dance needs a body. Spirits only have bodies when they have successfully possessed their mediums. The purpose of the ceremony, for the spirits, is to be provided the space and means with which to dance. As I heard so often, "a dancing spirit is a happy spirit."

The living also need the dead, and this is perhaps more widely understood. They want to convey respect, be healed, express their desire for protection and recognition, and shape a better future. People try to communicate very specific things to their spirits, and they use the elements of performance to do so. By playing for them, dancing with them, and granting them the accompanying respect, they help ensure social continuity and security.

Ndau mediums possess spirits who, in turn, possess them. By conducting ceremonies, publicly and privately acknowledging the authority of the spirits, and continuing these vibrant interactions, Ndau communities ultimately take possession of their own history, gain some control over their present, and find direction for the future. The madzviti do not protect ancestral spirits selflessly. They need to feel respected and they need to dance. Each community's respective desires, to dance, on one hand and to ensure that the midzimu are protected, on the other, are compatible, even reciprocal. Each is served in performance.

The interpretation of purpose that people and spirits acknowledge in one another's' signs and actions is necessarily an acceptance of agency as well, for only agents can act with purpose. Acting with intent, or signaling with purpose, includes the expectation that the intended recipient of the sign will interpret the signs as anticipated. When the Horus Farm women played and sang, they expected the spirits of Gaza Nguni soldiers to hear them, understand the invitation, and wake up. Successful interpretation depends on the intentionality that the knower can attribute to the known (Viveiros de Castro 2004, 469). Hoping for a specific interpretant, acting appropriately, and having that effect come to fruition feels good. This "final interpretant" moves this semiotic exchange on to a new purpose, represented with new signs, ultimately contributing to ceremonial success . . . or not. As with any complex set of sign-object relations rooted in experience, in the indexicality of the moment, these hoped-for interpretants, are not foregone conclusions. Music and dance are perhaps perfectly suited to frame experiences that follow certain expectations or conform to well-established habits, but they are rooted in the here and now rather than the generality of symbolism that dominates language.

MEDIUMS, MUSICIANS, AND DANCERS

The dead are the most obvious focal point of the ceremony. Everyone's attention is on their potential arrival, their presence, and their imminent departure. The purpose of attending is to ensure the spirits' arrival. Realizing this purpose determines whether a ceremony is a success.

Unlike familial midzimu ceremonies, which few people are expected to take part in or attend, madhlozi ceremonies are communal events. Bringing community members together, ensuring broad participation, and making people feel welcome matter, but it is always in the service of the spirits. The relationships between the living and the dead, though they extend beyond the boundaries of the ceremony, are most publicly manifest in the moments when spirits possess the bodies of their host mediums, moments of musicking. Relationship habits cultivated during years of ceremonial practice become the focal point of collective action. Beyond the benefits of attendance and participation writ large, there are two main roles living participants can fulfill: those of spirit mediums and musicians.

Mediumship is a specialized skill. Although everyone who identifies as Ndau can potentially become a medium since everyone is born with a spirit, in practice few actually cultivate that relationship in such a way that serving as a medium becomes a core part of the self. Musicians, on the other hand, fill a range of roles with varying degrees of specialization that offer opportunities for everyone, including visiting ethnomusicologists. Few learn to play the drums or lead the singing, but anyone can clap, sing response parts, pick up the makosho, and move with the dancing spirits. Jennifer Kyker argues that the musical and social groove produced by interacting instruments and voices performs ideal relations grounded in values of "dialogue, tolerance, and mutual respect" (2016, 20). Multiple sound sources and vocal parts interact dialogically to serve the spirits in order to ensure security in the future and joyful experiences in the present.

Ngarife Matabuka is a spirit medium for a dzviti in the Muzite village nestled against the border with Mozambique. When I asked him why the madzviti arrive and whether they have anything to say, he responded as follows:

> When they awaken at your homestead, it will be like this: you brew beer. When you brew beer now, you would have fallen sick but the sickness is bed-ridden sickness, you are sick from wounds because when you have a dzviti the sickness is from wounds and blood. Let us say you were stabbed with a knife. You try to go to the clinic and they bandage the wound, they try to put medication and it does not work. And they say, Ha! Let us try.

I suggested brewing beer, but he responded,

> No, they say, Let us go and ask the healer. When they get there, the healer says, Brew beer for *madhlozi*. Alright, they brew the beer now. When they finish brewing the beer they go to divination, like you pour the beer for divining. . . . They would enjoy the divining and the healer.

Illness is a well-established signal that a spirit is communicating to either say that you should become a medium or to inform you of some spiritual slight for which you need to make amends (Gelfand 1962; Bourdillon 1987; Lan 1985). The dzviti spirit follows a similar sequence but uses a signal more indicative of its militaristic heritage, a wound. Through divination, the healing of a n'anga, and eventually a ceremony (brewing beer), the prospective medium can either accept his or her new role and placate the spirit or risk the consequences.

Matabuka's family has lived in the Muzite area for generations, and though his identity as a dzviti medium distinguished him, it was nothing unique or particularly remarkable. It was a part of who he was; he was born with it. His relationship with his spirit connected him to the community around him, the historical events from which his family emerged, and the spiritual community as a whole. The habits he has learned through this relationship shape these moments of intersubjectivity that define spirit possession. The spirit awakens, emerges, or arrives within him: kumukira, kubudira, and kusvikira. The medium is awakened within, emerged within, or arrived upon: kumukirwa, kubudirwa, and kusvikirwa.

The relationship between a medium and his or her spirit is a core characteristic of the medium, a stable aspect of her sense of self. People are born with spirits and attribute distinctive skills or personality traits to the madhlozi spirit resident within them. Thus, the relationship itself matters. Mediums are unique in that they cultivate the relationship they have in skilled and focused ways.[24] It is true that they are sometimes coerced into doing so, as with Jabulani Mulambo, but they do it nonetheless. The self, in this sense, is not the atomistic individual that often appears in English-language scholarship. The self is rooted in relationships: kinship ties, shared totems, the ritual friendship of *husahwira*,[25] and spirits. These relationships define Ndau selves.

Subjectivity, habits of the self, engaged in the here and now, also include intersubjectivity, the moments when one's subjectivity is shaped by the lived engagement with others. Intersubjective habits are familiar relationships as they are experienced. As with all madhlozi spirits, the focus during ceremonies on madzviti relationships with mediums such as Matabuka can be profoundly effective and valuable because they reinforce the intersubjective habits that define and renew community via communitas as they are performed. Madhlozi ceremonies entrench intersubjective habits between the living and the dead as essential aspects of self and identity.

As the visceral, even brutal, connection between sign and object in the knife wound that Matabuka describes above reveals, habits that inform ceremonial action, spirit possession, and intersubjectivity are rooted in signs, and those signs are material. Whether sound waves, the synapses of thought, or a knife to the hand, there must be something to perceive before a sign can lead one down the signifying road to the nineteenth century, for example.

In each stage of the madhlozi ceremony, the sonic, visual, and tactile clues signify and reify centuries of history and layers of social coherence. The chigejo skirt, the snapped greeting, the spear, and the makandira drums extend these same influences, historicizing the present and perpetuating the past. The connections between the objects represented and the musical, performative, and visual signs described above directly shape people's experiences.

Although music's importance in a ceremony can be overvalued, the relationships described above between mediums and spirits are best facilitated by musicking in ritual. Without drumming, signs lose power. Madhlozi spirits need to hear the drums, not only to possess their mediums, which is possible without music, but to dance, which is not. If possession is a skill and a habit for both medium and spirit, drumming and singing help each focus on possessing as an act. It catalyzes that experience. Madzviti drumming affirms the intersubjective relationships of participatory music more than the drumming for the other madhlozi spirits described here in part because it requires several drummers to attain the required rhythmic density. Each spiritual performance practice has numerous contributors to the overall sound, since anyone in attendance can grab a gosho rattle, clap along, sing, or dance, but madzviti music is distinct in that the texture of the drumming is preferably divided among at least three to five players. It is only when each person's relatively simple rhythmic pattern comes together with the others' to create a single processual sign that madzviti drumming is at its most powerful. This dense texture is taken a step further when the dancing spirits strike the ground with an audible stomp.[26]

The makandira are frame drums (gandira, singular) played only for madzviti.[27] This exclusivity contributes to a strong indexical association between their timbres and rhythms and the spirits. This connection is so tight that local n'angas, like Mudiwa in Buffelsdrift, hang the drums from the walls in the huts in which they practice to help with healing. Ambuya Jaisi, a n'anga from the Matsetso village in Chimanimani, uses the dzviti's drum during divination sessions in which she throws *hakata*, "bones."[28] Ceremonies employ drums of multiple sizes, which vary from one community to the next. Each gandira is made from a circle of thin wood with two crossbars in the back and a goatskin head attached with wooden pegs and is anywhere from eight to twenty-four inches in diameter (see figure 3.3). One drum is never enough, so it is more productive to think of them collectively.

Each drummer holds the crossbar in the back with one hand while holding a stick in the other, typically their strong hand. She can then use the fingers

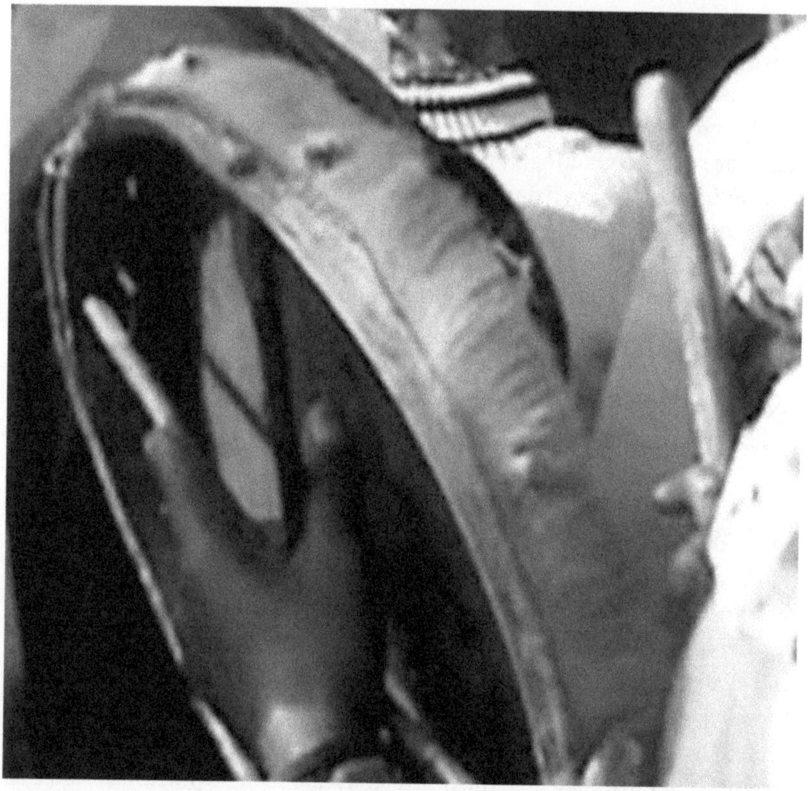

FIGURE 3.3. Crossbar and hand position on a gandira

of the hand holding the drum to tap the back of the drumhead and either dampen the sound, fill in the spaces of the beaten rhythms, or change the pitch of the drum. For instance, the sounds of the two loudest makandira played at Horus Farm roughly corresponded as shown in figure 3.4. The higher pitch is played by dampening the drumhead from behind with a finger. The differences between these pitches are never as clear as those found in zvipunha and mhongo drumming, but they contribute to the overall texture and help emphasize certain drum strokes more than others. This, combined with the stick work on the face of the drum by three to six drummers simultaneously playing slightly different patterns, creates a dense rhythmic texture based around a driving duple rhythm (see figure 3.5).

Makosho rattles are ubiquitous in Shona and Ndau indigenous music (in the former they are called *hosho*). In contrast to Shona mbira music, here multiple performers each play a single gosho simultaneously when performing

FIGURE 3.4. Relative tones of the makandira

for the madzviti. Gourd makosho are still played, but most of the performers I saw in Horus, Holland, Muzite, Daisy Hill, and Bangwe used a small insect repellent or motor oil can filled with resilient canna lily seeds called *hota*. Some players play an intricate pattern, whereas others simply emphasize the beat. Still other participants double the makosho by clapping their hands (maoko).

Madzviti songs seem always to be duple. Translated and transcribed into Western notation, this rhythm is a sequence of 2/4 bars, usually occurring in cycles of two or sometimes three. The makandira and makosho all establish clear duple patterns that exhibit none of the polyrhythm or asymmetry that marks drumming for the zvipunha or mhongo spirit. This rhythmic sign is also an index of Gaza heritage in South Africa, because the performance practices are iconic (signifying resemblance) of rhythmic tendencies in Zulu, Swazi, and Shangaan performance practice.[29] Madzviti rhythms, instrumentation, and timbres reflect the listening habits and taste of the spirits being summoned and serenaded.

During the heart of the ceremony, when dancing is at its peak and everyone is engaged, songs can last as long as thirty minutes. This length alone suggests that the purpose is a heightened experience for everyone involved, during which people focus on the intersubjectivity of the here and now. Other potential signs matter less, and semiosis is reduced to the immediacy of the moment as an experience of secondness takes hold via flow and communitas.

But not every performance serves a communal purpose so directly. Madzviti ngoma are striking in that they often have an audience of one. Multiple drummers, makosho players, singers, and more passive attendees engage in an ongoing and synchronized call and response for the specific purpose of singing to a single dzviti spirit.

Madzviti songs are usually sung in Zulu or Swazi as an appeal to the spirits' original language. The language that is sung usually corresponds to the different madzviti spirits associated with Ndwandwe, Zulu, or Ndau members of the Gaza Nguni army. Mudiwa describes the language used as ChiShona Chikuru, or big Shona. Lyrics often consist of declarative or imperative statements directing the spirit to wake up, do something, respond to the singers' requests, or depart. Songs serve a purpose. Despite using symbols (as linguistic expressions tend to do), ngoma lyrics are driven by indexicality, with understood connections to specific spirits (via naming), specific interests (via imperative verbs and description), and specific times and places (via language use).

Because these songs are often directed at individual spirits, their names are frequently sung during performance. Matabuka translated from the original Swazi several of the songs that his spirit sang during a ceremony in Muzite.[30] His spirit sang "Me, I am a Mthethwa, I am a Zulu" in order to introduce himself to the other participants and assert his own history.[31] Other songs used that day were sung to and for Mulaleni and Mtombeni. People even sing in the second person to reflect the perspective of the spirit himself, thus representing the spirit's own desires to express his strength and authority. Enos Simango taught me a ngoma in which people sing "Wachekwa banga roMudondo (You were cut by Mudondo's knife)." Naming practices like this, and shifts in perspective, connect lyrical practices to particular objects, moving beyond the general to the specific.

Singing brings the spirits and sends them off again, connecting the living with the dead by means of shared purpose and experience. Later in the Muzite ceremony people sang, "I am home [*kanyi*], this place where I am, it is home." This both welcomed the spirit's arrival on behalf of the living participants and served to thank the living for holding the ceremony on the spirit's behalf. In a sense, people used these songs and the ceremonial frame to harness their madzviti's power and contain their aggression. People in attendance, primarily women, forcefully sang a song from the perspective of the spirit that said, "Let's go! I'm about to leave." As the song drew to a close, the possessed medium ran out of the ceremonial space and down the path. Songs performed for the purpose of communicating a specific desired behavior to a specific spirit can be surprisingly short. "Siya Hamba," notated in figure 3.5, urged Matabuka's spirit to depart the space and his medium. Once the spirit got the message, the song was over, less than two minutes after it began. Shortly thereafter Matabuka returned, without his spirit, to participate in the rest of the ceremony. The singers would use first-person pronouns as a way to guide their spirits' actions, and the spirit would usually dutifully oblige.

When people want to invite the madzviti spirits, everyone enters the roundhouse, usually in the late afternoon. The house, regardless of size, always ends

FIGURE 3.5. "Siya Hamba"

up crowded, full of people sitting and singing, playing drums, dancing, or watching, clapping, drinking beer, and commenting on the proceedings. The makandira players, singers, and makosho players are usually women.

As the ceremony progresses and the drumming intensifies, more people join the singing, and the mediums dance more aggressively. As Samson Mapfumo described it to me, the effort to "wake up" the spirit (kumutsa) is sometimes literally performed by people beating the madzviti rhythms onto the head of the medium to shake up a stubborn spirit. Such action reflects either the value of viscerally embodying the rhythmic catalyst for possession or inspiration through iconicity by representing the spirit to itself as violent. Musicking communicates respect.[32] A dzviti spirit that feels disrespected can be a dangerous spirit. The living are responsible for creating a performance environment that facilitates the spirits' arrival and eventual dance.

Many of the participants don't speak Swazi. Although the Gaza Nguni influenced local language, Ndau is closer to Shona than to Swazi, Zulu, or Ndebele. Shona or Ndau can be used to help the singers get their bearings before singing in Swazi. When describing the song about the setting sun, Matabuka said, "Singing in Shona it says, I am leaving you, the sun has gone down." I asked whether that meant the spirit speaks Shona and he replied, "No, no, those who sing . . . it will start [the song] . . . so that you know which song it wants; it gives you [the start of the song] so that you know."

Matabuka said that every spirit "has a song for leaving and for waking up." For instance, "Siya Hamba" tells the spirit Mtombeni that it is time to leave in what Matabuka identifies as Zulu.[33] Matabuka translates *Siya Hamba* into Shona as *Ndava kuenda*, or, "I am going." The singers all join in the collective signal that the spirit should leave his medium's body. The cycle is six beats long and could be transcribed as 12/8, but unlike most 12/8 patterns in Zimbabwe (such as the mhongo drumming described in Chapter 5), this does not invite polyrhythmic juxtapositions of twos and threes but, rather, is a series of duple patterns: 4+4+4/8.

When dancing in the courtyard, the madzviti didn't organize themselves or stand in formation. They congregated in front of the drummers or wandered the yard authoritatively. Madzviti moved minimally to the music before launching into energetic bursts of movement highlighted by stomps and leaps. Spirits occasionally danced together but typically kept to themselves. None of the living participants joined the dance. When they weren't dancing, the spirits wandered the grounds with their heads held high, brandishing their

Key to Dance Notation: (= right arm up;) = left arm up; ( ) = both arms up; _ = thrust arms; □ = small jump; ■ = stomp jump; ◇ = small step; × = high step; . = shuffle step

FIGURE 3.6. Gandira accents and corresponding dzviti steps (dance transcription inspired by those of ethnomusicologist Louise Meintjes [2004, 186])

spears, pouring water over their heads, and feigning stabbing gestures, much to the children's delight.

Unlike the zvipunha's music, with its comparatively spare texture owing to the use of a single drum, the madzviti performance is a dense, unceasing performance texture that seems iconic of the spirits' aggression and flamboyance. The dominant gandira player will often interrupt the flow of drumbeats to play along with and emphasize the steps of the dancing dzviti. In figure 3.6 accented strokes correspond with the dzviti's stomp. The final stroke ends the dance, at which point the spirits pause, drink water from their ubiquitous katende kemvura, and prepare for the next song.

The lead gandira player during "Siya Hamba" plays two distinct patterns, each iconic of the spirit's steps and indexical of purpose. During the first, the spirit shuffles his feet, stepping lightly and looking toward the other spirits and the women performing behind him. The shift to the second dense pattern on the gandira coincides with the spirit's more aggressive steps. The most frequent step is a strong stomp in which the spirit lifts a knee above his waist

Key to Dance Notation: (= right arm up;) = left arm up; ( ) = both arms up; _ = thrust arms; □ = small jump; ■ = stomp jump; ◇ = small step; × = high step; . = shuffle step

FIGURE 3.7. "Siya Hamba" with dance steps

before striking the ground with authority. That is the foundation of much Ndau dancing and certainly of muchongoyo, whose drummers describe the stomp as strong, even important (Perman 2010). Once the purpose of possession has been realized, attention shifts and the makandira-driven texture triggers aggressive dancing (realizing a new purpose). Shortly thereafter, people say goodbye in sound, each spirit receives the message, stops dancing, and departs his medium's body.

Multiple experiences—possession, collective dance, and joy or excitement—emerge from the signs of performance and the ways in which these signs "bear the weight of history" into the present and shape purposeful, collective action. Songs for the purpose of directing the dzviti can be quite short, with the purpose easily fulfilled. Songs for the purpose of collective experience and enjoyment can be much longer, both because the purpose is the experience itself but also because these kinds of heightened experiences are difficult to simply generate.

Affective Objects

As I watched my video of the ceremony in Muzite with Matabuka and Pileni Dube, they explained to me what the spirits were doing and singing. These explanations were typically accompanied by quick affective asides as they laughed or cringed in amusement at their own spirits' dancing during the ceremony, something neither of them had ever seen in this way before. During one moment in the ceremony, while watching their spirits dance and interact with the living on my camera's tiny screen, Matabuka said, "I feel troubled; he is finally leaving." The moment was fleeting and ambiguous. Before long they were both telling me about the dangers of fake spirits, Samson Mapfumo's playful attempts to join in, and the specifics of the dance. Matabuka couldn't put into words quite what he was feeling, or why, but the emotion he felt in this moment was a direct consequence of the presence of the madzviti, the collective purpose of bringing them to the present, and the ceremonial practices that facilitated the successful realization of this purpose (among others).

Although affect theorists sometimes dismiss the "meaningful" nature of affect, numerous approaches to emotion insist that emotions are about objects (Damasio 2003, 41). Emotion-appraisal, the second step of emotional experience, involves the physiological appraisal of signs and the objects for which they stand (Damasio 2004, 5). The objects represented are valued in ways that affirm, threaten, expand, or reduce valued aspects of the self, reliably evoking an emotional response. When addressing Damasio's claims, Nussbaum (2001, 19) argues that emotions involve judgments, relating objects of importance to our well-being and lack of control over the outside world. The ways in which signs reflect objects, and the manner in which those objects are valued, shape experience. Purpose frames how objects are appraised and how they may or may not be valued.

Interpretation often relies on the ways in which similar signs related to objects in previous iterations. Peirce called the sign's prior relation to an object its ground. In part, the grounds of interpretation for the ceremonies at Horus and Muzite were previous ceremonies. Some responses are habitual, some action-oriented, and some more vague and nascent, moving toward affect.[34] A challenge in any semiotic frame during which habits of interpretation are relied upon, but in which experiences of immediacy are best generated through indices of the here and now, is balancing the predictability of habits and symbols with the desired unpredictability of indices. This is at the heart of recent ethnomusicological literature about participatory performance, in which music and dance connect people intimately and nonsymbolically (Turino 2009, 13). Signs also connect to other concurrent signs to helpfully and indexically point to the same objects, specific spirits, for instance. Thus, pasts can be known, recalled, or learned. Purpose can be revealed, rebuffed, or realized. What is known can be modified, what is unknown can be learned. Change can happen.

As manifest, known, and respected through purposeful song and dance, spirits are real. They are the objects of semiosis and the cause of ceremonial action. Doubt is rare, because their ontology is unquestioned. The connection that makandira drums, the rhythms played on them, and stomps have to the spirits for which they are performed is taken as real, and this reality is confirmed and reestablished when the spirits arrive and dance. When possessed by the dzviti spirit Mtombeni, Matabuka is "awakened within" (kumukirwa) by his spirit; the intersubjective presence of their relationship comes to the fore. Matabuka's experience is defined by this aspect of himself, which he welcomes. Everyone working together toward a common purpose, brewing beer, playing drums, preparing food, dancing, singing, and acknowledging their spirits through performance, thus experiences these moments together; they reaffirm relationships that have consequences for social life beyond the frame of the ceremony.

But dynamic objects, however much their reality is accepted and however causal they are of the signs that follow, are also open to reinterpretation through those very representations. Contemporary spirit mediums and adherents recognize and exploit the strength of their former nineteenth-century rulers. By inverting an asymmetrical power relation and becoming the sole vehicle to the corporeal for the ephemeral spirits, the Ndau reconfigure themselves into a position of power. This is not a relationship of dominance and subjugation, just as the nineteenth-century dynamic between locals and Gaza Nguni was never completely one of coercion; rather, the living and the dead are in a relationship of mutual dependence. Just as the madzviti spirits need living mediums in order to be embodied, to dance, and to essentially live again, so too do the living Ndau rely on their cosmological neighbors, the madzviti, for the protection of both themselves and their ancestors.

The Gaza Nguni, by all accounts, were aggressive foreign occupiers. MacGonagle writes that their rule cast a "shadow of tyranny" (2008, 31). In Tsonga communities, the dzviti spirits must be exorcised (Johnston 1972), yet the Horus and Muzite communities, located close to the former Gaza headquarters near Mt. Selinda, invite them eagerly. Considerable time and resources are spent to ensure a successful and well-attended ceremony. How might the madzviti's return and request for a goat contribute to this seemingly positive relationship? It is a noticeable gesture of generosity for a community of spirits famed more for ferocity. Witnesses must appraise the objects (the spirits) anew in the face of signs such as this. To be sure, madzviti are still feared. They are still dangerous. But they also protect the midzimu and heal the sick. Ceremonial moments of reconciliation like the goat sacrifice, over time, contribute to a redefinition of the dynamic objects being represented, changing the ways in which history is understood and lived. The interpretation of immediate objects as they are represented in signs can inform the dynamic objects that lead to future signs and semiotic interpretations.

Spirit possession is a form of history, as powerfully illustrated by Lambek's work in Madagascar. He writes, "Ancestral practices enable both a polyphonically historical consciousness and an energetic means to influence how change takes place" (2002, 263). There is a powerful connection between the living and the dead, the present and the past, which renders local historical understanding distinct from that found in societies where historical awareness is based on literacy or even memory, which is partial and unreliable (Crapanzano 2004, 160). The Ndau need not rely solely on their memories of past struggles since they can revisit the actors from those eras during a single ceremonial night. Because narratives of perpetual, teleological progress and texts cementing the past are not common here, people rely on the spirits who lived through these dynamic periods for both their past and their future.

Although the future is unknown, the past is known, and actors from those pasts protect and guide the living when properly respected and appeased. The clearest difference between these cosmological interventions with the past and more orthodox approaches to the historical record is the dialogic nature of Ndau historical understanding. Communities can literally interact with those who preceded them. *Dialogic* might not actually be the best word. *Intersubjective* may be more accurate, not only because these interactions are lived in the moment but also because these relationships are not driven primarily by language or dialogue. "They don't have to talk to you." Why talk when you can dance? Not only are these cosmological practices relevant to Zimbabwe's current struggles, despite being framed as anachronistic by local cosmopolitans and zealous foreign activists, but they also are essential for ensuring an eventual resolution. Masiza relies on his ancestors for security in everything from successful trips to relatives' homes to productive harvests. He and his cohort rely on the spirits for survival itself.

Semiotic objects are only known as represented in interpretants. One can't be significant without the other; sign, object, and interpretant always go hand in hand in hand. The foundation of past experience, historical understanding, and purpose informs the way signs are understood, how the objects signified are appraised, and what their effects (interpretants) might be, but in practices dominated by iconic and indexical processes of signification, little is given. Interpretive moves (Feld 1984) can shift the foundation on which subsequent interpretation takes place. Experience shapes the manner and extent to which the objects of signs can be known. The objects of history, embodied in spirits, must be experienced anew and continually reappraised to remain relevant to the here and now. But these histories and the purposes connected to them are the roots of ceremonial action.

The dimensions of value that are at stake during a ceremony can make events both unpredictable and emotional. What is real or not real? What is desirable or not desirable? What is dreaded or not dreaded? When someone, living or dead, does something with the intention of signifying purpose (such as playing a drum, taking snuff, or wounding a potential medium), the interpretant is not a given. There are multiple possibilities as others react to the sign as it signifies purpose as object. Desires are expressed, histories are represented, and these sign-object relations beget new signs as they are interpreted. Thus, regardless of the resilience of the histories being performed or the values being purposefully emphasized, success comes down to the signs themselves. At Horus Farm, when the madzviti left late that afternoon and the sun set behind the trees to the west, it was a sign for everyone, living and dead, that it was time to invite the zvipunha.

CHAPTER 4

Evening

Zvipunha, *Signs, and Transformative Experience*

It was now dark. I was seated next to Masiza again in the ceremonial house, clapping and singing along with everyone else. The drumming had succeeded and several zvipunha spirits were playing in the center of the circle, babbling away with one another, shoving dirt in their mouths with both hands, and acting very much like children with their faces covered in food. It was a striking shift from the sheer aggression of the madzviti, who had departed only an hour or two earlier. We were about to leave the house and dance outside for a couple of hours before inviting the mhongo spirits, but the zvipunha wanted to share some food first. Each chipunha (singular of the plural zvipunha) stepped through the crowded room with a wide shallow basket, offering groundnuts (*nzungu*) to everyone. The room was quite dark, so it was hard to see. One spirit caught sight of my unexpected face in the gloom as she offered us the basket. Her eyes grew wide, she gasped in terror, squealed, and leapt across the room to cower behind the skirts of the women seated there, stepping on heads and hands along the way.

This chapter is about a moment, one that preceded the episode just described and made it possible, one in which the zvipunha ceremony at Horus Farm transformed from one of adequacy and rote performance to one of spiritual awakening and joy. It is about how and when musicking is deemed effective and how semiotic transformations make such evaluations possible. These transformations also make spirit possession itself possible. If chapter 3 focuses on how semiotic objects provide the roots of action and chapter 5 is about how the effects of signs reveal the fruits of action, this chapter is about action itself and the importance of the now in shaping experience. As I explain the role of signs in interpretive experience, I highlight three moments that occurred during the ceremony at Horus Farm with Davison Masiza. Such moments can slip by quickly but transform individual experiences socially, emotionally and, ultimately, spiritually. In my analysis, as I pull these moments from ceremonial experience, they appear as ruptures. But as lived, they are indistinct from the other moments that went before and after. In haecceity there aren't sequences of moments, there is continuity.

From my ethnomusicological perspective, every emotional experience is inevitably personal, physiological, and cultural. Each of these dimensions is dependent on semiosis. Emotion cannot be detached from signification unless signification itself is stripped of its complexity and rendered narrowly linguistic.

Thus, signs matter. Emotional experience always begins with affective perception. The objects of semiosis are materialized in the signs that represent them. Signs trigger interpretive experiences and lead agents to signified objects via significant effects. Perception begets affect begets emotion. Emotional experience begins with the perception of signs, always. There are no exceptions.

The key moment during the zvipunha portion of the ceremony emphasized in this chapter was musical. Late in the evening, long after the music had started and mediums had begun dancing but before the zvipunha had arrived, Davison Masiza played the drum and everything changed. The basic rhythms, gestures, dance steps, and melodies were familiar, iconic to what we'd been hearing and seeing over the past hour, yet now we felt them differently. The perceived evidence of competence, energy, and purpose in Masiza's drumming drove the proceedings forward. Spirit possession, enthusiastic dancing, and joy followed. This moment made the ceremony successful. The success of VaMasiza's playing was heightened by what happened before this and confirmed by what followed, but the indexical now of this precise moment was what made it possible. As in the ceremony itself, in which Masiza's transformative playing followed a long period of ineffective playing, I deliberately defer describing Masiza's impact. It is essential to understand the spirits, their drumming, and the nature of sign-object relations before his impact can be fully understood.

Zvipunha

As the sun set over the hills to the west of the former Horus Farm and the madzviti left their host mediums, the ceremony seemed to take a deep breath.

People chatted, rested, and got something to eat or drink. Masiza and I were given *sadza* (the staple cornmeal porridge) by our hosts in the main house. The mood was relaxed, but I was still buzzing from the musicking that had ended just moments earlier. Eventually, somebody gathered up the madzviti paraphernalia, replaced the makandira drums with a single *chigubhu* drum, and laid it on its side; the ceremony continued. The house was crowded again and even darker than before, the single candle on the wall looking lonely in the gloom. The space was again organized with men seated hierarchically on the bench, women clustered on the floor along the opposite wall, and a narrow space in the center for dancing. A young man, Zivanai,[1] settled at the chigubhu, which looks like a military bass drum, two women picked up the makosho rattles, and we began to invite the next group of spirits, the zvipunha.

When describing how zvipunha ceremonies typically begins, Enos Simango told me,

> They say, Today there is beer that was brewed for the zvipunha dance. . . . Those who get possessed by the chipunha . . . are not called chipunha they are called *mapunha*. . . . They say, We have come to call you, we have our beer for the zvipunha so we need someone who can get possessed by a chipunha here. They then come with those who accompany them. Those who accompany are bodyguards of the zvipunha now. . . . People come now in their numbers because it starts at a certain time. Those bodyguards now are told, Enter the house now. When they enter the house now they put a little bit of tobacco . . . they put a wooden plate or a *chimusani* . . . the reed baskets are placed there. . . . She starts being given those she sees as the little ones . . . from those who started, the elders who are said to have started awakening a long time ago. There are those who awakened, there are generations all awake now.

The zvipunha I encountered share numerous characteristics: they act like children, are identified as girls, possess female mediums, and are important to all local events associated with fertility, including childbirth, harvest, and funerals.[2] I understand them as spirits of social continuity. Zvipunha are spirits of women and for women, nurturing pregnancy, harvest, funeral rites, and fertility. Collectively, they suggest a shared core identity as something akin to "outsider mothers," women who lacked children in life, cannot be affines, and effectively are working to right the wrongs of their lives as spirits.[3] Whether described as girls, elder aunts, or rain spirits, the widely divergent descriptions of zvipunha in the literature and in my fieldwork reflect connections to motherhood, fertility, and a need to nurture.[4]

Simango says that *punha* means "girl" in ChiNdau and that these spirits "were called zvipunha because they were girls who played with children." They are also called *zvisora*, depending on where you are in the Chipinge District and whom you ask. I encountered both terms with almost equal frequency, but the community at Horus preferred *zvipunha*, so that is what I use. For Ambuya Mazveshe, "Zvipunha are zvisora." As with all local spirits, they are neither static nor monolithic; there are multiple orthodoxies of interpretation at play. The people at Horus Farm trust them and rely on them. They aren't relics or theatrical characters but beings with agency, desires, and relationships that continue to change.[5]

Although zvipunha are frequently played for on their own, outside of general ceremonies, our collective effort was a predictable response to the madzviti's departure. People typically prepare to invite the zvipunha once the madzviti depart from their mediums. Playing for the zvipunha is an expected interpretant to the signs of the madzviti's departure.

Zvipunha spirits exclusively possess women.[6] Simango told me that "men don't do that." In life, they were young girls during the formative days of Chipinge's early Ndau communities who died before marrying and giving birth. They were often acknowledged as among the oldest madhlozi spirits in the ceremonies that I attended. These two facts are not unrelated; they speak to the zvipunha spirits' most important role in Ndau society, a nurturing protection of fertility.

Simango, whose mother had a chipunha, described them as the spirits of housemaids who babysat young children, *manheni* (from the English *nannies*). He said, "Zvipunha . . . is danced by nannies who used to play with the children." They were the unwed caretakers of ancestral Ndau children. Without direct descendants, they could not become midzimu. In 1934 the Swiss ethnographer Henri Philippe Junod, paraphrasing an informant, described them (originally in French) as "Spirits of the VaKaranga in relation to the mapendji. They are soothed by offering them a sort of sticky fruit called gufa, together with sound. We put on long fringes of pearls and dance with a kind of cane called midozo" (1934a, 280).[7]

Reverend Charles Blakney shares a revealing story that he was told in the 1960s.

> They say they lived in the Port Victoria [*sic*] district, where they were orphaned as children. They wandered from place to place, scratching for food, living on crabs and such wild things as they could gather. Finally, they died of malnutrition. As spirits, they became attached to the trek

> wagons of the Afrikaans settlers (who were moving through Karangaland in the 1890s) and followed them to Gazaland, where the VaNdau live. Here they found mediums to rise in. The story is plausible enough, historically, but the sad story of the neglected little girls is what identifies the cult mood and attitude. (1969, 101)

The spirits of these young girls indirectly allow communities to interact with their own forerunners, people who lived and died prior to the more salient historical moments that followed. They even speak their own language, Chingotoro, which indexes antiquity to their living interlocutors.[8]

As with all madhlozi, the connection between zvipunha and familial heritage is complex. Mulambo said that "a person [who] is possessed by this one is not her child but the child of her relative. So they are unable to speak about things of the dzinza lineage, but she becomes a visitor who comes, yes, she comes to help [the child or woman giving birth]."[9] Without that familial relationship, the living person cannot serve as a medium.[10] Her outsider status, in this case, simply confirms that she did not become an ancestral spirit after death because she died before she was married or had children. In life, however, zvipunha were intimately connected to the ancestors of the contemporary communities they now protect as caretakers.

Zvipunha can be silly, tempestuous, messy, and mischievous. They squeal in delight or fear, dance with childlike abandon, and eat anything from dirt to crabs to *derere* (okra) with both hands.[11] Simango told me that they try to eat live crabs if their attendants don't prevent them.[12] Chikumbo said, "When a person is possessed by zvipunha they usually do silly things which you won't like. Eating mucus from young children's nose, they go and suck that from their nose, they like that. And catching locust and eating raw locust. These are the zvipunha. . . . They are used for frustrations." They like to play with *magagada* leg rattles and often wear them when dancing. Mutwanhi said, "They are young children, those who possess. The dead ones awaken and they like to play with these rattles." Their emotions are never far from the surface. They were children in life and act like children in death.

Simango covered many of these points in his basic description of the zvipunha and their ceremony:

> The nannies act like little children, the girls acted like little children. Yes, now they clap like this [like a child]. As it starts when she is here, the grandmothers sitting there and it awakens, saying, Haaa. People now look. . . . Doing what she used to do, cooking matumba rumba. Do you know matumba rumba? So they . . . what they did—do you know *butu*? Butu,

> when you grind sorghum and do this. . . . That is their sadza that they would be cooking now. They take wild okra, the one you prune in the wild, that is the one they eat the sadza with, that is the offering. One can take a pot, take them like this and run away with it. They run away and they cry, Hiiii. Others cry, Hiiii, saying the pot has been taken from them. So that is when they console the child, singing, Hush, don't cry, punha, mother has gone to the river, mother is coming, punha, iyeeee iiyee iyawo.

Simango credits his mother's chipunha with helping raise him. As spirits the zvipunha continue the responsibilities that they had as nannies and caretakers when alive. Their childlike behavior intersects with a mature ability to nurture. An explicit interest in the well-being of the living is evident in their ceremonial actions, as when they fed groundnuts to participants as described at the outset of this chapter. Mudiwa explained, "They help, the zvipunha, to protect the mother's children. While she is at the house where she got married, she . . . is pregnant. The chisora [chipunha] will be the one taking care of the baby until the child is born." They may display signs of immaturity, but their need to nurture is sincere and highly valued.

Women are responsible for the majority of the semiotic labor necessary for a successful zvipunha ceremony. At Horus Farm, men often sat along the benches inside the house, occasionally singing but generally staying quiet while the women sang, played makosho, clapped, danced, and became possessed.[13] Rennie (1985, 180) and Blakney (1969) emphasize the importance of the zvipunha to Ndau women as a tool for complaint and a response to patriarchal control, going so far as to say that men are excluded from zvipunha dances. Yet men provided support at most zvipunha ceremonies I attended by playing drums or singing. Whether this reflects a change over time, a regional difference, or simply an earlier misinterpretation is unclear. Whenever I witnessed women gathered together to sing, they would at some point sing zvipunha songs.

Zvipunha apparently age, unlike most other spirits. Madzviti, mhongo, and midzimu are generally thought to remain the same age as they were at death. Everyone agrees that the zvipunha died young and continue to act like little girls. Mutwanha said, "It can be an old spirit but it died as a child, it awakens as a child." But Chikumbo and Wilson Simango, another n'anga from Chipinge, maintained that the zvipunha spirits continue to age after death.[14] They suggested that the spirits want people to think they are still children in order to hide their true identity and power. They are playful, energetic, difficult to understand, and very fearful of strangers, including visiting researchers from the United States, but are they ultimately powerful and necessary. As

Wilson Simango explained, "The spirits speak like little girls [but] the spirit grows up after death. They talk like little children, to confuse others so that they don't do what they are doing."

Since the zvipunha offer continuity with the distant past via previous caregiving, it is unsurprising that they assist in fertility and facilitate both pregnancy and childbirth for contemporary Ndau women with experience and knowledge. In Ndau families, young, unmarried girls often provide childcare as nannies and maids. Zvipunha protect children just as they did in life, ensuring social continuity. They help children and adults so that they don't miss their mother and father (or the ancestors).[15] But this protection is not guaranteed. It must be nurtured by brewing beer and dancing.

The zvipunha's role as protectors is a status they share with other madhlozi spirits. Chikumbo said, "This young family woman is now possessed by that spirit. If she has children, that spirit now says, these are my children I protect from danger. . . . She [the chipunha] is a soldier who guards for children." When a girl becomes a chipunha, Mulambo said, "she becomes a soldier." Enos Simango, Wilson Simango, and Mpande Chikumbo all call them *mabodyguards*, marking a similarity between their role in aiding childbirth and pregnancy and the explicit protection of midzimu and the living by the more militaristic madzviti and zvaayungu. Just as the madzviti and mhongo spirits are characterized as soldiers for the ancestors, so, too, are the zvipunha described as soldiers for the children. Chikumbo provocatively explained that when a person's mudzimu wants to fight, "he sends an army of his zvipunha, girl spirits. They are about to fight. During the night, they come and they make love to you. You are weakened. They come naked, they are being directed by this one. These zvipunha, those girls who died without having been married. They sleep with you, that is a strategy in order to weaken the enemy. The man when he tries to use his juju, he is weak because of that strategy."[16]

Chikumbo's explanation lends weight to the suggestion that zvipunha are only pretending to be young. The strength and will required to protect the ancestors, guide childbirth, nurture the living, and assist with the harvest requires powerful spirits. The living must serve the spirits well, by playing for them and giving them space to dance, in order to receive their protection. The living and the dead protect each other. Thus, just as Chikumbo and Simango referred to the zvipunha spirits as bodyguards (soldiers for the children), Enos Simango referred to the living attendants to the spirit as the bodyguards for the spirits. Drumming is essential to achieving this reciprocity. Simango said, "To pay for the spirit's protection we brew beer. When we brew beer, we should hit the drum that we can say, This beer is yours."

Moment 1: Drumming for the Zvipunha

Zivanai tapped the side of the drum, cutting through the surrounding conversations. Women sang, filling the texture with overlapping parts. Masiza shouted encouragement—"You play that drum!"—as others laugh good-naturedly. The proceedings had just begun and the mood was relaxed. Zivanai was a novice drummer, so he played when expectations were low. The men split their focus between the drum, the lingering conversation, and the beer. They only sang occasionally, but the women sang, played multiple makosho within the basic eight-pulse phrase, and clapped. At first, the drumming never continued for more than twenty or thirty seconds, alternating with primarily women's voices on the far side of the room. Some mediums danced in the center.[17]

The pattern from the drum rose above the texture of voices, feet, shakers, and clapping: ♪♩♩♪♩ (1_2_x_1_x_1_2_x_), in which the eighth note gets the pulse and each *x* represents a rest. Again and again we heard this eight-pulse sequence, first tapped against the side of the drum as people chatted, shuffled around, and settled in, and later on the head of the drum: ♪♩♩♪♩ | ♪♩♩♪♩. Each token established, then confirmed the type; a pattern emerged. Once the pattern was in our heads and we no longer needed the actual strokes in order to hear it, Zivanai shifted into the now-anticipated sonically dense zvipunha pattern, and we were off. Makosho rattle players, people clapping, and singers added to the texture, filling the responsorial spaces with dancers stepping as indicated and mediums beginning their work. These women danced nimbly to the rhythm, working to integrate the sounds, smells, sights, and gestures into a whole effective enough to call the spirits down and induce possession. The drumming held it all together.

Masiza and others tried to help Zivanai along, but soon their constructive criticism became too much to ignore. Zivanai stopped. "You were slow." Others yelled to the host women, "The beer is good, but there is so little." The women eventually stopped as well, needing the drum to return and the complaining to subside. Zivanai started again, much as before. Everyone remained in high spirits, even if the beer wasn't quite plentiful enough and the drumming had yet to inspire the mediums or their spirits. The singers and makosho players diligently carried on.

When people invite the zvipunha, they typically play the chigubhu (or *tangi*), a cylindrical double-headed drum tuned to a different pitch on each side. In zvipunha, it is placed flat on the ground and only one head is used (see figure 4.3).[18] Some people occasionally add a second drum, a small *chimu-*

dumbana.[19] Mai Matiti, a respected n'anga and musician in Daisy Hill, uses this drum to either support the basic beat and patterns of the makosho or double the patterns of the larger chigubhu.[20] When everyone has gathered in the house, someone starts singing or playing. Sometimes, this initial bravery is met with disinterest and the lonely man or woman who started things off will just stop, maybe trying again in a few minutes.

To my ears, as Zivanai played, the ceremony proceeded appropriately, but there wasn't much energy. Nothing was particularly wrong, but things weren't progressing especially quickly, either. The collective mood was pleasant but static. The dancing of the mediums in the center was half-hearted and thus, unsurprisingly, the spirits had yet to wake up. It was more like work than joy.

The zvipunha drummers at this ceremony performed three basic phrases. Because Zivanai was not considered an expert drummer, he relied on the simplest patterns. The indicative zvipunha rhythm is typically an asymmetrical, syncopated eight-pulse sequence that starts just before the beat. To begin, the drummer plays this gesture on either the rim, as Zivanai did, or on the head of the drum.

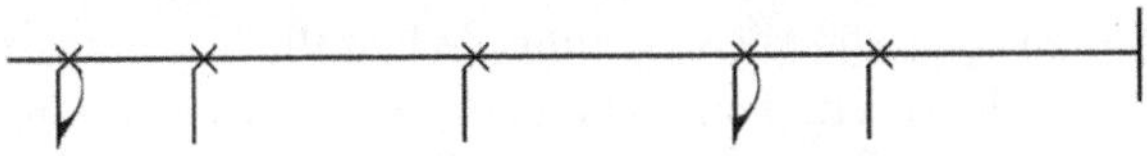

FIGURE 4.1. Basic zvipunha rhythm

Although I was taught to play it as written in figure 4.1, and this is my understanding of how it is heard, this actually aligns with the beat given by the makosho as shown in figure 4.2.

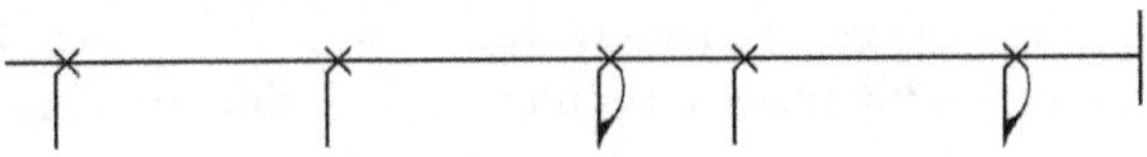

FIGURE 4.2. Basic rhythm on the beat

This phrase operates like a timeline, organizing other elements of performance. Drummers usually start with this and return to it at moments of ambiguity or insecurity. It is a simple phrase that signals the *intention* of inviting zvipunha spirits. Playing this basic part once everyone is participating becomes a signal to focus attention, tighten up collaborative parts, or reenergize the singing; it serves as a deictic reference to imprecision. This isn't always true, of course; it is not a symbol. Returning to this simpler part can also give the drummer a breather without compromising the integrity or energy of the performance. VaMasiza returned to this part more often near the ends of pieces than he did at the beginning.

As with all Ndau performance practices, there is significant regional diversity, and the range of patterns that drummers might play for the zvipunha can vary considerably. These variations are usually closely related to the eight-pulse patterns outlined here. This was true in Horus Farm, Holland Farm, and Muzite, where I conducted the majority of my research. But the Matiti family, who knew some of the people attending the Horus Farm ceremony, played both twelve-pulse and eight-pulse phrases for the zvipunha. Mai Matiti's twelve-pulse pattern resembled that of the mhongo. When the muchongoyo team from Bangwe took a break from a muchongoyo demonstration to play zvipunha for me, they employed a four-pulse pattern that took greater advantage of the possibilities of the multi-stick, multi-drum muchongoyo drums being played at the time. Both Mai Matiti's twelve-pulse phrase and Masiza's eight-pulse version employed alternating two- and three-pulse rhythmic motifs.

At Horus Farm this eight-pulse pattern permeated the entire zvipunha ceremony, whether sounding on the chigubhu, makosho, or maoko or as implied by established patterns and vocal rhythms. When the instruments shifted to different parts, this pattern would cue the spirits and signal intent: ♪♩♩♪♩ (1_2_x_1_x_1_2_x_). Asymmetrical and audible regardless of the texture, this phrase indexes timing, cycle, and purpose.

Once the performers are in sync, the drummer shifts to a new phrase to fill out the texture. For these patterns he or she uses one elbow to press the head of the drum to change its tension and alter its timbre and tone (figure 4.3), thus producing either two or three clear tones. The simplest version thus alternates between high and low using the elbow to generate frequent iterations of a simple two-pulse pattern: high-low, high-low, high-low (figure 4.4). Skilled drummers prefer a version that adds a third tone, complicating the texture and reinforcing the 3+3+2 timing of the initial zvipunha pattern. Depending on how one hears the patterns, either descending or ascending in pitch, this pattern can either be heard in synchrony with the makosho or out of phase (figure 4.5). Experienced drummers shape this phrase into different variations. This version is more difficult to sustain and synchronize precisely because it is difficult to consistently render three discrete tones using one's elbow, though experts like Davison Masiza, Mai Matiti, and Ambuya Mazveshe have little difficulty. Beginners like Zivanai stick to the simple high-low phrase. These sonic differences shape meaning. Whereas Masiza's three-tone pattern can convey competence and an ability to awaken spirits, the two-tone

FIGURE 4.3. Mai Matiti demonstrating drumming technique

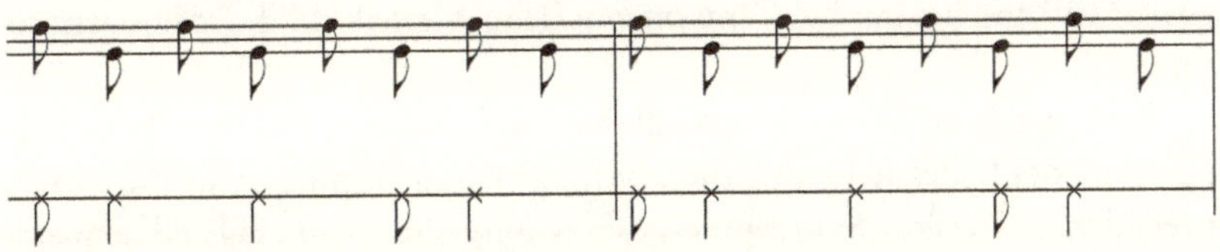

FIGURE 4.4. Two-pulse pattern

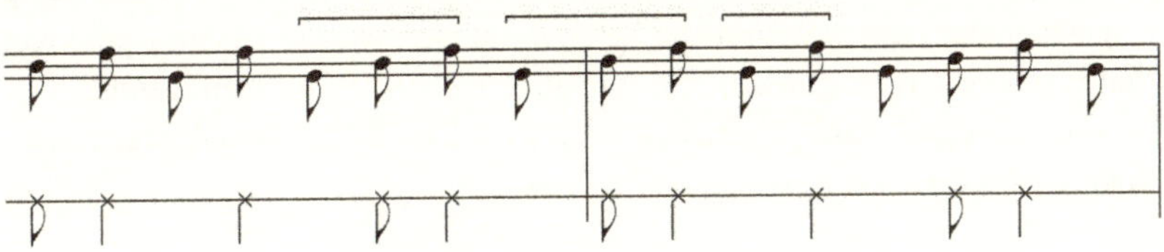

FIGURE 4.5. Three-pulse pattern

pattern conveys a lack of competence and an inability to easily summon spirits, altering the collective expectations of performance.

Makandira drums are reserved specifically for madzviti spirits and dances and *mateza* drums are exclusive to mhongo, but zvipunha have no specific drum of their own. Makandira and mateza drums are such reliable indices of their associated spirits that their very presence becomes powerful. The zvaa-yungu are young, so it is unsurprising that they are still "drum-free." But the zvipunha are, as Chikumbo put it, "ancient spirits." Although they are essential to events that are necessary for the survival of local communities, their rhythms are played on a chigubhu or even a mhongo deza if that is what is available. But the chigubhu is also common in muchongoyo and *chokoto*. The key signals for zvipunha musicking, therefore, are the 3+3+2 timeline and the use of the elbow technique. Spirituality here is marked less by the object than by the technique. Until the drummer places his or her elbow on the drumhead, it has nothing to do with zvipunha spirits. Drumming makes it spiritual.

Zvipunha songs are often simple, such as one Enos Simango taught me: "Nyarare kuchema punhawe, mai vaende kumvura punha woye, amai achauya punhawe (Hush the crying, young girl, mother has gone to the water, young girl, mother will come, young girl)." Short lines of text are filled out with one or more lines of vocables that contribute to a dense overall texture, such that the lyrics are often buried in the texture. Another "zvipunha lullaby" from Mai Matiti and her family, "*Nyarara kana* (Hush, small child)," demonstrates this well.

These songs creatively index lullabies and dance music simultaneously (Turino 2008), ideally linking the soothing zvipunha spirit to the movement needed for possession. Sometimes vocables dominate the singing and no words are sung at all. Lyrics obviously have meaning here, with layers often synthesized as "deep Ndau." The layering of vocal and percussive parts matters in ways that are consistent with that in other parts of the continent, contributing to participatory textures and the "groove" at the heart of musical practices that is so effective in generating both spirit possession and communitas. But for the moment I want to focus on what I took to be the central, salient moment of the ceremony.

Moment 2: Drumming to Possession

Davison Masiza began to play, skillfully changing the tone of the drumhead with his left elbow to play three-tone zvipunha patterns with the stick in his right hand. Because he is a skilled drummer and powerful singer, his attendance at ceremonies is greatly appreciated. Like Zivanai, Masiza only used one drum. He oscillated between three tones while others clapped and moved with the standard zvipunha timeline. Once he got going and the women sang, the mediums danced again, using quick steps in time to Masiza's playing with few of the big gestures or high stomps I saw in the madzviti dance. The movements were similar but less demonstrative. Against the darkness and the flickering shadows of the candle, the central space of the house was crowded with women inviting the spirits to emerge via dance. The sudden musical cohesion encouraged prospective mediums to dance with intent. Over the course of the next hour zvipunha spirits possessed several women as the intensity in the house rose with each successive possession.

Mediums react differently to the foregrounding and embodiment of awakening spirits. Some respond violently, falling to the ground and shaking in response to the conflict within them. Others react subtly with the confidence afforded by experience, barely missing a beat as they dance. Each woman's respective experience as a medium was evident to all as the spirits took control. Some, in piques of hunger, grabbed handfuls of dirt and shoved them into their mouths as a child might. Finally, after all the spirits had arrived, the music stopped and we went outside. Once there, the spirits danced again. We sang and clapped anew, someone new played the drum, and they danced for hours until, satisfied, they left their hosts and disappeared.

When Zivanai played, everything looked and sounded like a productive zvipunha ceremony, but the zvipunha themselves never awoke. The spirits weren't inspired by the signs being offered. Why was that? Much of the reason rests on how the relative skill of the drummer shaped the semiotic interpretation of the others. Everyone's response, including the spirits,' was defined by his or her expectations. Zivanai's drumming sounded fine but remained iconic of the desired objects, incompletely representing the desired objects. These objects included the purpose of invitation, the desire for possession, the spirits themselves, collective performance, and past instances of successful performance. Notice that many of these objects are closely linked with anticipated effects (interpretants) of these signs: possession, dance, participation. Even the spirits are interpretants of drumming. Their absence is an effect shaped by the less-than-ideal sign-object relations in evidence before Masiza took over.

When Masiza played the drum thirty minutes after Zivanai began, the sonic and affective impact was dramatic. Masiza's obvious skills catalyzed the pace of possession, consequently intensifying the singing, dancing, and overall energy in the house. Although in a successful ceremony each semiotic element is integrated, it was these signs (Masiza's drumming), at this moment, that triggered the sequence that led to eventual success. The moment he took his place at the drum, the desired effects of possession and participation became not just possible, but probable. It is significant that the only change I noticed was Masiza's playing. Superficially, there was little difference. Both drummers played "correctly." Both rendered tokens of the type. Yet the visual and sonic responses to Masiza's playing became, in turn, the signs to trigger spirit possession and the arrival of the zvipunha, a process of semiotic chaining central to any goal-driven participatory event. Understanding why requires a fuller explanation of what exactly a sign has the potential to do within a Peircean framework.

Signs

As a reminder, a sign is anything that is determined by an object and has an effect or interpretant in a person (Peirce 1992, 478).[21] Signs are one's gateway to reality. The interpretant binds the sign to its object. As I follow the semiotic experience, signs begetting signs begetting signs in the form of interpretants, I am the initial agent. Over the course of this particular evening's events, the number of agents eventually expanded beyond the people participating to include the spirits. At some level, these musical signs were about the spirits. Each living participant had his or her own semiotic experience, but it was the spirits' interpretations that ultimately defined the success of the music and the ceremony. Because they awoke and danced, it succeeded; the collective purpose was realized. Ritual performance is designed to help mediums focus on their relationship with the zvipunha, help the spirits understand the sincerity of the invitation, and facilitate their awakening via possession. Focusing on the intersubjective habit of human-spirit relationships allows spirit possession to take place.

Defining life as constitutively semiotic does not mean life is constitutively linguistic (Kohn 2013, 9), particularly ceremonial life. These events are richly multisensory because signs are multimodal and material. The living and the dead *hear* the drum, the makosho, the sounds of dancing feet, and layers of sung messages; they *see* the movement of the dance, the spirits' gestures, the expectant crowd, and the paraphernalia that look so familiar to the spirits as they awaken; they *touch* the mediums' clothing and the ground beneath their feet;[22] they *taste* the food and water on offer, the okra, crabs, dirt, and groundnuts that the spirits consume greedily; and they take the snuff (forya) that is indexical of spirit as mediums breathe it in.[23] One's encounter with the sensory material of the zvipunha ceremony in signs unfolds in multiple ways, employing the full range of semiotic processes that potentially are in play.

THE SIGN-OBJECT RELATIONSHIP

Peircean theory usefully distinguishes between three basic sign-object relationships: icon, index, and symbol. Each refers to a different way in which a sign represents an object; each refers to relations that connect meaning to interpretation to experience via the effects they have, the interpretants. The ways in which those interpretants relate to the objects represented determine the path taken, the semiosis to follow, and the experience of participants. Semiosis is unceasing, at least when the agent in question is awake, not in a possession trance or otherwise indisposed. Beginnings and endings become acts of interruption, and satisfied purposes close off one semiotic chain, only for a new one to take its place.

ICON: SIGN OF RESEMBLANCE Icons represent objects "only insofar as they resemble them themselves" (Peirce 1998, 460). Zvipunha mediums dress like spirits. They mimic them. They wear wraps appropriate to the spirits' status as child-rearers, with a *mubereko* cloth used to carry children on the back and a spirit-specific apron.[24] They keep their heads covered as nannies do as an index of their modesty and carry long *midonzvo* walking sticks as they dance. Early in the ceremony, these indices of women and elders linking modesty and authority (through co-occurrence) collectively generate an icon of the spirits being invited. When the spirits do arrive, people want them to feel comfortable. They are dressed for success, so to speak. This begins with resemblance; mediums should look like zvipunha spirits, as icons.

Iconically, there are a number of interpretive moves that can happen immediately.[25] Some signs sound and look like signs that one has encountered before: the way the drummer sets his or her elbow on the drum head, the signature zvipunha rhythm, the gathering of people inside the house, the familiar faces nearby of men and women in their usual places. Kohn (2013, 31) describes these likenesses as signs in which the differences they might have from the objects represented are ignored. The differences between this event and others, between the mediums and the spirits they look like, and between novice and skilled drumming don't yet matter. Everyone is establishing form, rendering their collective imagination, and imitating well-known types.

None of these signs is very effective in isolation. People drink beer, carry walking sticks, or take snuff in myriad contexts. But when framed by the house, when preceded by madzviti, and when attended to collectively, the meaning is heightened.[26] Each of these signs is iconic; a woman carrying a walking stick and wearing a mubereko *looks* like a chipunha; a drummer with her elbow on the head tapping out a 3+3+2 pattern looks and *sounds* like previous instances of zvipunha drumming. This is necessary. On one hand, all indexical signs are built on iconicity. On the other, ensuring that these signs are eventually understood indexically, as connected to and experienced with the objects represented, is a necessary step for ceremonial efficacy. Ceremonies transform icons of possibility into indices of actuality.

INDEX: SIGN OF CONTIGUITY Indices represent objects "by virtue of a real connection with them" (Peirce 1998, 460): contiguity. Grunts (kugaudza) and spirits go together. One accompanies the other, and so the grunt becomes a reliable indicator of possession. But a medium can't just grunt and become possessed. In isolation, this icon of a reliable index loses the sense of authenticity that genuine indexicality provides. A lot has to happen in the ceremony before a grunt indexes anything. What I first heard when the drummer began playing for the zvipunha was that this pattern was different from those heard for the madzviti: 1_2_x_1_x_1_2_x_. The difference was timbral (the edge of a big drum rather than the head of a frame drum), temporal (this was slower), and rhythmic (the asymmetry of the threes and twos versus the relentless madzviti duple). These are all qualities manifest in the instance, or qualisigns in a sinsign. When recognized, these differences index change. This recognition became a new sign in the chain almost immediately. Quite quickly this difference was ignored and the iconicity between this drumming and past zvipunha drumming took over. I recognized the form.

There are numerous ways in which a sign can indexically connect to its object. Beyond the role indices play in shaping ideas of reality as they shape habit, Turino highlights two indexical functions: pointing (deixis) and metonym (2014, 196). I interpret these as types of indexical connections and add a third, the replica index. Peirce's only distinction between different kinds of indexicality includes genuine and degenerate indices.[27] Genuine indices are in existential relation to their objects, as with deixis. Degenerate indices refer to secondness as reference only (Peirce 1998, 274), as with metonyms and replica indices. As with other Peircean trichotomies, deixis, metonym, and replica index reflect three nested ways in which a sign can index the object it represents.[28] Deixis attends to the here and now, metonym recalls complex associations rooted in the past, and replica index brings shared understanding and purpose together.

The first element in this trichotomy is deixis: pointing. All indexical signs are deictic.[29] Directing one's attention and forcing oneself to focus is essential to ceremonial efficacy. Pointing to purpose contributes to the eventual realization of that purpose. Resembling a ceremony generates different results than becoming one. A grunt points to possession as possibility, based on a learned association of the sound and the awakening spirit. The grunt indexically predicts the arrival of that which is not yet present, the spirit (Kohn 2013, 37).

The second is metonym. Each object used to collectively present an icon of the chipunha spirit is a metonym of that spirit: the mubereko, the mudonzvo walking stick, even the elbow on the drumhead. For Peirce, each is a degenerate index since the object is not in existential relation to the sign but is simply referenced (1998, 274). Thus, metonymy depends on context, habits, and memory, drawing on past deictic instances of contiguity that inform present interpretations of metonymy. As these associations are repeated and confirmed over time, the recognition of the spirit that each represents becomes habitual, even conventional. Many of these repeated associations become the conventional indices that confuse definitions and descriptions of symbols. The mubereko is part of a nanny's outfit, standing for the whole that preceded it as synecdoche; the elbow on the drumhead always accompanies zvipunha drumming, and this association heightens the anticipation of the zvipunha's arrival; and the grunt eventually is taken as actually being caused by the awakening spirit. It is the effect of that spiritual cause. Metonymy brings previously generated indexical associations between medium, ancestor or spirit, and sound together anew.

Third is the replica index. Peirce calls general signs "legisigns" and their instances "sinsigns" (1998, 291), an iconic token-type relation. Form recognition is based on this iconicity. When the deictic and metonymic attributes of a general sign bring its associations into the immediate present with the *purpose* of replicating it, it becomes indexical. The legisign, as object signified, carries its own expected associations, which it is *intended* to signify. This purpose of replicating assumes the existence of the legisign replicated, so it operates indexically (Short 2007, 212). Unlike symbols, when the legisigns of replica indices are intended to signify, the object is not assigned by a rule (222).

SYMBOL: SIGN OF STIPULATION Symbols, the third type of sign-object relation, represent their objects when "factitious habits of their interpreters insure their being so understood" (Peirce 1998, 460): stipulation. Given that symbols depend on definitions, it seems ironic that Peirce had such difficulty;

he defined *symbol* at least ten different ways over the course of his career. A consensus definition remains elusive. Its vague ubiquity in everyday English clouds attempts at theoretical precision.[30] Symbol's similarity with Saussure's sign leads to frequent elisions of the two systems, obscuring *processes* of semiosis in favor of the semiotic taxonomies that rightly frustrate critics. Symbols are general signs for general objects. This definition is open enough to inspire multiple interpretations and vague enough to cause confusion with legisigns. Equations with social convention loom over explanations of the symbol, casting shadows that obscure symbolic utility and distinction.

Symbolic relations reflect a different form of connection between the sign and the object than do icons and indices. Whereas icons are understood with resemblance and indices with proximity, brevity has muddied the waters for symbols. I align myself with three mutually compatible definitions from Turino, Cumming, and Short, who define symbols based on linguistic definition (Turino 2014, 197), stipulation (Cumming 2000, 93),[31] and a rule of interpretation (Short 2007, 221). The symbol is not the rule of interpretation, as Peirce occasionally implied, but requires such a rule to function symbolically (221). Although it is theoretically possible to *stipulate* a sign-object relation or *assign* a rule of interpretation with something other than language, that has yet to be demonstrated, supporting Turino's narrow interpretation. These approaches have yet to sway anthropological interpretations of the symbol and remain overshadowed by descriptions of symbols as conventional, arbitrary, embedded within systems of signs, and general. None of these descriptions are wholly inaccurate, but neither are they sufficient or unique (Deacon 2012a, 11). Indices can be conventional and exhibit "systematicity" (Tomlinson 2015), icons can be arbitrary, and all legisigns are general.

THE INDEXICAL NOW AND HAECCEITY

Turino (2014, 196) describes the "indexical now" as instances when signs are used to direct attention to the future and maintain attention. Like surprise, indexical nows draw the perceiver's attention by pointing to that which is not yet present. They index the proximity of possibility; it is not yet known what will happen next, but indexical nows set up the anticipation that something will happen.

There is a second species of indexical now, less analogous to surprise, in which the moment is not a sign of a not-yet object but the object of a right-now sign. This second species operates like an "accumulation of nows" (Agawu 2016b, 343). Signs with immediate proximity to the here and now, pointing unequivocally to "this moment," alleviate the possibility of surprise or reflection; "there is only presentness" (343). This kind of indexical now generates a form of secondness essential to participatory ceremonial practices like the madhlozi ceremony.

Indices of the here and now forcibly draw attention to the immediate present, a deixis that has become predictable through decades of ceremonial action: haecceity.[32] Peirce defines *haecceity* as "hereness and nowness" (1982–2010, 6:205). Haecceity is irreducible, particular; it simply is (6:205). More easily said in ChiShona or ChiNdau with *izvozvi*, *zvino*, or *izvinozvi*, haecceity is "pure secondness" (6:206). For Short and Peirce, haecceity precedes spatiotemporal location (Short 2007, 50; Peirce 1982–2010 6:455). When experiencing secondness, one loses that mediated sense of time and place, only snapped back by thirdness. By definition, haecceity is the absence of generality, and thus the experiential absence of iconicity and symbolism, which have nothing to do with the experience of hereness and nowness itself. Haecceity actualizes the possibilities of music and spirit as instances in the here and now (Short 2007, 78). It makes the uninterrupted contiguity of signs with here and now the foundation of experience itself, hence the potential generation of trance and flow. In moments when one's experience is encompassed entirely by a lived engagement with another, whether in Turner's spontaneous communitas, as lovers, or a medium with her spirit, secondness becomes the root of sociality. In spirit possession the past acquires haecceity, viscerally embodied by the dead possessing the living, and becomes an authentic, unquestioned fact.

When Masiza yelled "You were slow" to his young predecessor our collective attention was drawn to that moment, but it detracted and distracted from the collective purpose, pulling us from the moment but hopefully ensuring that future moments would become more effective. Conversely, when Masiza hit the drum and launched into Zvipunha patterns, our attention was drawn in and focused on the indexical now of our collective performance, potentially even losing recognition of moments at all, absorbed in the extended here and now in a shared space of participatory flow.[33] Through well-established participatory practices and the cultivation of communitas, attention to the now remained focused and heightened until time had passed, the spirits had arrived, and the ceremony succeeded. The musical challenge is to heighten attention to the now and shape a state of being (secondness for some, firstness for others) that stays in the moment until the purpose of the event, whether spirit possession, healing, or a shared performance experience, has been realized.

Terrence Deacon (2012a) rigidly demands the proximity of the object to the indexical sign; absent objects suggest symbolic mediation. I do not make the same demand of indexicality. It unnecessarily limits indexicality to only the most immediate and genuine deictic representations and defines all signs that are reliant on memory or imagination as symbols. I would amend Deacon's claim that nothing is indicated without the immediacy of contiguity (21) by arguing that nothing is indicated beyond a possibility, an idea, or a memory as immediate objects. The possibility of an awakening spirit is not to be taken lightly, nor is it a general, abstract quality. The specificity of visiting spirits is what makes the signs that represent them so productive.

Deacon goes to great lengths to point out the centrality of the non-intrinsic (meaning, purpose, and so on) to phenomena, a characteristic he defines as "ententional." Inspired by Deacon's (2012b) book *Incomplete Nature*, I ask whether an ententional index is possible. As Tomlinson points out, indexical associations require the capacity to learn from experience (Tomlinson 2015, 190). Remembered associations allow for indexical connections to objects that aren't physically present. Metonyms index objects that aren't physically present via experience and memory. The lack of proximity does not negate causality. Degenerate indices are ententional indices. Zvipunha drumming is indexical of the spirits before the spirits are there. They point the way, so to speak. Even without proximity, the deixis predicts their potential arrival as a possibility. It is one sign for the living listeners and another for the spirits.

Few of the signs I have described thus far are symbols, although most of the information about these signs was given to me via symbols during interviews and conversations. The generality of symbols thus provided an additional layer of mediation between the ceremony and my description. Symbols also shape the historical, political, and spiritual contexts of understanding and expectation within which signs are experienced. I admittedly afford symbols cursory attention in this text and prioritize the icons and indices that inform musical and spiritual experience. As general signs for general objects, rooted in arbitrariness, predictability, and rules of interpretation, symbols work because people agree that they work. Generality and predictability make it difficult to ground symbols in the here and now. Once you do, the words become indexical and you have the symbolic begetting the indexical. The use of symbolic language was important, but not exclusively so. I don't mean to disregard symbolism, but symbolic thought creates separation (Kohn 2013, 49).[34] It removes the thinker from the proximity of the here and now. Ceremonial engagement necessitates resistance to this separation. The conventions at the heart of this ceremony were not symbolic.

Purpose

The iconic resemblance of this ceremony to previous ceremonies makes it knowable. In this limited sense, this event is a replica index of the "zvipunha spirit possession ceremony." It is a token of the type or legisign it is *intended* to signify. One could argue that every sign has a legisign, but the purpose is not always to signify. Short divides Peirce's category legisign into two parts: legisign and legisign (G). The G stands for "general" (2007, 210). Legisigns (G) are not replicas, even if they have instances (210). Ritual is different. The reiteration of ritual moments and acts has a purpose: to replicate. But that is not the only purpose. One purpose is to invite the spirits to possess their mediums and provide space for their activity, especially dancing. Yet another is to inspire people to dance, and this activity should continue long after the spirits have arrived. The ultimate purpose[35] is to strengthen the community and ensure the future.[36] It is to make people safer. In Nussbaum's (2001) post-Aristotelian thinking, the purpose is (collective) human flourishing. The future of the community is at stake, and the way somebody plays the drum influences that future.

While the purpose is not *solely* semiotic, the representation of the legisign in this instance is deliberate, and it shapes how the ceremony is experienced. The purpose of the initial token-type association is semiotic. Drummers want to represent and conform to a certain genre, rendering the replica of an anticipated type. People understand what to do next owing to this resemblance. They also understand what to do next because they talk about it. Symbols and their unique power to communicate predictably and generally are obviously essential *almost* every step of the way.

Eventually, differences between this instance and past instances must be attended to. As ceremony as type is acknowledged, that acknowledgment becomes a new sign, triggering a new effect, and that initial token signifying type moves into the past. The here and now is what matters, focusing on the indexical now. Simply representing ceremonies iconically and ceremonial drumming as a type has limited utility; rote repetition won't inspire the spirits.

Each iteration of the basic zvipunha pattern (1_2_x_1_x_1_2_x_) helps establish a type. People respond to the sound as representative of this well-known sign. The type is what functions as the initial sign for the spirits. This new pattern indicates the zvipunha because it is similar to past instances of drumming that were used to invite zvipunha. For most attendees (other than small children and, initially, me), this type already exists as an idea. Within the context of the ceremony, this legisign is indexically connected to both the spirits being invited and the invitation itself. Its representation signals purpose. The pattern must become an index of the zvipunha.

When Zivanai played, the pattern was not yet interpreted as being caused by or co-occurrent with the spirits, but could be eventually.[37] At that point, the connection remained mere possibility. In order for possession to happen, the drumming must cease to be mediated by the generality of legisigns and be experienced as pure secondness. This possibility is rooted in iconicity and is a necessary step for everyone, including the spirits. Experience suggests the close proximity of the drumming and spirit possession. Interpreting the sign as such, recognizing the link between sound and spirit, bonds the sign to its object: the effect of recognition connects sound to spirit, sign to object.

This is somewhat analogous to stage smoke during a play. Stage smoke is iconic of the type "smoke from a fire" that then signifies fire itself as a mere possibility.[38] It works dramatically because of the audience's established association of smoke with fire. It is iconic of the instances that established that association. The difference here is that, to continue the analogy, we want to actually set the stage on fire. One weakness of theorizations of spirit possession as a form of theater or drama is that smoke on stage never leads to actual fire. A blank from a gun in a play ideally won't actually injure anyone. If the ceremonial musicking doesn't eventually awaken spirits and lead to their visceral presence as actual agents, then the ceremony is a failure. The goal is not to mimetically represent an idea but to change things: to bring spirits who weren't there before, invigorate relationships between participants, and productively engage the ceremonial goals so that the future is better. The goal is to transform these icons of possibility into indices of actuality.

The cyclic form, repetition, driving beat, and density of texture in Ndau ceremonial performances all contribute to an ongoing sense of the here and now that can engender experiences of secondness and firstness, flow and trance. These features are typical in musical practices in which participation is the point (Keil 1987; Turino 2009). The purpose is to minimize the mediating reality of thirdness (semiosis) in order to generate more immediate, visceral experiences. The capacity for performance to do this is grounded in haecceity, hereness and nowness. Participants ideally don't reflect on the past or orient their listening toward the future (Turino 2014) but concentrate on the vibrancy and vitality of the extended present moment.

Awareness of purpose is not enough to engender possession and shape a positive experience. It is neither magic nor a trigger. Possession takes effort and is a skill that can be improved (Becker 2004). The drum pattern's similarity to past ceremonial action guides everyone's behavior. It inspires clapping, makosho playing, and singing. Sometimes singing precedes the drumming. The melody's previously established indexical connection to the drums, rhythms, and spirits similarly inspires participation. This participation is what matters, at a minimum. It is necessary, but by no means sufficient. It is difficult to musically generate an experience that is unique enough to be grounded in the here and now and familiar enough to be predictable in such a way that success is assured. If everyone's individual contribution collectively generates a sensory sign that simply aligns with the previously established type and it is the type itself being engaged, the odds of enthusiasm and spiritual participation via possession become less reliable. Initially, everyone depends on iconicity, perhaps even mimesis in the sense used by the anthropologist Michael Taussig (1993).[39] That is what happened at the start at Horus Farm.

In some music, the primary goal is participation (Keil 1987, Turino 2016). Following the trail blazed by Keil, Turino, and others, the values and expectations of participatory music making are better understood than ever. It can bring people together, reinforce interpersonal relationships, and integrate participants into the potential success of the event in which it occurs. Spaces in which participatory practices are consistently engaged can also be the primary contexts in which community is performed and made manifest, generating tangible communities rather than imagined ones. "Good" performances in contexts like this are not defined by an autonomous aesthetic standard but by effectiveness (Perman 2011b; cf. McAllester 1954). If the desired effects emerge, the performance is good. Quality need not be based on competence, skill, or virtuosity; it just so happens that skilled drumming and singing are more likely to be effective. When fully engaged, Masiza often shouts brief words of critique to the performers like "you are slow" or "things are not good," in order to improve the performance by focusing attention on the task at hand and the audible flaw, whether due to incompetence, inattention, or exhaustion. Phrases such as this index a desire for change. They say something about the future, in which more skilled drumming would be necessary to ensure ceremonial success and participatory intersubjectivity. Superficially similar, the sounds to follow were understood quite differently. This difference meant something. Possession and participation are not easy. Realization of social values is unlikely without hard work. Collective affective experience must be shaped over time through diligence.

In an environment like the zvipunha ceremony, the habits that matter the most are tied to one's relationship with others: musicians, dancers, and spirits. These intersubjective habits shape experience. Music and dance are used to heighten these encounters. If the tempo lags or the drumming is imprecise, it can be hard to move in sync, sing with joy, or draw out the spirit. That is what happened during this event. Initially, our collective music making comprised a sign that was an obvious token of the intended type but never elicited the effects that people wanted. Over time, the relation between these musical signs and the effects they had changed the ways in which the same signs related to the objects they were intended to represent. This is why Zivanai's novice playing never fulfilled its primary purpose; the spirits never arrived. So he stepped aside and Davison Masiza took over.

Unlike Zivanai, who took breaks and changed patterns once it was clear that things were not working, Masiza kept playing until the spirits had danced. As Turino and Keil argue, participatory music is evaluated along different dimensions of value than presentational music. The ways in which these musical signs are interpreted along these dimensions of value shape how they are understood and felt.

Masiza himself, as with many musicians who play during ceremonies, wasn't focused mainly on these broader expectations, goals, or values, but he had certain musical expectations that needed to be realized. If the music improves, the rest will take care of itself. The indexical connections are so strong that if the signs are right they predict the future.

A Transformative Moment

When Masiza struck the drum, everything changed. The drum shifted from resembling expected patterns and inspiring rote participation to replicating shared legisigns, triggering authentic understandings of intent—the desire to invite the spirits—and generating a successful, collective, participatory experience. The intersubjective habits and experiences could be considered as a form of communitas but also heightened attention to the here and now. His drumming shaped an extended indexical now.

Indexicality is the most important mode of representation in ceremonial experience.[40] When signs are interpreted as being directly connected to the objects represented, the connection can feel immediate and visceral. Because indices are unpredictable, they shape reality.[41] During this ceremony, the sound of the makosho indicated a desire to sing and play for the spirits. Words of encouragement for Zivanai indicated an interest in pedagogy and practice. Each stage of the madhlozi ceremony employs signs that are indexical of ceremonial space, spirits, and communal intent. There are obvious iconic and symbolic processes at work as well, so it is reductive to limit ritual to indexicality, but beer, snuff, walking sticks, mubereko cloth, drumming patterns, dance steps, language, and the space itself all operate indexically for the spirits. These signs rely on established associations as metonyms for the spirits, their ceremony, and the desires of the participants. They are conventional signs that rely primarily on indexicality.

In semiotic terms, Zivanai's playing remained iconic of many of the objects anticipated by participants, offering little about reality in the here and now. In their generality, icons and symbols move separately from the moment-to-moment experience of the world. Icons cannot offer information, rooted as they are in similarity, whereas symbols rely *exclusively* on previously determined and agreed-upon objects. They function symbolically precisely because the objects they represent are predetermined.

Eventually, the differences between reality and the ideal were recognized and were interpreted accordingly as indexical of inadequacy. Instead of displaying sincerity, competence, and precision, inspiring movement and energy, Zivanai's two-tone drum strokes indicated inexperience and inadequacy, inspiring an eventual desire for change. Spirit possession ceremonies take time to develop, so everyone is more patient with novices performing during the early stages such as this. Less value is placed on skill because there is not yet much expectation of success. Aside from Masiza's more skillful rendering, the simple addition of the third tone opened up an entire realm of potential meaning rooted in experience and assurance. As events transpire, expectations change. The more valued the spirits' presence becomes, the greater the need for musical skill.

THE SEMIOTICS OF GROOVE

Different grooves are generated by the subtle relationships that each of a player's drum strokes has relative to the others and to the established beat. Zivanai's strokes fell slightly behind the beat. It was easy for the dancers to follow, but there was little to drive them or initiate an increase in energy. Masiza's strokes anticipated the beat ever so slightly. Playing that disrupts the beat by dragging or rushing interrupts habituated entrainment by directing attention away from that entrained and anticipated now, undermining the possibility of success and leading to a fuller awareness of when and where one is, which undermines haecceity, or a focused sense of here and now. Conversely, Masiza's precise playing directed attention to the immediate present.

This difference is difficult to demonstrate visually, but there are other differences that can be shown more easily. Masiza struck the higher-pitched strokes with more force than his younger counterpart did and initiated a slightly faster

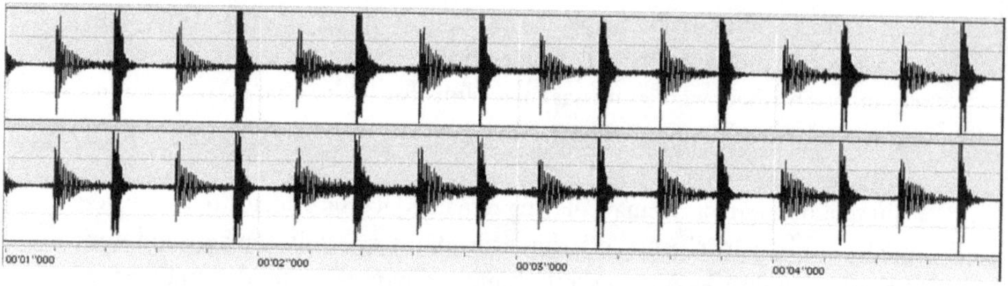

FIGURE 4.6. Novice drummer's waveform

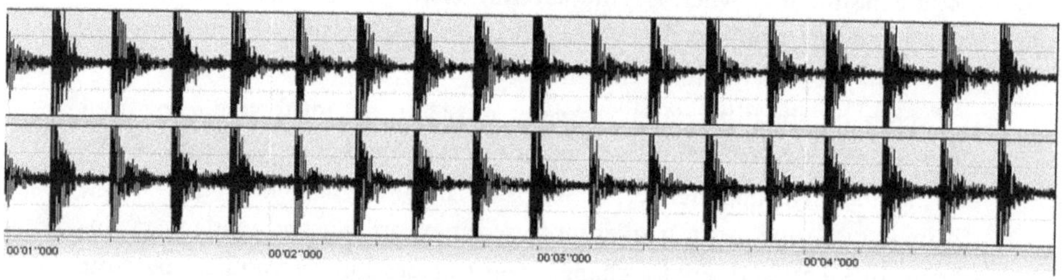

FIGURE 4.7. VaMasiza's waveform

tempo. Before he began, people were playing at approximately 126 bpm.[42] When Masiza played, the tempo increased immediately to 132 bpm. The faster tempo and stronger beats created a denser texture that is a reliable platform for participatory performance and ceremonial efficacy (Turino 2008, 44). Because Masiza played with more force, his playing exhibited a slower rate of decay, further reinforcing the dense texture. Zivanai's thinner sound envelopes were emptier and undesirably transparent. Zivanai's playing is reflected in a waveform showing amplitude over time in figure 4.6.

The darker, flatter shapes mark the sharper, higher tone of the two that Zivanai played with his elbow pressed against the drumhead. Notice how much softer and less defined the initial, lower tone of each two-pulse sequence is. Figure 4.7 shows Masiza's drumming. Each drum stroke is consistent when compared to Zivanai's strokes. This consistency, the drive elicited by the faster tempo, fatter sound envelopes, and the slight anticipation of his strokes all contributed to the increased sonic density and relative energy of his playing. Masiza's skill is more easily demonstrated if we focus on the amplitude of just four drum strokes (see figure 4.8).

Each of Masiza's strokes looks the same, whereas Zivanai's lower tones on pulses one and three lack a defined attack and are audibly softer. The effect of these subtle differences is striking. Differences in texture contribute to

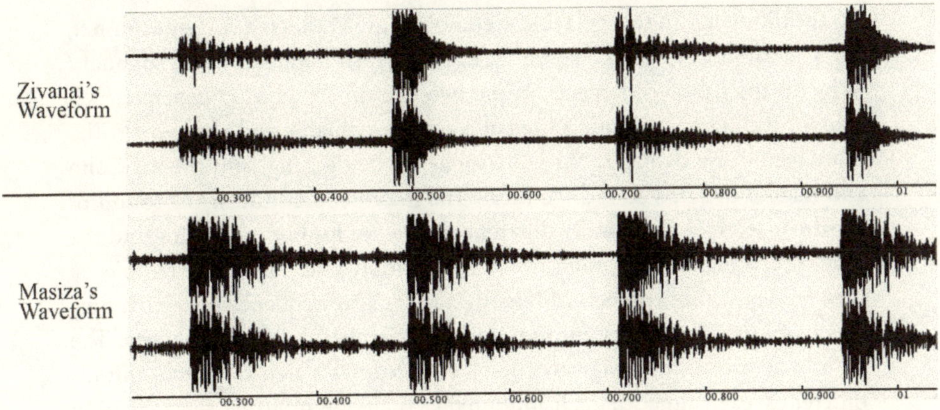

FIGURE 4.8. The waveforms of both drummers

radically different interpretations. One inspires pedagogy, a casual engagement with the event's purpose, and a thirst for beer. The other leads to spirit possession, enthusiastic participation, and nurturing protection from happy spirits. These two instances are obviously not the same sign, although they sound similar and are played for the same purpose. That they are interpreted differently has to do with the ways in which each sign represents its object. Each sign's relation to its effects relates significantly to each sign's relation to its object; there are relations between relations. Much of the difference, I argue, is a shift from iconicity to indexicality.

TRANSFORMATION

Semiosis depends on transformation (Kohn 2013, 50). Icons cannot generate many interpretants. After recognition, they remain general and inert. It is difficult to feel connected to an icon because connection itself is a property of indexicality. When the music simply sounds *like* zvipunha drumming or references form, that's all it can do, sound *like* something. That makes it hard to generate new interpretants like spirit possession. In order for the Horus Farm ceremony to succeed, something needed to change. The drummer could suddenly improve, the community could shift their expectations to devalue the spiritual, or someone else could take the drum and drive the music forward, draw people's attention, and trigger new effects that ultimately lead to possession and success. When VaMasiza sat at the drum, among other phenomena, the formerly iconic associations that the sound of the drum had with various objects quickly became indexical. They transformed.

The difference in their playing seems obvious. Masiza is a better drummer, and you can hear it. You can even see it. But why should that matter so much? Why do the subtle differences in the two drummers' playing generate such profound differences among the collective participants and the spirits? The same people are dancing, the same songs are being sung, and the makosho and maoko patterns sound identical. The microscopic shift in the sound of the drum led to a profoundly different experience for both the living and the dead. Precision became profound. It is not simply that signs relate to objects; they represent those objects differently and, as a consequence of these differences and the effects they inspire, lead participants to different objects. The path of semiosis, from sign to effect that becomes a sign to effect, unfolds differently each time for each interpreter. There are multiple signs eliciting multiple effects based on their connection to multiple objects. These differences make a difference.

Everything in Peircean semiotics is nested. This elegant feature helps organize what can initially appear a complex system. Every symbol has an indexical and iconic component within it; every index has an iconic component. Even legisigns are nested. The song "Nyarare kuchema" is nested within zvipunha songs nested within madhlozi songs nested within Ndau spiritual songs nested within Zimbabwean songs.[43] It is helpful to continuously remind oneself of the basic categories of Peirce's phenomenology: firstness, secondness, and thirdness. Three always contains two always contains one. One cannot contain three. This plays out in time as well. Symbolism emerges from indexicality; as those indices become conventional, agreed-on, general, and assigned via a rule of interpretation, they become symbols. But indexicality matters more in ritual because it shapes experience *now.* As memories of past associations are referenced on the basis of their similarity to the present, indexicality emerges from iconicity.

It may seem counterintuitive to think of indexicality as emerging from iconicity, but that is precisely what matters here. During previous ceremonial experiences, playing and possession coincided and formed an indexical association. This history informed the response to Masiza's playing and focused our collective attention through causal connections to objects that would have gone unnoticed previously. Whether it is the needed connections of intersubjectivity or the sincerity of invitation, spirits, performers, and mediums, all needed to feel a direct connection. Masiza's drumming, as it connected indexically to ideal relationships between musicians and dancers, mediums and spirits, predicted the zvipunha's arrival (Kohn 2013, 35). When playing elicits spirits and their presence is felt as real, the semiotic association of performance and spirituality is taken as true. These kinds of connections are hard to fake but also can't be taken for granted or assumed. Unlike symbols, predictably representing objects via rules of interpretation and collective agreement, these sound-spirit connections must be manifest in the instance indexically.

The shift to indexicality during Masiza's playing generated a signal for spirits and mediums alike because of its purpose to inform, an intent to signify, rather than a cue's incidental indexicality (Huron 2015, 2). When a zvipunha medium dresses like her spirit, the similarity, the iconicity, is general and doesn't initially represent the actual spirit. But the act of dressing adds an index of purpose to the embodiment of mimesis. Zivanai's playing represented the *idea* of collective music making and zvipunha more than it was *felt* to represent a manifestation of that ideal. Resemblance to spirits, to ceremonies, and to performance, then, recall the associations that those resembled performances had. Sounds that are iconic to past sounds allow the associated possession of those past sounds to become possible in the present.

When Masiza picked up the stick, played, and inspired those around him, the improved timing was an index of their synchronicity, felt and understood as such, an index that is based on the interpretant effects of his playing. The index here is the connection of the sign, in this case Masiza's drumming, to an object (skill, a desire to invite the spirits, an expectation that others will perform) that is understood to have effected that sign. Icons aren't understood or felt in that way.

A token instance represents a type because it is similar to that type that was developed through repetition. All sinsigns are iconic of legisigns. But that is incomplete. In cases like the zvipunha ceremony, more is needed to convince spirits that the community's invitation is genuine, to make the collective music making appealing, and to ensure ceremonial efficacy. The legisign of the ceremony must be replicated convincingly (for both the living and the dead) and must be indexically understood as causally connected to the desire to invite, the intent to perform collectively, and the need for the spirits. In order to do this, the instance must also represent its type, its legisign, indexically. The purpose of the sign, in this instance, is to replicate the legisign "zvipunha ceremony" as type. Token-type iconicity, the pointing index (deictic) that characterizes all indices, and the association of drumming as metonym of ceremony, metonym of spirit, and metonym of the Horus Farm community all are necessary to understand the instance as a replica defined by ceremonial type. It is not enough to be similar to a ceremony, nor is it enough to interpret the general type, so the transformation from iconicity to indexicality stops short of transforming into symbolism. The playing needs the immediacy of the here and now in order to be felt as real, as visceral. Indexicality requires the ability to learn from experience, apply what is learned, and match that experience to the present (Tomlinson 2015, 190–91). Indexicality is iconicity transformed (191).

Although the present drumming sounds like past drumming, the mediums look like other mediums, and the sonic relationships of the participants diagram past musical relationships, there is purposeful intent to replicate something challenging and ephemeral beyond resemblance. People want to direct the attention of the zvipunha spirits to what is happening here, at Horus Farm, now. The zvipunha must recognize this purpose and recognize the co-occurrence of these real-time events and the ceremonial types being deliberately signified. In this way, the iconicity between this event and past events, the mimesis of these mediums and the spirits being invited become indexical and felt as something real and true, more than imitative. Experience shifts from the generality of legisigns to the specificity of the instance. Beyond simply imitating the past, it is a deliberate act of *creating* the present: this ceremony, these participants, this moment. Now![44]

Hearers know quite a bit about the systems of relations that define the spirit world as well as the music performed for them. But I stop short of interpreting the zvipunha pattern as a symbolic legisign. It works as a legisign, certainly, but I doubt the presence of a "rule of interpretation." These systems of relation are indexical, not symbolic (Tomlinson 2015). The object is not stipulated but remains predicated on past events, iconic to past indexicalities, so to speak. The convention of using drumming to invite spirits isn't enough to ensure that a rule of interpretation is followed. It must be felt as indexically connected by all involved, but especially the spirits, in order to trigger the semiotic processes necessary to result in possession. Neither the generality of the symbol's sign nor object is rooted in the here and now. The trance that enables possession, the visceral experiences of ceremonial action, demand and depend on a heightened awareness of the here and now. Symbols can't inspire ecstasy. They are meaningful, predictable, and flexible, but inert.

Moment 3: Ethnographer as Sign

The zvipunha were fun to watch. They acted like little girls, spoke in childlike voices, ate with both hands, and moved with childish gestures. By the time all the mediums were possessed, the energy in the room was palpable. Those of us who had arrived late had to mind our toes, attentive to the possibility that a dancing spirit could step on them during the excitement. When the chipunha caught sight of my face and fled across the room to cower in the safety of the women working for her, VaMasiza could only laugh, relishing the moment. Perhaps the clearest evidence of their antiquity, aside from people's explicit assertions, was the zvipunha's reaction to me. My presence was disruptive of zvipunha ceremonies because, as Masiza bluntly pointed out, "Zvipunha are afraid of white people." Masiza said they feared me because they had lived and died before Europeans had penetrated into Chipinge; thus they had never seen a white face before, and, of course, because they were little girls. Madzviti and mhongo spirits never really paid much attention to me. The zvaayungu were actually quite at ease with me. But I was a sign of the unexpected and the unpredictability of ceremonial experience, even for spirits.

That moment when the spirit recoiled resonates with me personally for two reasons. First, it marked my outsider status and reinforced the realization that categories of identity and difference were negotiated through events such as this, as people's own pasts were recalled and relived. Second, it confirmed the chipunha's relation to care as her efforts to nurture the collected participants were disrupted by the unexpected, and mitigated by the women who protected her. Negotiating difference and cultivating the sociality that defines a successful event helps the living come together during these communal moments and shared experiences, but it helps the spirits as well. To put it bluntly, they have needs, too. Jabulani Mulambo explained, "After we have brewed beer we beat the drum and we say, The beer is yours. It is given food while the person is possessed, the zvisora eat okra. . . . It [the chisora] is given traditional beer and it eats. Then you call others with zvisora from other places . . . so that it eats . . . and so that it has friends."[45] This particular ceremony was less charged with a task than are those tied to childbirth, funerals, or harvest, but care was manifest in the passing of groundnuts and the attention paid to every individual. Caregiving emerged as a tangible response to the chaotic moments of history that ultimately led to the zvipunhas' becoming spirits (Kleinman 2014, 125). In ritual, it restores order with love, resilience, and service (125). The living and the dead care for one another.

The living pay for this care with beer, a metonym for all that a ceremony entails. Mulambo said, "To pay for that protection we will brew beer for them. After we have brewed beer we beat the drum and we say, The beer is yours. . . . You say to it, We thank you for all you do for us here with what you help us with." Brewing beer, singing songs: a small price to pay for protection, care, and social continuity. As Enos Simango put it, "We were raised being carried by a chipunha."

Looking ahead to Chapter 5, the spirits themselves are interpretants. They are effects of the signs that preceded and predicated their arrival. Every interpretant is also a sign. The multivalent zvipunha here signify multiple objects. They signify success and confirm the effort put into playing and singing an invitation to their arrival. When the spirits fail to arrive, as I was told countless times, it is a troubling index. One can't be sure what the object is in such a case and may have to consult a healer or another spirit to find out, but it is assuredly problematic. There is no coincidence. Rural Zimbabwean communities are semiotically attentive and consistent in that signs are indicative of something intentional; bad luck has causes; failed possession has reasons. So the spirits' mere arrival is worthy of celebration. The goal is to placate the spirits and provide them an opportunity to dance, so their arrival is a confirmation of that purpose.

Signs come together to form complicated sign complexes, but there is also a linear process at work. Drumming leads to better singing and clapping, which leads to more inspired dancing, which leads to spirit possession. Each effect becomes a sign for the next effect in the chain. Drumming was the ground, the foundation, for eventual ceremonial efficacy. It was the difference between the two drummers' playing, the discrepancies in their participation (Keil 1987), that led to the differing experiences of everyone participating. Yet while I'm sympathetic to ethnomusicologist Charles Keil's assertion that socially valuable music should be out of tune and out of time (1987, 275), Zivanai's "out of time-ness" undermined its social value and decreased others' personal involvement. Masiza's energized precision was an essential catalyst to the efficacy of the collective experience. His strokes were clearer and more intricately combined. The sonic density enhanced by his playing, regardless of how subtle, had an important and noticeable influence on the pace of possession during the ceremony.

Everyone agreed that things improved once Masiza began playing. But the reason things improved is not that the drums sounded inherently "better" but that Masiza's playing demanded more energetic attention, inspired more attentive dancing, and was, consequently, more *effective* in initiating possession and spiritual dancing. Judgment of performance skill was based on participatory efficacy. Masiza more effectively facilitated experiences of pure secondness, indexing the values-based expectations of danceable drumming, sonic and social density, and confident participation. He also appealed more directly to the spirits' desires, and that appeal was evident in their imminent arrival. The equally important contributions of others were improved because of Masiza's playing. The key was transforming resemblance and possibility into haecceity, the immersive experience of presentness without mediation. The generality of icons, legisigns, and symbols all faded into the background. With skilled playing, enthusiastic participation, and collaborative performing, the next step in the sequence became inevitable. With signs such as this, there was only one possible interpretant: spirit possession.

CHAPTER 5

Overnight

Mhongo and the Effects of Performance

Samson Mapfumo hosted a ceremony at Muzite on my behalf. His generous gesture provided my first opportunity to see the mhongo and hear their rhythms. Although all of the necessary preparations had been made and spirits possessed their mediums as expected, the mood was lighter than is often the case during ceremonies. For one thing, owing to a combination of my own clumsiness in introducing myself to the Muzite community and the tense political climate that permeated early twenty-first-century Zimbabwe, the local headman required that the entire ceremony take place over the course of an afternoon instead of overnight. For another, because VaMapfumo had in part offered to host the ceremony so that I could film, the daylight hours were more accessible to children, and he garners such respect in his community that more than a hundred people came to watch the unexpected afternoon of dancing and see the muyungu filming in the center of it.

I sat among the elders on the edge of a wide open outdoor space. As I watched, engrossed in conversation with a neighbor, peals of laughter from the gathering children pulled my attention away. As two men drummed sincerely and several mhongo spirits danced in their characteristic shuffle, VaMapfumo strutted around the ground, flamboyantly tossing the sacred *chingunda* wig he wore on his head back and forth as he playfully and dramatically mimicked the dignified dance of the spirits. In the midst of a sacred event, with real consequences for the families involved, in a climate compromised by political tension, there was still room for whimsy.

This chapter does three things. First, it introduces and describes the mhongo spirits, their performance, and the intricate drumming that brings them to dance. Though similar to the madzviti and zvipunha spirits, there is something different about the mhongo and the music with which they are associated; their drumming is more complicated and multi-faceted and their dancing looks more solemn. Second, this story is examined from the perspective of semiotic consequences: the effects or interpretants of signs. Whereas previous chapters focused on the way signs and sign-object connections inform experience, this chapter emphasizes the next step in that sequence: the interpretant. Intepretants are also signs, and understanding them as such provides a powerful tool in elucidating how meaning can be made musically. One of these interpretants (or effects) in this case is possession. Third, the chapter demonstrates how emotion itself is meaningful and explains how these semiotic processes, as experienced, shape the emotional experiences of the participants. In order to do that, I return to my model of emotional experiences and explain how different musical and ceremonial contexts can lead to very different emotions and feelings.

I compare the Horus Farm ceremony that has framed the narrative thus far to two atypical performances of music intended for mhongo spirits. These performances, one hosted by VaMadzitya and the other by Ambuya Mazveshe, were unusual in that each host actually hoped to avoid spirit possession, which is typically the goal, although they did so for different reasons and in different ways.[1] In each case, the shifting interactions of participants' respective desires, expectations, and habits shaped the contrasting events that followed and people's subsequent emotional responses. Meaning is not fixed, despite the conventions of ritual. The way these conventions are manipulated, intentionally or not, has important consequences for the efficacy of ritual practice and the ability of the living to control relationships with their spirits. I explore the way signs of performance are interpreted along dimensions of value, namely, desirability and possibility. These values, as interpreted, shape specific effects, or, in Peirce's terms, interpretants.

Interpretants, Emotions, and Feelings

Experience involves the unceasing evaluation of signs. In semiotic terms, the central element of meaning is the effect of a sign, any effect. For simplicity's sake, I equate a semiotic effect with an interpretant that "encompasses the concepts of interpretation and meaning simultaneously" (Turino 2014, 202). Most of the signs in operation during a mhongo ceremony are icons and indices and are not operating symbolically. They do not represent a predetermined, general, and fixed object that is agreed upon. Their meaning comes from the effects they have. Thus, when Masiza strikes the drum and a spirit medium begins to dance, the drumming meant that she danced. That's it. The sinsign, the instance, is what matters; a chain of signs to interpretants is freed from generality. Habits of entrainment ensure that generality no longer determines experience. Surprising effects and semiotic manipulations can bind unexpected objects to familiar signs. In each case below, it also means that music made people feel differently because of nonmusical factors.

Peircean theory brings the individual interpreter and the specific instance into the center of analysis through the interpretant. Every experience is partially unique, regardless of the predictability of the signs involved. Rather than relying on a fixed and arbitrary binary sign—the signifier and the signified—interpretants rescue the distinct processes of musical meaning from an unnecessary equation of meaning with language.

Peirce divides interpretants in three different ways corresponding to the nature of the interpretant itself, the interpretant's relation to the sign's representation of its object, and what is evoked in the interpreter. Like most Peircean hierarchies, each of Peirce's subdivisions of the interpretant is a nested trichotomy tied to firstness, secondness, and thirdness. First, Peirce distinguishes between three kinds of sign-object-interpretant relations as one of three trichotomies of the sign: rheme, dicent, and argument.[2] The distinction between rheme and dicent, rooted in the difference between the possible and the actual, is particularly useful in highlighting how music shapes different emotional experiences, as will become clear in the cases investigated below. A rheme is a sign that is interpreted as *possibly* being tied to its object. All icons are rhemes. A dicent is a sign that is interpreted as *actually* being connected to its object, typically an index. The distinction between the possible and the actual exposed by rheme and dicent is helpful in explaining why music makes us feel a certain way and how authenticity informs those feelings (Turino 2008). Arguments, signs of law (Peirce 1998, 292), are third. Peirce fortuitously defines them in a way consistent with everyday English vernacular usage.

Dicent and rheme highlight the nature of response more than they do the nature of the sign. Whether people and spirits interpret signs as authentic dicents or as potential rhemes has profound consequences for the ritual success of ceremonies. When a medium dancing with the intent of inviting and awakening a mhongo spirit grunts, the grunt is either interpreted as actually caused by the struggle of the spirit's awakening (a dicent) possibly caused by this struggle, or possibly caused by deception but initially simply similar (a rheme); this distinction can have important consequences as participants trust the spirit implicitly, test the veracity of the spirit's identity, or dismiss the medium's efforts as insincere.

Second, Peirce (1998, 498) distinguishes between immediate, dynamic, and final interpretants. The immediate interpretant addresses the "interpretability" of the sign. The dynamic interpretant is the actual effect of a sign in the interpreter and is the most relevant for my purposes. The final interpretant reflects how a sign should and will be interpreted given enough time. The teleological nature of semiotic experiences demanded by an acknowledgment of final interpretants is a productive way to think about the role of purpose during interpretation. Denise Gill (2017), for instance, writes about the affects that people *should* feel in Turkish musical experiences and the impact of these affective expectations. The distinction between how musicians and listeners feel in the moment relative to how they will eventually feel based on collective expectations speaks to the potential theoretical utility of distinguishing between immediate, dynamic, and final interpretants. More succinctly, the immediate interpretant is what might be, the dynamic interpretant is what is, and the final interpretant is what ought to be.

Finally, Peirce (1998, 409) distinguishes between three kinds of dynamic interpretant: emotional, the energetic, and logical. My interpretation is consistent with Peirce's but also corresponds with the recent neuroscience of emotion, the anthropology of feelings, and critical affect theory. Emotional interpretants are affective (vague sensation, blushing, accelerated heart rate), energetic interpretants are active (turning to look where someone is pointing, stepping when the drum's cue is heard), and logical interpretants are symbolic (agreeing with someone, reflecting on the events at hand). The emotional interpretant is a necessary component of semiosis, which I equate with affect (Deleuze and Guattari 1987; Stewart 2007).[3] All interpretants include affect. Thus, interpretation is affective; it begins with affect. This assertion is key to my synthesis of affect and meaning.

The analysis to follow is obviously partial; it is focused on a narrow selection of signs and objects. There is always more to be said about the sounds themselves, the words that can be sung, the gestures and movements of the mediums, spirits, and other dancers, and the broader political, historical, and social contexts and constraints of each particular performance. But a narrow focus on a few key signs illuminates the emotional, and ultimately social, consequences of specific changes.

The ways in which drum sequences played during mhongo ceremonies are interpreted differ in each of the three events I discuss, leading to very different musical and emotional experiences. Normally, the sequences played on sanctified mateza drums are interpreted as dicent indices of the spirits. That is, everyone is so familiar with them that they are interpreted as actually being connected to the spirits and a desire to convene with them. The spirits' arrival becomes an interpretant of these musical signs. How the drumming relates to the spirits' arrival as it relates to the intent to invite them (or *not* to invite them) shapes how the drumming is experienced and made meaningful.

In chapter 2 I defined emotions as "processes of response to and appraisal of signs that signify objects of value and thus effect changes in the body and habits of the self" and introduced the four stages of the semiotic chains felt as emotional experiences: affect, emotion-appraisal, feeling, and emotive. Each step leads to the next just as signs lead to effects that become new signs. Effects (interpretants) keep the chain moving, shaping semiosis as experience.

These processes influence one's self and sense of identity by hardening, softening, or dismantling the edges around valued habits and ideas. The struggle between expectations, desires, and ideals becomes a call to action grounded in the values and sense of morality that shape how emotions feel, drawing on important negotiations between the possible and the actual that expressive practices like music are so well positioned to negotiate.

Performers deliberately signify certain habits and expectations in order to shape emotional experiences. Musicians knowingly (and unknowingly) play with the habits, expectations, and ideals of performance, leading to expected and unexpected consequences. The conflict in values that informs these consequences trigger neurophysiological appraisals that people feel according to their habits, which are shaped culturally and personally over a lifetime. The reasons why communities engage in spirit possession practices, the anticipated and desired end goals, inform the way performance signs are evaluated in real time. When Mapfumo wore the wig and brought some whimsy to the ceremony, he disrupted the habits of response for seasoned participants, generating laughter. He also revealed the comfort of realized expectations in an event with relatively low expectations. Once the spirits had arrived and danced, as they were doing in the midst of his flamboyant act, their collective purpose had been realized. Responsibility shifted. It was Mapfumo's party, and he wanted to entertain the children, who usually are asleep by the time the mhongo arrive. The disruption of habits by the unusual circumstances of the event changed things. Because the spirits were happy, things changed for the better.

Episode 1: Horus Farm

It was close to midnight. The zvipunha had left and already seemed like a memory as the evidence of their recent presence was swept aside. Everyone took another break to drink, eat, and stretch their legs. Although two dif-

FIGURE 5.1. Davison Masiza playing the mateza

ferent types of spirit had come and gone, the proceedings were only getting started. The mhongo spirits, the next to arrive, always danced for a long time. When people returned to fill the ceremonial house, Masiza took his place at the three tuned drums of the mateza,[4] which someone had already heated by the fire to achieve the appropriate tension and tone on the goatskin drumhead (see figure 5.1).

Masiza played well. He and the woman using the two smaller *zvimudumbana* played polyrhythms unique to mhongo spirits while several men and women dressed as the mhongo were dancing in the center of the house. Their dance, dominated by small steps, shuffles, and turns, always seemed restrained compared to those of their spiritual neighbors, the madzviti and the zvaayungu. Occasionally they would dance on their knees, swaying and turning with gestures associated with the nzuzu mermaid spirits who assisted their possession. As the energy intensified in the room thanks to the drumming, singing, and our collective clapping, the mediums danced more demonstratively. Their spirits soon awoke within them with similar signs of trembling, shaking, and falling. Some of the possessing spirits visibly struggled with the effort of possession. Soon there were more than ten mhongo spirits dancing.

The spirits asked that we move outside, and before long people were dancing, singing, clapping, and drumming again. The mood grew euphoric. People shouted encouragement to the dancers and comments of playful ridicule, interjected ululations (*kupururudza*) and whistles of admiration (*mheterwa*), and collectively sang with increasing strength. The drummers sat only inches from some of the dancers. Some of the spirits knelt on mats before the elder men and ululated in greeting as they bowed their heads. The elders clapped slowly and respectfully in greeting, and the spirits bowed and ululated in response. But their ululation was only marginally similar to that typically heard from the women at key moments of numerous social gatherings. They warbled slightly and, it seemed to me, gurgled.

As the sun rose over the hills to the east, everyone danced even more vigorously than they had been for the past six hours. Their enthusiasm was almost aggressive. Participation was more widespread now as both men and women engaged in the performance. Approximately one hundred of us gathered together just outside the house where the ceremony was started. The space outside was still roughly gendered as it had been inside, with the women standing and dancing on one side and men on the other, but a man and a woman played the drums, both male and female mediums danced, and men and women contributed to the dancing, singing, and collective effort, which seemed more balanced than either the madzviti or the zvipunha portion of the event had been. People crowded around the drummers and dancing spirits, tightening the ceremonial circle, unifying everyone in an intimate shared space. Some of the unpossessed participants joined in, performing the same dignified moves as the mhongo. Aside from the chingunda wigs and ceremonial paraphernalia that the spirits wore, the easiest way to tell the living from the dead was their comportment. The spirits were reserved. Their dance was quiet, almost still. The living jumped, shouted, smiled, and showed off, boisterous and creative in their movement as the ceremonial responsibilities of the preceding hours faded with success from people's minds. There was a small space in front of the drums where dancers would occasionally enter to do a step, but for the most part everyone danced in their own space, shuffling along with the quick tempo at about 200 bpm.[5]

The spirits bobbed up and down as they stepped subtly to the sounds of the drum, adding shuffled steps that coordinated with the rhythms of the mateza. Whenever Masiza ended a cycle with a rest the spirits would pause or turn and then continue dancing with the next cycle. They rarely engaged with other participants, preferring to keep to themselves. They danced in place, spun like mermaids, stepped in sequence to the drum, and rarely uttered a sound, except for two male spirits who played whistles throughout. The living danced with enthusiasm, enjoying the celebratory mood. The spirits seemed happy, at least, happy enough to dance for hours without interruption or complaint. The musicians were playing fast and everyone was engaged. Masiza kept everyone going with the quality of his playing. He playfully wore a wig as well. Given that he'd been playing the drums, off and on, since dusk, his energy was remarkable. He was having a wonderful time playing as hard as he could, shouting praise at the dancers, and singing along whenever his breath allowed.

Every so often the drummers would stop and everyone would start talking at once. The mood remained elevated; the spirits waited for people to stop arguing about what to sing next, whether anything was missing, or who had derailed the performance. A couple of minutes later, Masiza would start the pulse again, singing, drumming, and clapping followed shortly thereafter, and the spirits began to dance again. The sound must have carried for miles. Shortly thereafter, people returned to the house and played until the spirits left, much as the zvipunha had. Everyone was exhausted. The mhongo dancing had been invigorating. Happy spirits, happy dancing: the ceremony was a success. After hours of collective ceremonial labor, this was the payoff. Every phase of the ceremony thus far had been more successful than anticipated, and the only thing left to do was express their shared joy and whimsy through sound and movement.

MHONGO SPIRITS

Mhongo are crucial to local healing practices and dominate madhlozi ceremonies, connecting the Ndau to their VaDanda neighbors in Mozambique and mermaids from the coast of the Indian Ocean. Mhongo are perhaps the most powerful spirits in Chipinge, a focal point of every ceremony I attended. During ceremonies in which multiple types of spirits emerge, the mhongo dominate the spiritually significant overnight hours, evidence of their importance to the local community.

Mhongo present a marked and placid contrast to the potential volatility of the madzviti. As Mpande Chikumbo, a former mhongo medium, often succinctly reminded me, "Madzviti destroy, the mhongo preserve." The threat of the madzviti must be contained, whereas the promise of the mhongo must be nurtured. Indeed, mhongo are intimately linked with the ability to heal and the skills of the n'anga herbalist and healer. For Chikumbo, that which they were either protecting or destroying was "culture," a concept that, in Zimbabwe, typically refers to practices and objects that were considered outside and prior to the realm of the modern, the European. Like their predecessors that day at Horus Farm, the mhongo share roots in the southern African turmoil of the nineteenth century.

Disagreements about the terminology and identity of mhongo spirits can be confusing because they have multiple names and descriptions depending on geographic origins and the circumstances of death. Chikumbo said, "They call the spirit mhongo, the VaDanda. The Vashuma . . . some call it jukwa. It is the mhongo. Some call it muvhimi, the hunter." Because it was the most common definition among my informants in Muzite, Chipinge, Holland, and Birchenough Bridge, I restrict my use of *mhongo* to the category of spirits who participated in the ceremonies I attended at Horus Farm and Muzite. The Chipinge n'anga Joseph Mutwanha explained that "when you have been possessed by people who come from near the sea there, for example, those who come from Mozambique further there, that is what they call mhongo." Wilson Simango said, "Mhongo are of the water."

Closely associated with nzuzu mermaid spirits, these mhongo originated in the Danda region of Mozambique and were also under the authority of the invading Gaza Nguni armies.[6] Jabulani Mulambo, another Chipinge n'anga, explained further: "They [the VaDanda] are there. To be a Danda is the same as saying a person dies in Mozambique that we do not know and he/she comes to us because he/she would have left their ancestral lineage because they would have done bad things to him/her. So he/she has gifts that they have such that wherever they land they are able to find help." The spirits typically speak ChiDanda, the lingua franca in the Danda region, linguistically similar to ChiNdau, and enjoy the *mbira dzaVaNdau,* an instrument that my mbira teachers Masiza and Zombiyi Muzite Gwenzi claim originated in Danda.

VaDanda currently tends to refer to people in the lowlands of Mozambique east of the Ndau in the highlands of eastern Zimbabwe and western Mozambique. Because these ethnic markers emerged in response to this political history and the following era of colonial rule, it is unsurprising that there is disagreement about membership and boundaries. Lowland Ndau in the Save Valley and Highland Ndau near Mozambique's border have very different ideas about who is considered Ndau, just as they collectively think of their ethnic identity differently than do those in Mozambique's Ndau communities.

Danda was one of several secondary states along with Teve, Sanga, and Shanga that were formed in what is now Mozambique when Portuguese pressure splintered the hinterlands of the Monomutapa Empire, one of the most influential early kingdoms in southern Africa (Rennie 1985, 167).[7] The Danda District lies between the Zimbabwe-Mozambique border and the Indian Ocean on the path taken by Soshangane during his migration with the Gaza Nguni north into Zimbabwe. Most of the people I spoke with agreed that the mhongo who have so much importance in the Zimbabwean Ndau cosmological framework originate from Danda, such that many of the spirits are called VaDanda. Danda is often described as a "subdivision" of Ndau to "distinguish inhabitants of the coastal plain from those of the highlands, who were called Ndau" (MacGonagle 2007, 49). MacGonagle distinguishes *Danda* as a "political" ethnic marker, whereas *Ndau* is a more general term. In my research, Zimbabwean Ndau used *Danda* to describe communities to the east in Mozambique, reserving *Ndau* for themselves.

The VaDanda who died during this early history have since reemerged as mhongo. Chikumbo told me, "Because this was the Monomutapa Empire, in the process of fighting some were dying without children. It is those people who died without family who come as spirits who they call mhongo." The mhongo identified as VaDanda are closely connected to mermaids, or nzuzu, who traveled to Zimbabwe with the VaDanda spirits inland from the Mozambique coast.[8]

NZUZU

Nzuzu are mermaids. They are neither midzimu nor madhlozi but comprise a category all their own; they are powerful spirits. Chikumbo described the nzuzu as the "mother spirit of all spirits," explaining that "the njuzu now finds a place to go and he is the one who trains the ancestral mudzimu spirit survival techniques and how to coordinate these other, smaller spirits." Cryptically, Mutwanha said that "njuzu is a person but he isn't a person." They live in pools and lakes throughout the Ndau-speaking region, traveling from pool to pool in dust devils, the little whirlwinds of dust and air common during the drier months.[9] Whenever women see one of these dust devils pass by they begin singing and ululating to greet the traveling nzuzu. Some use *mhongo* simply as a synonym for *nzuzu*, but this seems incorrect. Wilson Simango bluntly said, "Mhongo are not njuzu."

Ambuya Mazveshe told me that "nzuzu and mhongo spirits are related." The relationship between them is unique and of central importance to Ndau cosmology, particularly in relation to healing. Ndau n'anga, local healers, often are mediums for mhongo spirits and rely on those spirits for their skills, although these healing powers are technically granted by the nzuzu, not mhongo themselves. Enos Simango was taken by a nzuzu spirit in 1947, when he was a young boy. He was under water for days before being returned. The mermaid took his tooth and Simango acquired the abilities to work as a n'anga.

This symbiotic relation manifests itself explicitly during possession. These powerful mermaid spirits help mhongo spirits to such an extent that both possess the mhongo's medium together, which is why some people confuse the two. The mhongo spirit only possesses the medium's head and shoulders because the nzuzu spirit is beneath it, supporting it both literally and figuratively. As Chikumbo explained to me,

> Now, this is a combination of two spirits. Yes, there is the mermaid spirit; the mother spirit of all spirits. It is the mermaid. Yes, the njuzu, it is the mermaid spirit. . . . The man[10] goes to a traditional healer. The traditional healer says, Why can't you first of all appease the mermaid? If you do that the mermaid will know how to prepare the way for any other spirit that comes after him. . . . That spirit which is talking is upheld by the mermaid. The mermaid is fortifying the lower end so that no other spirit can go in this one which is still talking, Get away! The mermaid is in control. And if another spirit wants to come the mermaid will say, Not you. She wants the order.

Thus, mhongo mediums at Horus were actually possessed by two spirits simultaneously, mhongo and nzuzu.[11] For the n'anga Mudiwa, "MaDanda are together with mermaid spirits."

This relationship is an extension of the mhongo's long-lasting association with mermaids owing to their proximity to the ocean during their lives. Because of this relationship, mhongo spirits often make gurgling noises akin to the fishlike sounds of the mermaid and have noticeably fishlike movements in their dance. As a visible marker of this, mediums possessed by a mhongo typically wear a fiber wig called a chingunda as a sign that their hair grew long while they were living in the water (see figure 5.2). They sometimes dance with freshly cut branches and always wear red as the madzviti do, for it is a spiritually significant color in much of Zimbabwe. Ngarife Matabuka, the Muzite spirit medium, told me, "Mhongo usually wears a cloth with drawings of a lion."

Nzuzu spirits grow in the water and learn from older nzuzu who live there, as my conversation with the Chipinge n'anga Wilson Simango and Chikumbo reveals:

> WILSON SIMANGO: You see, that child now who dies as a baby is buried in the river. Now that spirit develops into a njuzu and the hair now becomes long because of living in the waters.
>
> TONY PERMAN: Is that why mhongo wear wigs?

FIGURE 5.2. A mhongo with a chingunda wig playing a whistle

MPANDE CHIKUMBO: Yes, trying to bring that similarity with the njuzu. So you see, that baby who is one day old, he has died. Or is three days old, dies, and has been buried in the riverbed. This is the tradition here. A baby is buried along the river. That spirit now grows in the water. In a spirit now. And that spirit, when it manifests itself to people, it has got long, long hair.

Thus, like the zvipunha, nzuzu spirits grow after their deaths as infants to become powerful spirits.

In May 2005 a young boy disappeared while swimming at a dammed lake on the edge of Chipinge. Rumors began to circulate that the nzuzu in the lake had taken him. Workers whom I met in the Ministry of Education, whose offices overlook the lake, watched the events that followed with curiosity and amazement. A few days after his disappearance people ran to the nearby police station, claiming that the boy was at the lake, or, to be precise, on the lake. On top of the water in the middle of the lake, the missing boy was sitting in the lotus position. He apparently looked healthy and calm as he sat on the water's surface. The police found a rope and managed to pull him in. Unfortunately, as soon as the boy reached the shore he violently threw up blood and died almost immediately, confirming suspicions that it had in fact been the nzuzu that had taken the boy. The police had pulled him to shore before the mermaid had finished passing along her healing gifts. Mpande Chikumbo, who worked in the ministry, told me that a nzuzu had recently returned to the previously unoccupied lake.[12]

MaDanda are not the only mhongo spirits, although they were the only ones who participated in the ceremonies I describe here. Several people stressed that there are a few different types of mhongo, depending on their specific origin and whether they are male or female. Some are even Ndau spirits who choose not to become midzimu despite having children. Chikumbo told me:

> Here is an ancestral spirit. But in his home his children possibly do things he does not want. They use *mbanda* juju to try to invite him into the home. He then says, No, I cannot stay in this home. The children are doing medicine that I don't like. I can't work here. I can't do anything in this home. He leaves his home, this old man's home, and comes to my home as a mhongo now, to me. Leaving his family there although he had a wife and children and starts giving me those jujus and things he was using. He does not want [to become mudzimu] because his children are disobedient or they are doing things he does not want.

Jabulani Mulambo confirmed that there are several Ndau spirits who choose not to become a mudzimu when they die: "It is actually an ancestral spirit and it would be called mhongo because it has come to me. When he goes to his children he becomes an ancestral spirit now, so he doesn't want to give them the gift he has. They offended him before he died so he got angry and so he then goes to an alien and gives them help because his own family offended him." Thus, they choose to become mhongo spirits and direct their family's behavior that way. These spirits are overshadowed by the dominant mhongo archetype, but as Chikumbo suggested above, sometimes the VaDanda spirits are also disappointed by their descendants. As with virtually every feature of this particular cosmos, there is little unanimity. Different spirits have different levels of presence from one community to the next, much as each specific community has slightly different histories, despite general trends that are shared throughout the region.

Their status as healers and protectors gives the mhongo considerable authority during ceremonies. After the aggression of the madzviti and the youth of the zvipunha, their mature serenity can be a comfort to the ceremony's participants. Perhaps for this reason, mhongo dominate during the midnight hours, usually dancing past dawn the following morning. Despite their relative placidity and protective nature, their power is still nothing to be taken lightly, as Simango's anxiety and caution during our interview suggested. Mhongo have a responsibility to ensure that the communities they visit remember and sustain the cosmological practices that have served them well. Much as they heal the ailing body with the medical practices of the n'anga, they heal an ailing society by teaching the proper ways to respect and honor spirits, thus restoring equilibrium to the community. Their authority goes a long way toward ensuring that the practices of the previous generation continue, thus encouraging a certain level of practical conservatism.

DRUMMING FOR THE MHONGO

"And the mhongo, they are characterized by two things: observance of the culture and dancing. If you hit the drum and mhongo comes, before talking to you he has to show you one thing by his dance. It's a powerful dance." Chikumbo told me this as we were discussing mhongo. This is why these spirits show up; this is why they've always shown up. As previous chapters have demonstrated, people and spirits tend to interpret signs on the basis of experience with similar signs. Mhongo drumming is a common enough category of performance that its objects and effects are predictable, though by no means fixed. Mhongo drumming is a general sign, or legisign, intended to trigger spirit possession. It exists in order to engage with mhongo spirits. That is its purpose. The way in which musicians engage with this purpose shapes their results. These sounds made by these drums lead to spirit possession frequently enough that participants expect the spirits to show up. Sounds inform participants' expectations, which then inform the way events are understood and felt in the moment.

Performers employ numerous multisensory semiotic modes to ensure that these expectations are realized, iconically recalling past successful events and indexically re-creating conditions that appeal to the spirits and ensure their arrival, leading to the multisensory experience of the typical mhongo ceremony. Contextual circumstances can change the way these collective signs may be interpreted, but when done well, desirable outcomes become probable outcomes, and positive feelings of community, accomplishment, spiritual support, and joy emerge. If the signs are performed in such a way that the intended objects are signified, desired effects like possession become more likely. The spirits' manifestations are interpretants of the drumming and singing. The invitation to those spirits is an object of the drumming, and their arrival is directly connected to correct drumming.

Masiza describes the spirits' dance steps as *kutenderera mvura* (turning in the water). He explains further,

> They will have a basin of water because it is of the water, because the mhongo is a mermaid. You know that, right? Yes, they live in a pool of water. They will have basins of water being taken out and dipped into the water. Yes, that is of the water, *vakatendera dziyawe*. Dziya, they mean pool of water, they will be circling around [the basin] and they see it as a pool of water now and they say, *Titi titi titi. Yakatendera dziyawe.*

There is nothing aggressive about their dance as they shuffle quietly in time to the music, turning occasionally as cycles come to a close, pauses in movement and sound aligning with one another.

The four or five bowl-shaped mateza drums are so significant and indexically tied to mhongo spirits that, within the Ndau communities in which I lived, they are ideally only played during ceremonies and can only be made if requested or permitted by the mhongo themselves. Both the drums and the patterns played upon them are more complex than those associated with the other spirits. Each drum includes a small hole near the bottom in order for water or beer to be poured inside. Before they are used, a special naming ceremony is held to "christen" the drums, offer them to their spirits, and prepare them for eventual ceremonial use. Beer is poured inside each drum as an offering to the nzuzu who assists in the process of mhongo possession. This beer (or water) is also used to fine-tune the drum if the head was overheated when prepared for use. The drums' round and shallow shape is openly intended to iconically mimic the pools in which the nzuzu spirits live.

One person plays the three larger drums, called *muoshwe*, *mukati*, and *mudyi* (literally left, center, and right), and a second performer plays one or two smaller drums, the *zvimudumbana* (see figure 5.3). They work together to generate a rhythmically complex foundation for the singing of other attendees and dancing of the mediums and spirits. Using polyrhythmic layers of twos and threes, mhongo drumming needs to hold people's interest for the long overnight hours of the ceremony.

As in zvipunha drumming, there is a signature rhythm for mhongo spirits (shown in figure 5.4) that signals to both the living and the dead that the spirits are being invited. This rhythmic motif can be played by either drummer with his or her sticks against the rim of the drum. Dancers can also start things off or join in by clapping. Once the pattern and tempo have been established, each drummer plays more idiomatic patterns.

The zvimudumbana are played in numerous ways, but typically players choose one of two basic patterns depending on their skill level. Beginning drummers usually play a basic three-pulse pattern on a single chimudumbana

FIGURE 5.3. Ambuya Mazveshe playing the mateza

FIGURE 5.4. The basic mhongo rhythm

drum of R-L-pause, R-L-pause. Once the lead drummer joins in with the styles described below, the two-against-three pattern emerges more clearly. Skillful drummers use both zvimudumbana to play patterns such as the second one in figure 5.5, filling out the texture and contributing to the desired sonic density.

Once the zvimudumbana pattern is established, there are several styles available to the lead drummer that correspond to different repertoires of mhongo songs and can be reserved for specific times of the ceremony, as demonstrated in a pattern played by Masiza and given in figure 5.6.

Each style generates a different type of tension within the resulting texture and relates to the dancing in different ways. Style A accommodates the most flexibility and creativity on the part of the drummer, as the sequence of tones can vary considerably from one cycle to the next. Each cycle ends with a pause, indicated by the rest at the end of each measure. The dancers also pause here, often turning quickly before dancing along with the next cycle.

FIGURE 5.5. Common zvimudumbana patterns

FIGURE 5.6. Three styles of mhongo drumming (each line represents a different drum)

The pause coordinates the dancers and drummers, connecting them temporarily and intersubjectively. The ideal effect is one of synchrony. Masiza said that this dance move, the turn during the pause (indicated by an eighth rest in style A), marks the nzuzu's influence, iconic of a fish turning in the water. In Style B, the drumming provides a perpetual drive to the texture that elicits heightened dance energy and can enliven the proceedings. These two styles, the most common, comprise the vast majority of mhongo drumming I heard. Style C was played less frequently. The constant two-beat alternating tones sounds a little like zvipunha, but the implied beat from the other drums and the basic rhythm in the makosho and singing creates a clear rhythmic tension between the duple and triple rhythmic textures. I only actually heard this style during demonstrations from Masiza, never during an actual ceremony.

In all mhongo drumming there is a perpetual tension between rhythmic motives centered on twos and threes. A classic figure in polyrhythm throughout the continent, it is this tension that, along with the more melodic drumming passages, makes mhongo so musically rich. Madzviti and zvipunha drumming are not organized around polyrhythmic tension in this way. I argue that the complexity of mhongo drumming allows the mhongo portion of the ceremony to remain interesting during the long overnight hours. Mhongo spirits will often stay and dance for more than seven hours, much longer than the other spirits do.[13] It is important that the music engage the living enough that they continue to participate even as they grow weary with exertion.

The rhythmic figures in mhongo drumming do not shift, nor do they in any of the other madhlozi dances. There is, rather, a constant tension between simple rhythmic motives (two and three) that provide a foundation for innumerable vocal, drum, and dance options that can contribute to a vibrant, polyphonic, and dense texture. Steven Friedson (1996, 158) compares the "acoustical illusions" of *vimbuza* drumming with optical illusions, suggesting that shifting rhythms provide the space of encounter for spirit, drummer, and singer, calling it the sonic equivalent of a Necker cube. Similarly, Martin Scherzinger (2012, 105) suggests an iconicity between the "phantom" likenesses audible during mbira music with the spiritual transformations that mark ancestral spirit possession ceremonies in which mbira music is played. The rhythmic tension in madhlozi drumming is only accounted for in part by an iconicity with visual illusions. The inherent tension is analogous to the "in-betweenness" that Jankowsky (2010) foregrounds in his analysis of spirit possession in Tunisia.

This tension is audible in style A in figure 5.6 once the chimudumbana enters with the fast, repetitive three-pulse part that overlaps with the mateza's duple patterns. It is this density of texture that is highly significant, in conjunction with a musical space in which to dance. In many ways the specific melodies of the songs, the intricacies of improvised drum lines, and the meanings of the texts are secondary to a rich, dense texture that creates a frame for intense dancing and participation.

Despite the complexity of mhongo drumming relative to that of the madzviti or zvipunha, it is not a virtuosic practice. Skilled drummers such as Masiza are recognized and admired for their skill because they can facilitate ceremonial efficacy, as we have seen, but their virtuosity is not essential for the ceremony to proceed smoothly. This was never more apparent than at the times when I was encouraged to play, despite my nascent skills. Since the role of the drummer is to frame the other elements of participation and engage active involvement from as many people as possible in order to encourage spirits to dance, exceptional skill is primarily manifest in a nuanced sense of time, consistency during performance, and stamina. Virtuosic variations can make performing more interesting for people, particularly during a long ceremony, but these potential exhibitions of virtuosity (as, for example, figure 5.7) are symptoms of extensive playing rather than prerequisites for effective playing.[14] More than signifying participation, performance is constitutive of it.

FIGURE 5.7. Excerpt from "Makwitika"

Episode 2: VaMadzitya

Tendai Chitopo and I heard the drums long before we arrived. Their sound cascaded along the valley as the sun set, while we sat in the living room at Chitopo's home, where I was staying. We were at the Muzite primary school, where his home was, nestled on the hill with a beautiful view of the valley and bright green tea estates below. Mozambique was just visible beyond the next hill. The school serves children on both sides of the border, operates as something of a cross-border center of gravity, and was my home away from home while I lived in Chipinge. VaMadzitya, a local n'anga who lives down the hill, had graciously invited me to a ceremony at his home.

The proceedings were in full swing as we arrived, greeted everyone, and entered the ceremonial roundhouse. The mood was light, the beer was flowing, and the music was flying. It was still early, so nobody expected the spirits to emerge just yet. As if to prove that, I was invited to play the drums. The focus remained on joy, play, and dance. At the time, I was unaware of the complexities behind this seemingly straightforward ceremonial experience.

Within a few hours the affective intensity heightened and shifted as more experienced drummers took their seats at the mateza, mediums became the featured dancers, and everyone figuratively rolled up their sleeves. The strength of the playing and singing ricocheted across the Muzite valley as the combined drumming, dancing, singing, snuff taking, beer drinking, and participatory activities triggered the spirits within their mediums to awaken. The spirits soon possessed their hosts and the ceremony became a success, realizing and affirming the typical values of a mhongo ceremony. Unfortunately, this is exactly what VaMadzitya was hoping to avoid. Although he was the host, he was really hoping that the mhongo would stay away.

In the days before the ceremony, for which VaMadzitya had spent considerable time and money in preparation, a member of his family had passed away. Bereavement in these Ndau communities is typically accompanied by ceremonial abstinence; the drums should remain silent and indoors as a gesture of respect to the deceased and the spirits involved. This madhlozi ceremony had been planned for a long time, however; VaMadzitya and his family felt it was important to conduct the ceremony and play for the mhongo. Given the harsh economic conditions prevailing in Chipinge in 2005, he said, he wouldn't be able to afford a ceremony like this again for quite some time. The expense the family had already gone to in preparing beer and providing food for the whole community was not something they could abandon lightly. The stakes were high and VaMadzitya was trapped in a difficult situation.

Even on the afternoon of the ceremony, no one was sure if the drums would be played. On one hand, people were grieving and wanted to respect the deceased with quiet drums. On the other, people were anticipating the ceremony both for the respect it demonstrated to the madhlozi in question and the opportunity for celebration and communal joy these ceremonies typically afforded. Despite his ambivalence, the ceremony went ahead as planned. It was, to all appearances, a typical mhongo event.

When we arrived at the beginning of the ceremony, the stakes remained low; there was nothing to indicate the conflict behind the host's façade. But as the evening progressed, the mood changed, while events unfolded as one would have normally expected. The anticipated effects triggered by these signs then led to interpretations of those effects that compromised their value. There was a conflict between the *typical* purpose of playing these drums and the intentions of VaMadzitya and his family. The conflict between the probability of spirit possession and the desirability of avoiding it was untenable

Spirit Possession and Intersubjectivity

At face value, spirit possession is a straightforward process within these Ndau communities. There are spirits, in this case mhongo, who need to possess living people, their mediums, in order to dance, be content, and continue providing the services on which people rely, such as powers of healing and protection of ancestors. Once they are made aware of the bond they have with their spirits, those mediums can ensure a mutually beneficial relationship by adhering to whatever restrictions the spirit requests concerning specific foods to eat or avoid and other lifestyle choices and ease the process by utilizing tried and true methods of possession. This is where music and dance are so valuable. One does not *need* music in order to become possessed, but it certainly makes the task easier. Even if both the spirits and the community want spirit possession to take place, it still takes work. The spirits want to feel respected, loved, and needed. Thus, it is important to have as many people participating as possible as an index of intent, sincerity, and respect to the spirits being invited. This has the added benefit of strengthening the ties that bind the living to one another, whether through family relationships or residential proximity. Possession is not automatic because the spirits need to interpret these signs of intent and desire as being real, as dicent signs.

Two forms of intersubjectivity are desired and employed to ensure the smooth awakening of the spirits and the success of the ceremony: that between living participants with each other, ideally manifest as a form of communitas, and that between the medium and his or her spirit. Spirits also relate to one another, but that is beyond the control of the people involved and usually assured if the ceremony is successful.

There can be other goals, but every ceremony is intended to strengthen the community via productive interpersonal relationships engendered by participation, and every ceremony is expected to result in spirit possession. Whether the music is considered good or not is largely based on whether these anticipated effects emerge. As an inextricable part of the sign, the interpretant determines how a sign is evaluated and engaged. Spirit possession and communitas are both performed manifestations of intersubjectivity. These relationships and the habits involved, as they are lived in real time, are important components of ceremonial life.

Drummers, mediums, spirits, and other participants form their relationships in part by relating to one another in the moment during a ceremony. Community is an interpretant of ceremonial performance, just as pies are interpretants of ovens. In order to encourage collective flow, or communitas, performances like those for mhongo spirits incorporate multiple components to entice experts and novices alike. The drumming is difficult, particularly over the course of the long ceremony, but hand clapping, singing, and dancing are all almost immediately accessible. I participated in the first ceremony I attended at Muzite. I didn't do much more than clap my hands and sing the occasional vocable, but I was a part of the proceedings. Ceremonial success is built on such participation. Community is partly created in these experiences. Community, as a process, emerges from shared experiences, relations, and habits. Expressive practices like music and dance allow for fuller integration of community, beyond the linguistic. Thus one effect of good drumming is the lived relationships that define community. Done well, the habits instilled by performances such as this shape the communal relationships that continue after the ceremony is over.

Mhongo ceremonies are moving in part because they focus on intersubjective habits that can reinforce these very communities as communitas. Performance in mhongo ceremonies reinforces intersubjective habits between the living and the dead that shape self and identity. The communitas that emerges from collective participation and purposive ceremonial action not only helps ensure possession but feels good because it alleviates any potential conflict between the ideal and the actual.

Spirit possession is also a form of intersubjectivity, reflecting the relationship between the living medium and his or her spirit, a bond that has been a part of the medium since birth. As the Chipinge n'anga Jabulani Mulambo reminded me, spirits are resident within their mediums. Spirit and host are each quite literally part of the other's self whether or not the spirit eventually manifests via possession. As a reminder, one's skills, personality traits, or talents are attributed to one's spirits. Spirit and medium need one another if they are to flourish.

Among other things, musicking serves as the means to an end; it allows and invites both the medium and the spirit to focus on their shared connection.[15] With practice, mediums are able to focus on becoming possessed, a learned ability to cede agency to the spirit. In these terms, possession itself can be seen as a form of communitas, as a clear case of intersubjective positionality. The ways in which each relates to the other, and the focused concentration on this relationship, pushes everything else outside their focal awareness. Differences fade, and the spirit assumes control of the medium's body.

Ceremonies work because people engage collectively in generating signs that refer to objects that are intersubjectively shared, including the spirits, the histories from which they emerge, and the purpose of the gathering, in the hopes of generating new signs (that is, interpretants) that are intersubjectively expressed. Spirit possession is an interpretant of ceremonial action, the effect that *ought* to take place if the signs of the purpose of spiritual awakening as an object are performed appropriately. But the spirits are agents of semiosis, not merely its creation. One's relation to that spirit can be an interpretant of the ceremony, particularly as a spirit medium, but the spirit itself exists regardless of one's openness to the relationship. The conditions of the ceremony do not invent the spirits but, rather, open the way for the spirit to manifest within a medium. Possession is an interpretant of the drumming. Embodiment is an interpretant of dance. But the spirit is initially the object of the drumming, tied indexically to past instances before becoming an agent of interpretation, *choosing* to dance, *choosing* to greet, and *choosing* to feel offense at VaMadzitya's choice to carry on with a ceremony despite being bereft.

As the mhongo awoke VaMadzitya's face was visibly tense, accompanied by interjections of "*Maiwe* (Oh, mother!)" and hurried looks to family members that seemed to imply questions about what should be done. His anxiety emerged from the conflict between two accepted truths that contradicted one another. First, playing music during bereavement is considered disrespectful, so refraining from doing so at this time was a form of respect. Second, performing music in a ceremony is typically a sure way of showing spirits respect, so refraining from doing so could be received as a form of *dis*respect. The effort to satisfy both aims led to a period of ceremonial malaise in which the goals of ceremonial performance were only partially realized. VaMadzitya was hoping that the signs tied to drumming and ceremonial performance would be interpreted differently than in the past. He would have preferred that the sounds not be interpreted as indices of invitation and the desire for possession. But it wasn't entirely up to him. Some of the performers, some of the participants, and, most important, the spirits interpreted these signs as they thought they should, as indices of ceremonial intent and purpose. As the evening wore on and the actual (dicent) connection between ceremonial drumming and satisfied spirits came to the fore, the playing became enthusiastic and the drummers' playing became an interpretant to the spirits' actions rather than VaMadzitya's.

In the end, the effort to respect the spirits was most effectively practiced via the established and true means of drumming for them. So the hosts went ahead with the proceedings hoping that the drumming could remain respectfully quiet, that the volume could be taken by the spirits as an index of the sincerity of their grief and as respect for their loss. But signs like the sounds of the mhongo drum combined with the availability of alcohol, food, and snuff have worked for decades to trigger very specific, deeply ingrained habits of response. Simply asking the drummers to play a little quieter did little to undo years of habit formation. Thus, despite the Madzitya family's hopes and concerns, their ceremony evolved very quickly into exactly what they expected but feared, a full-blown, successful, and loud mhongo ceremony. The habits of performance shaped by years of practice during other ceremonies eventually overwhelmed any efforts on the part of the hosts to resist the inevitable consequences. The complex swirl of anxiety and anguish, tied to loss and concern for appearing disrespectful, mixed with the collective enthusiasm and joy typical of a mhongo ceremony such as this, led to a complex and emotional event. For the hosts, trapped between two difficult options, the conflict between the highly probable but undesirable expectation of spirit possession and the highly desirable but improbable ideal of their absence, led to frustration, anxiety, and even fear.

After the ceremony was over, VaMadzitya and his family were resigned to the realization that they would likely have to host an additional ceremony to appease the spirit who may have been offended and repair the damage. He knew that the consequences could be severe, although he never specified to me exactly what he was afraid might happen. A ceremony done with the best of intentions had slipped avoidably out of their control such that success from one perspective, when considering the *immediate* goals of a mhongo ceremony, defined failure from another perspective, when considering the responsibilities of bereavement. For VaMadzitya, this was frustrating. Sadly, it only made the sorrow that accompanies the bereft more acute.

Episode 3: Ambuya Mazveshe's Home

Ambuya Mazveshe lives a short walk from the Muzite Primary School, where I was staying with Tendai Chitopo. She is a masterful drummer, skilled healer, and powerful singer, and she is very worried that my interest in her skills is due to my role as a potential spy rather than as a researcher. Unbeknownst to me at the time, Samson Mapfumo had gone to see her earlier in the week to vouch for me and assure her that my presence had nothing to do with either the United States or the Zimbabwe government. Mapfumo is one of Muzite's most respected elders. His timely and gracious intervention had convinced Ambuya Mazveshe to talk with me and play mhongo for me the following evening; he had convinced her that I was harmless. I fumbled along with my myopic city-corrupted night vision with the headmaster of Muzite Primary School, who had graciously agreed to accompany me. In exchange for the caustic home-distilled *sope* grain alcohol that almost everyone in Muzite over fifty seemed to love, Ambuya Mazveshe and her friends had agreed to play some ceremonial songs for me, including madzviti, zvipunha, and primarily mhongo pieces. It took my eyes a moment to adjust to the flickering light of the sole kerosene lamp illuminating the room as I saw a dozen women singing and a few drummers playing in the corner. At first, everything sounded like a typical mhongo performance, but the timbre wasn't quite right. Instead of the signature round drums reserved for the mhongo, each drummer was striking the dented side of a plastic jerry can, normally used to hold water or black-market petrol.

Ambuya Mazveshe was concerned because we were not setting the stage for a ceremony and we weren't properly preparing any of the local mediums for possession. Owning a mateza, the set of ceremonial mhongo drums, is, for her, no small thing; they are imbued with spiritual power. After having them made, christening them with beer, and holding a ceremony to name them, one should play them only for ceremonies.[16] It didn't seem right to her to play them for me in a recording and drinking session. Ambuya Mazveshe didn't let this stop her performance or her hospitality. She and James Mabuyawa gathered all of the plastic jerry cans, brought them inside, and played the mhongo rhythms on them. Because the cans were of different sizes, they worked surprisingly well as an approximation of the five tuned drums of the mateza, despite the unattractive timbre. Once the players got going I occasionally forgot that they were playing plastic jugs rather than the actual mateza, which sat unused in the next room.[17] That surprising choice had a direct impact on the nature of the performance and everyone's response to it.

As with VaMadzitya, Ambuya Mazveshe and her friends preferred that the spirits for whom these songs were normally sung would stay dormant. They were demonstrating these songs specifically for me, so they wanted the spirits to stay away. They hadn't made any preparations for a ceremony, hadn't invited the whole community, and tried to avoid inviting the spirits to an event intended for my benefit. That's how I found myself trading moonshine for music made with makeshift plastic drums.

Ambuya Mazveshe understood the tight indexical connection between the drums and the spirits and took the necessary steps to eliminate this kind of interpretation, the dicent. She and her friends wanted to uncouple a familiar and trusted indexical connection and rely solely on resemblance, on iconicity, without indexically replicating the constellation of signs that lead inevitably to spirit possession. She wanted to avoid the semiotic transformation that defines ritual success. Thus they didn't bring the sacred drums. She also avoided other indexical cues to those spirits such as the wigs, fabric, and ceremonial beer and eliminated the possibility that the spirits would feel disrespected if their drums were played in a nonceremonial context. The plastic "drums" now served as a sign of resemblance, an icon, rather than one of contiguity, an index. The visitors responded accordingly. The jerry cans didn't sound too bad, actually; they certainly were good enough to get everyone singing and otherwise participating. But their pedestrian ontology and lack of sacred indexicality ensured that the spirits didn't show up or involve themselves. They weren't invited.

VaMadzitya's and Ambuya Mazveshe's ideals and habits were at odds; they were at conflicting points along the dimensions of value marked by desirability and probability. But Ambuya Mazveshe changed the signs of performance rather than simply hope for the best. She and her friends sonically represented the music associated with the mhongo spirits without representing possession or the spirits themselves. In Peircean terms, they wanted to detach the dicent.

The difference between the impact of VaMadzitya's actions and Ambuya Mazveshe's choices can be helpfully clarified by the difference between effects of signs that work as rhemes versus those that work as dicents (Turino 2008, 16–20). Rhemes are only signs of a *possible* connection with the object signified, whereas a dicent is interpreted as *actually* being connected to the object represented. When a sign is understood as a dicent, the interpreter doesn't really have a choice but to believe it. Habit and sensory evidence force a certain interpretation. That is the foundation of truth within the Pragmatist tradition that Peirce helped initiate. Short argues that, "perception . . . is like a door forced open against our resistance to it, while imagination is like a door that we force open against the flood of current sensation" (2007, 77). Imagination is a choice; perception is forced. Ambuya Mazveshe freed the imagination of her fellow musicians by removing the indexical connections they would have been forced to make by habit. Her intervention loosened the typical ceremonial constraints that informed possible interpretations, leading to unexpected effects. These new interpretants became signs in the chain of semiosis that now represented unanticipated objects. The experience unfolded quite differently as these new possibilities emerged.

This semiotic manipulation changed the nature of everyone's experience. Most of the other signs that contribute to the joyous atmosphere of a typical mhongo ceremony were there, such as alcohol, darkness, spirit mediums, and enough participants to play, clap, sing, and ululate. As a result, the possibility emerged for a socially edifying and joyous occasion without the gravitas of ceremonial performance. By removing indices of the spirits and their ceremonial associations, while still retaining sonic iconicity, Ambuya Mazveshe and her friends were freed from the responsibility and sincerity that inevitably accompany mhongo spirit possession. They were free to reimagine the music's purpose. Everyone was liberated from typical ceremonial constraints and the accompanying emotional expectations. Freed from the habits and ideals of sacred performance, their singing became rambunctious and playful. The power and specificity of indexicality gave way to the freedom and possibility of iconicity.

With deliberate effort, Ambuya Mazveshe and her friends dissociated the sounds they intended to produce with their drums and voices from what David Samuels calls the "historical sedimentation of meaning." Samuels is referring more specifically to language and "semantic purification" as "stripping away material and indexical meanings of an utterance, leaving pure semanticity" (2006, 531–32). Ambuya Mazveshe and friends didn't focus on language and ultimately relied on what I might call "pure iconicity," but the impact of avoiding historically determined meanings is similarly profound. They avoided specific indexical connections of these sounds that they and their spirits were habituated to call forth and the specific sociocultural processes that this repertoire normally participates within. They closed off certain emotional possibilities in order to ensure less likely but more appropriate ones. She saw the typical outcome of mhongo drumming, spirit possession, as undesirable.

She anticipated these expectations, based on habits from experience, and did something about it, reducing the probability of those unwelcome effects and increasing the probability of other effects, turning this event, over time, into a surprising and joyous experience. Participants started singing bawdy songs, playfully introducing other ceremonial drum genres, laughing, shouting, and raucously enjoying themselves, all emotive expressions of this unanticipated joy and freedom.

Emotional Experience

At Horus Farm, at VaMadzitya's home, and at Ambuya Mazveshe's home there were emotional components of the events that not only were inaccessible to the ethnographer because language and observation fall short, but are also quite likely inaccessible to the participants themselves. When possessed, when grieving, or when laughing, neither linguistic nor neuroscientific description can account for everything. Ethnography can account in part for the causal absences ignored in science such as meaning, purpose, and intention (Deacon 2012b). The feelings of emotions are the interpretants that are most obviously defined by habit, cultural experience, and personal choice. Feelings are meanings and reflect purpose.

Superficially, the three performances sounded the same, but they inspired very different emotional experiences among core participants. Whereas VaMadzitya was eventually shaken by the possibility of spiritual retribution, troubled with anxiety about these consequences, and absorbed by grief, Ambuya Mazveshe ended the evening laughing, joking with her friends, and singing a wide range of songs, freely mixing sacred ones with secular. Masiza and the other participants at Horus Farm sent the mhongo away with a sense of accomplished satisfaction, ready for the zvaayungu and the next phase of the event.

VaMadzitya and Ambuya Mazveshe both tried to control the effects of their respective performances because of reframed musical purposes. They tried to manipulate the signs in order to avoid certain indexical associations that are deeply ingrained in Mhongo practices, but in different ways to differing degrees of success. These differences ultimately reveal meaning as the intersection of effect and purpose. Purpose does not dictate experience, but it certainly informs it. These are not denotational practices; meaning is habit-driven and experiential and thus very hard to control and manipulate.

For VaMadzitya, the drum's typical purpose overwhelmed his unusual purpose, leading to conflicting hopes and expectations. The habits of everyone at the ceremony and the familiar context of their engagement did more to determine the course of the proceedings than did the wishes of their frustrated host. This led directly to his feelings of anxiety. Despite the sorrowful atmosphere and expectation of ceremonial abstinence, despite his desire to mute the proceedings, his minimal intervention led the iconicity of this event to previous ones to call participants' habits, which are tied to the general signs of mhongo ceremonial drumming, into play. All of the elements of a successful ceremony remained, including the drums, the beer, the snuff, the mediums, and the participants. Unfortunately but predictably, events spun out of his control.

Conversely, Ambuya Mazveshe effectively avoided the signs that might trigger predictable responses, sidestepping the expectations of performed habits and avoiding the typical sacred signification of Mhongo drumming. She avoided indexing the ceremony as replica, circumventing its purpose of signifying. The legisign "mhongo ceremony" was iconically recalled without becoming indexically replicated. Her event transpired unpredictably because of this semiotic manipulation and evolved into a playful performance, stripped of ceremonial responsibilities. It retained the social, celebratory nature of a typical ceremony but avoided indexing the sacred.

Similarly, Enos Simango became aware of the potential for his own mhongo spirit to possess him simply by talking about it during our interview. He chose to temporarily end the conversation rather than give in to the inevitable chain of events he saw coming. His anxiety had fewer consequences than VaMadzitya's because it was about a potential future rather than a lived past. Simango saw spirit possession as undesirable, and so he did what needed to be done to avoid it.

Ambuya Mazveshe's performance was a success; she satisfied her purpose and achieved the result she desired, realizing her ideal. The ceremony at Horus Farm was also a success; it confirmed to participants' expectations based on habit and purpose. At Horus Farm, perhaps the most important effect was that the spirits were happy, which is comforting. It confirms and reifies important if elusive values. There was a conflict of sorts between people's expectations, ideals, and reality, but in this case, the ceremony went better than expected. Signs were interpreted such that the positive affect of these better-than-expected dimensions of value led to energetic dancing and focus: joy ensued. VaMadzitya's performance, unfortunately, failed. The stakes were much higher and he couldn't avoid the one effect of the drumming that would cause problems: spirit possession.

The first purpose of mhongo drumming is to frame the ceremony. It communicates a certain responsibility to people in attendance to contribute to the event's success. After that, it joins the food, the snuff, the dancing, the wigs, the space, or the people involved as one sensory mode among many. The second purpose is to communicate to the spirits a desire to invite them to possess the bodies of their mediums. That this particular music works for these particular spirits is a result of habit built through years and years of repetition. It just so happens that "good" drumming is more likely to succeed because it encourages participation and indexes sincerity. As shown in chapter 4, subtle signs of competence have a profound impact on success. But as Simango's experience shows, one doesn't need the drums or the music in order to become possessed. Spirits frequently arrive without a musical invitation. If the host of a ceremony has offended his spirits, they may stay away until reparations are made. Music does not define ceremonial experience, but it is a reliable tool for ensuring that people and spirits feel the way they want to feel. In other words, the specific sounds only matter as they represent certain objects and lead to certain effects. All three, signs, objects, and effects, are necessary.

CHAPTER 6

Early Morning

Zvaayungu *and the Shaping of Ndau Modernity*

The final spirits to arrive during the Horus Farm ceremony were the zvaayungu, young, impetuous spirits of soldiers who died during the war of independence in the 1970s. Their arrival kept the ceremony going and maintained continuity but also signaled the impending end of the proceedings. After only a couple of hours they departed, and everyone relaxed into a more playful, celebratory experience. The dancing, primarily in the form of muchongoyo, continued, but the spirits stayed away and the stakes remained low.

Unwelcome in many local communities, the zvaayungu were embraced in the newly resettled households at Horus Farm. That they found a welcome space to dance with the poor on one of Zimbabwe's famously resettled farms is perhaps no surprise, for these are the newest spirits of turmoil and an unresolved Ndau modernity. The zvaayungu should be understood as spiritual descendants of their ceremonial predecessors, especially the madzviti, but they are brash and exhibit little of the gravitas of their older spiritual counterparts. Their emergence, the ways in which locals perform for them, and locals' efforts to understand them expose the anxieties behind contemporary life in Chipinge and the inevitable confrontations with modernity. The zvaayungu reveal how the premises and logic of modernity have become locally specific within the conditions of postcolonial Zimbabwe and are understood historically and spiritually. I argue that one cannot understand the spirits without understanding how they are embedded within long-term processes in which they participate, that is, the continuity of semiosis as experience. They have a formative influence on the direction that the future takes.

Security, safety, and sovereignty have ebbed and flowed in the Ndau communities of Chipinge since the end of the Monomutapa Empire in the sixteenth century. This volatility continues into the twenty-first century. Even now, decades after independence, much of social, political, and spiritual life in Zimbabwe still is defined by the violent experiences of war that helped achieve that independence, the Second Chimurenga. More and more participants in political conversation are "born-free," but that status still marks them as outside the legitimate authority that participation in that war bestowed, although these dynamics play out differently in Harare, Bulawayo, the heart of Mashonaland, and in Chipinge (Mate 2012; Oosterem and Pswarayi 2014). After President Mugabe's unexpected fall from power in 2017, the controversial war veteran Emmerson Mnangagwa assumed the presidency and the old guard tightened their grip on power.

After suffering centuries of outside interference and authority, many Ndau communities treat the national government of Zimbabwe with a long-familiar distrust. As the soldiers of the Gaza state gave way to the colonial authority of the Portuguese and the British, who unwillingly gave way to the triumphant regime of Robert Mugabe and ZANU-PF, Chipinge communities have felt marginalized (Sithole 1999; Zamchiya 2013a). Residents like Claude Chizana, Vhukani Muzite, and Samson Mapfumo confront contemporary realities with clarity regarding their marginalized status, frustration with current events, and a willingness to do what it takes to survive. Life in Zimbabwe, like almost everywhere, has changed profoundly during these transitions. Christianity dominates public spiritual discourse, and monetary desires and a capitalist ethos of acquisition and modernity increasingly inform how people seek employment and spend their money (Comaroff and Comaroff 2014). Just as the spirits discussed in the previous chapters helped those participating in ceremonies deal with the dynamism and anxiety of these historical insecurities, so, too, do they confront the colonial experience. But the madzviti, zvipunha, and mhongo may not be equipped to fully engage with the dynamism of the late twentieth and early twenty-first centuries. Now, somewhat suddenly, there are new, confusing spirits to brashly and confidently force locals to confront these contemporary changes: the zvaayungu. After prioritizing the three key components of semiotic experience in isolation—objects, signs, and interpretants (effects)—in the previous chapters, here I address the presence of the zvaayungu by attending to the continuity of semiosis in experience and the agents of interpretation. Zvaayungu signify ambiguity about the past, dynamism in the present, and possibility for local people's futures. They participate in local engagements with modernity, the stakes of which have yet to be fully understood or realized.

The Zvaayungu Arrive at Horus Farm

It was late morning (after eight o'clock) at the end of a lengthy ceremony at Horus Farm. Everyone was tired from a long night of dancing but happy with how events proceeded. The sun had risen hours ago, and we were all seated around the last vestige of the fire, drinking beer and struggling to stay awake. There was excitement in the air because the madzviti spirits had unexpectedly returned to express their pleasure with the ceremony, dance, and sacrifice a goat to feed everyone in attendance in appreciation.

As we watched the spirits dance outside the ceremonial house, and shortly after the goat was corralled, VaMasiza pulled me aside and suggested that I get my camera out. He guided me away from the central space between the two main buildings where the madzviti were surrounding the goat to the back of the kitchen, just out of sight. We turned the corner to see two young women and a young man holding court, making demands of the women gathered deferentially in front of them. Their commands included a mix of Shona and English words. The male and female spirits sat on stools in the sun as women prepared plates of rice for them that they ate with a spoon, served glasses of Chateau brandy, and gave them Madison cigarettes. Dressed in their collared shirts and bucket hats, seated while eating, drinking, and smoking, they looked like honored guests. These are the zvaayungu (see figure 6.1).

Normally, zvaayungu spirits would have already arrived, publicly, but since people were delayed by the madzviti's unexpected return and the living and the dead both prefer that only one type of spirit dance at a time, they had to wait. Nobody wanted these spirits and the lingering madzviti to interact and potentially compete for our attention. Despite their proximity in the spirit world, it would be problematic for the madzviti to meet their younger spiritual counterparts. As Masiza and others told me, spirits prefer not to share time and space with other spirits. Several of the more experienced participants, worried about potential conflict, had quietly prepared the way for the impatient zvaayungu spirits to arrive around the corner of the roundhouse and out of sight of the madzviti spirits. One dzviti casually wandered toward us, seemingly unaware of what was happening, before a woman gently guided him away, saying, "Please leave here."

Once the madzviti had departed for the second time, people moved to the center of the grounds. The zvaayungu joined them and engaged with everybody; they were gregarious. They shook our hands, played the drums, clapped demonstratively, and danced energetically in a style reminiscent of madzviti's militaristic stomps but with flailing arms that conveyed little of the

FIGURE 6.1. Zvaayungu

madzviti's aggression. Unlike madzviti, zvipunha, or mhongo, these spirits interacted directly with the crowd around them, talking to people and urging participants to clap along, sing more loudly, or dance with them. The collective energy level rose in response to their encouragement. As the zvaayungu danced they would flail their arms up and down in time to the drumming. As vocal cycles came to a close, the spirits would sometimes jump up and down to cue the drummer to pause (somewhat like the ends of mhongo phrases), and then start again. They were brash and loud, like the youth they presumably were in life.

Continuity

There is uncertainty in zvaayungu possession. Even among long-term interlocutors there is little agreement or orthodoxy concerning their identity, at least not yet; much is unknown. The signs of performance can seem unstable when the objects signified are ambiguous or differ from person to person. The short-term effects are clearer than the sign-object relations that inspire them, which can seem counterintuitive, but the habits informed by experience with the spirits introduced in previous chapters assures some continuity. The iconicity of representations of zvaayungu spirits and preceding spirits includes familiar indices of possession on which a sense of authenticity relies. The long-term effects are still unknown. There are multiple possibilities in the objects signified, the interpretants to follow, and even the agents involved. The potential reality of these possibilities is itself an aspect of performance. In part, this chapter explores how semiotic instability can actually contribute to the making of new semiotic domains and realities.

People respond to indices of the possible on the basis of trusted habits of interpretation built from years of spiritual encounters and interaction. Possibilities are thus continuous with every other aspect of ritual, making this spiritual uncertainty at least potentially and partly knowable. Signs of zvaayungu spiritual performance are continuous with other signs, linking the past and future to the present, even imbuing signs of the past with that indexical connection to the here and now. Semiotic meaning (combining purpose, value, and effect) is embedded in each participant's experience and is continuous with the experience of others, shaped by interpretive agency and intersubjective engagement, with potentially lasting effects. Semiosis is a seamless continuity unless interrupted by analysis, flow, or trance.

I use synechism, what Peirce called "the tendency to regard everything as continuous" (Peirce 1998b, 1), as a way to keep my ethnographic explorations in check. It is important to focus on the details, the individuals, sounds, words, and gestures that play a role in ceremonial life. Description is the central method of ethnographic inquiry in ethnomusicology, but it is an act defined by choice. As the author, informed by years of ethnography and guidance by my teachers, friends, and informants, I choose which details to describe and which to omit. Yet rather than synthesizing multiple elements together into a narrative, descriptive writing is destructive, interrupting real-world experiences, stopping time, and erasing that which is unnoticed or deemed irrelevant, secondary, or epiphenomenal. Synechism acknowledges and resists this. Wholes precede parts. The ceremony at Horus Farm, as a whole, is one phenomenon. The signs, the moments, the people, all (and each) only make complete sense when their connection to other signs, moments, and people is acknowledged and considered (Short 2007, 81). Meaning is experienced as continuous. For Peirce (1931–58, 6:202), semiosis itself is continuity.

The zvaayungu are in between—past and present, black and white, modern and traditional, Shona and Ndau—but they also expose binaries as fictitious analytic impositions (see Jankowsky 2010). Their "in-between-ness" is the key to connection and continuity (Nancy 2000, 5). Zvaayungu combine black and white, connect tradition to the modern, and integrate past, present, and future. They connect the experiences of postcolonial modernity to the distant experiences of the nineteenth century and tie the modern to the historical, black to white. Their impact has yet to be determined, their role is still unfolding, but they reveal how these moments in Ndau history, the players in Ndau life, and the signs of Ndau experience are all connected and ongoing. Their ambiguity is meaningful.

Every sign is part of an ongoing relational process that is rarely completed. Signs connect to other signs and objects from the past and can combine with other signs in the moment before leading to new effects (also signs) in the future. Some signs emerge from complex systems (like languages) to be understood as such, some are embedded within other kinds of signs, and all of them connect with agents. Semiosis as the relation of relations is the key (Kockelman 2011). Signs relate to objects; signs relate to interpretants; agents relate to signs; agents relate to interpretants; interpretants as signs relate to other signs, these relationships relate to one another, and on it goes.

In order to relate to an object, a sign must be attended to and interpreted by a perceiver. Continuity is perhaps more easily understood in relation to a sentence or a sequence of music. Each element loses its ontological importance if removed. The whole also becomes a different whole if a "part" is removed. The synchronic and the diachronic need each other. The paradigmatic needs the syntagmatic. Signs are parts of continuities in part because one perceives not simply a sign but a sign-object relation, the specifics of which can differ depending on the effect of that perceived relation. There is no sign without the object represented or the interpretant engendered; no two are sufficient. Every sign is part of a triadic relation; thus every sign is meaningful (Peirce 1931–58, 1:345). The interpretant is the third, and it binds the sign to its object for an agent. Each binary relation relates to another binary relation. Without the third (which is the whole), each part is merely potential (Short 2007, 84). Continuity is the combination. The interpretant itself is a sign, continuing a chain of semiosis, sign begetting sign, but multisensory experiences like the madhlozi ceremony paradoxically slow down time and generate modes of being more akin to secondness, in the case of flow or communitas, or firstness, in the case of trance.

For the zvaayungu, that semiotic chain is still in process. The immediate effects are even now being evaluated, as are the objects that the signs of the zvaayungu potentially represent. The different interpretations that I describe below are part of this process, which could be quite different ten years from now.

Thus, signs don't live in isolation. Labeling a sign can provide an analytic opening, but taxonomic fixity can mislead. If one looks at the objects and interpretants of any sign, its roots and fruits, as well as the contexts in which it is embedded and nested, meaning becomes an ever-expanding site of experience tied to purpose, value, and effect. One gesture from a possessed zvaayungu spirit brings centuries of history into the present, brings multiple personal encounters into a glance, and informs the possibilities and judgments that guide the future.

I address three domains in which attention to continuity can be productive: time, the signs of performance (especially music), and community members (both living and dead). I continue the work of previous chapters by exploring the roots and fruits of semiosis, explain how details and specificity are nested within broader generalities, and consider how the relation between the possible and the actual is enhanced by attention to continuity. Meaning, whether defined as a means to an end, as purpose, or as an effect, must be experienced. In this way, the details of ritual, the sound of a drum, the taste of snuff, the look on a medium's face, connect with, participate in, and shape broader processes tied to community, identity, spirituality, and modernity. Perhaps the zvaayungu offer new continuities, reshaping old truths in order to undermine binaries otherwise accepted as oppositional.

CONTINUITY IN TIME

This sense of continuity is most intuitive when considering time; as Short writes, "What we experience as the present contains the dying past and an aborning future, and thus we have a direct experience of the passage of time" (2007, 82). This continuity is elegantly and viscerally embodied in Ndau spirits. The arrival of zvaayungu spirits in the twenty-first century not only connects and continues events of the latter twentieth century but also carries on paths, possibilities, and habits shaped by spirits from the nineteenth century and earlier that could only have emerged in the crucible of colonialism. The colonial legacy shaped the future in Zimbabwe before Cecil Rhodes ever set foot on her soil. That future is still being shaped, never fully taking form, with each arrival of the zvaayungu. Spirits participate in local communities' efforts to reconcile their past, understand their present, and prepare for the future. While potentially reductive and speculative, spiritual purpose is in part an unstated confrontation with modernity and its consequences for the communities of eastern Zimbabwe.

Not only do these spirits in the here and now come from multiple pasts, but they shape attitudes about and expectations for the future. Time blurs as spirits that emerge from multiple encounters bring those encounters into the present. Madzviti spirits bring their lives during the nineteenth century into the present. The zvipunha bring their experiences as nannies to the early Ndau to the lives of contemporary Ndau women. In this way, the past becomes vibrant again, renegotiated and reconsidered in the present to inform the future.

CONTINUITY IN SIGNS

Experience, meaning, and time emerge via signs and their relations to objects and interpretants. Focusing on the role of continuity in signs becomes a valuable lesson through which to understand how experiences such as the Horus Farm ceremony, the modalities through which they unfold such as music and dance, and the agents involved, including both the living and the dead, shape the future. Attention to continuity exposes the necessity of each of the sign's requisite parts (sign, object, interpretant, and agent). Meaning is never fixed but, rather, fluid.

In waking life, excepting unusual circumstances such as spirit possession or trance, semiosis is unceasing. Interpretants bind signs to objects before operating as signs themselves that beget new interpretants that become signs in a semiotic chain (Turino 2014, 203). The processing of signs transformed throughout life and in experience, from the ambiguity of iconic images to the visceral reality of indices to the predictable generality of symbols, shapes the habits of interpretation and culture. When the zvaayungu strikes the drum or drinks from a cup, connections of those acts to a series of objects, both tangible and otherwise, relate to effects of that sign-object relation that inform others' actions. Participants in ceremonies can exploit the unique semiotic potential of music and dance to facilitate specific kinds of experience and relationships, bringing invited guests from the recent past to the present. The future is an eventual interpretant of these semiotic chains, ensuring that acts taking place in the present have a bearing on what comes next.

CONTINUITY IN COMMUNITY

Finally, continuity emerges in community and the ways in which people living and dead relate to one another. I am not myself without the people with whom I engage. Spirits and mediums are, in more ways than one, part of one another (Peirce 1998, 2). They reveal continuity. Intersubjectivity emphasizes the social continuities at play in individual senses of self and identity. Viewing community through a semiotic lens reveals meaning as "bared name of our being-with-one-another" (Nancy 2000, 1). Ceremonies are invaluable, though not necessarily unique, in the efficiency and reliability with which they allow participants to experience something together as intersubjectivity.

In Ndau ceremonial life, this neighborliness extends beyond the grave into the past as a way to ensure the future. The most obvious forms of interpersonal community with respect to spirit possession ceremonies are the continuity of agency after death and the assurance of communal thriving from one generation to the next. Death is not a barrier here because of the possibility of continuing on as a spirit. In the Ndau case, people have spirits within them already, one intersubjective dimension of the self among many. Spirits are parts of selves. After death and the ceremonies needed to bring the spirit back into the family, this dynamic is perpetuated and inverted as people go from hosting spirits to being hosted themselves, perhaps as an ancestor or mudzimu, but some people come back as a number of madhlozi. The community with unknown boundaries, potential corporeal limits, and elusive distinctions becomes knowable in spite of everything.

Spirits of Encounter

For most participants, zvaayungu are the spirits of soldiers from the war of independence. Like other madhlozi, they are the spirits of social encounter. Since first emerging during ceremonies held in the 1980s, they have been a constant source of confusion, ambiguity, and controversy because they exhibit signs that combine Shona characteristics with European ones. Zvaayungu are the latest spiritual arrivals to emerge from the long series of social encounters mentioned in Chapter 1 that continue to shape the present through the intersection of memory, music, history, and spirituality. Salient historical encounters align with the key moments of spiritual emergence, as the roots of that emergence. Zvaayungu reflect the impact on local spiritual relationships of recent historical events tied to the end of Rhodesian rule and colonialism, the traumatic war for independence, and the internal political struggles that followed independence. Just as the traumatic encounters of the nineteenth century are embodied in the madzviti, the traumatic encounters of the twentieth are evident in the zvaayungu.

In order to explain how the zvaayungu acquire a tenuous place at the table during these ceremonies, I move back in time through a series of encounters that reveal their role. I begin with my own encounter before tracing the roots of their place in Ndau cosmology via the zvaayungu's meeting with madzviti spirits and local encounters with the soldiers of the Second Chimurenga. Unexpected encounters that shake the foundations of everyday life are the roots of madhlozi spirituality. The central role of the spirits that emerge from these moments of historical volatility in local life is indicative of the importance that these encounters can still have for people. As with all spirits, the circumstances of their lives inform the zvaayungu's personalities in death.

Encounter 1: The Zvaayungu and I

Seated outside the *mhatso* at Horus farm by the campfire with VaMasiza, the local chief, and some other men, I was exhausted from an evening and morning full of music, dancing, and drinking, and from the general activities of the ceremony. The sun had risen hours earlier, and we had been watching the recently arrived zvaayungu spirits dancing outside with interest. As usual, they were the last to arrive. Nothing I'd learned about the process of possession had fully prepared me for the audacious youth or mixed signals of the zvaayungu spirits. They sat in chairs or on stools (rather than on the ground), wore baseball caps or bucket hats and button-down shirts (instead of spiritually significant fabric), drank lager or brandy (instead of homemade ceremonial beer), and smoked cigarettes (instead of taking snuff). They identified themselves as Shona but adopted certain characteristics that are explicitly European and might be identified as modern.

Compared to the spirits who had already come and gone, their interaction with the rest of the ceremony's participants was unusual. For one thing, they were not shy. The confidence with which they engaged with their living interlocutors made them different from any of the other madhlozi spirit communities. Unlike the introspective dancing of the others, who seemed to dance with and for one another in spite of the presence of the living, the zvaayungu spirits engaged continuously with the living participants, dancing with them instead of simply near them; they were extroverts. All the deference and respect I had grown used to seeing in a recently arrived madhlozi spirit was gone, replaced by brazen confidence.[1] Whereas the madzviti, mhongo, and zvipunha spirits would kneel and respectfully greet their hosts with clapping or snapping (and largely ignoring everyone else), the zvaayungu would walk right up to someone, shake his or her hand, and say hello. The zvipunha were terrified of me and the mhongo and madzviti either ignored me or greeted me casually, but not the zvaayungu.

One spirit stopped dancing and approached me. Under the shade of a tree, I was more focused on the pot of beer being passed around than on the dancing taking place nearby, and it took me a moment to notice the spirit's approach. Many of the women and several men were still singing, clapping, and dancing with a group of zvaayungu spirits who had possessed their host mediums earlier that morning, but most of the people there had been dancing for far longer. They were tired and ready to eat, drink, and finally rest. The spirit approached me and Masiza, curious as to who it was who had been filming the ceremony. He greeted me with "Maparts ari sei?"

Chonapi Gwenzi, a musician from Buffelsdrift near Ngaone, the Mutema homeland, identified the zvaayungu's broken Shona as Chilapalapa, a pidgin language that emerged as a way for non-Shona-speaking colonial officials or farmers to communicate with their employees.[2] The n'anga Khosanai Wilson Simango identifies the language as Chingoto or Chiroro, but he dismisses the language as a lie, as a way for false mediums to suggest legitimacy. Chilapalapa is a humiliating language for many Zimbabweans, in part because it is so impolite, filled as it is with imperative verb forms. Otherwise known as Fanagalo, Chilapalapa is the language of colonial domination. The typical zvaayungu greeting, rooted in Chilapalapa, is "Maparts ari sei?," which means "How are your parts?" It is a surprising linguistic choice within the context of the deeply significant madhlozi ceremonies.

After greeting me, the spirit shook my hand, confirmed that I was in fact making a videorecording, and then told me he knew me. He said that I had killed him.[3] I had flown the plane that had dropped the bombs that had killed him during the war in the 1970s. Taken aback, I failed to respond, but the spirit filled the silence with a smile. He came back shortly thereafter with a clay pot of beer for "the one who had flown the airplane," a gesture of friendship unexpected after his smiling accusation. As I drank with Masiza and the other men, he rejoined the zvaayungu, the drumming began again, and they all danced for another hour or so. At that point they departed, and the ceremony was over.

The Unknown, the Possible, and the Actual

Who are the zvaayungu? Thus far, I've implied a certain interpretation, but their identity and ontology remain under discussion within the greater Ndau community. There are several approaches to this question. As befits a category of spirit of such semiotic ambiguity, they go by several names including *zvaayungu, zvivarungu, zvemaguru*, and *mabwacha*.[4] The root *-yungu* is also found in *Chiyungu*, an Ndau word for the English language like the Shona word *Chirungu* or the other Ndau alternatives, *Chingezi* and *Chingisa*. Someone referred to as a *muyungu, murungu*, or *mungezi* is thus an English person, but more generally the terms refer to Europeans or simply foreigners. Even Zimbabweans who have spent time abroad and exhibit characteristics or habits that reflect a cosmopolitan identity can be labelled with the plural, *vayungu*, which can be uncomfortable. It also implies that characterizations of "whiteness," "Englishness," or "foreignness" can have more fluidity or complexity than the English labels "white" and "black" might suggest. *Zvaayungu* can be translated as "things of the English, the European, and the white community," but because of the historical connection between whiteness and modernity, it can also imply "things of modernity." They are the spirits of this intersection between black and white, local and foreign, traditional and modern. They make up neither side of any of those binaries but the transformative emergence of their encounter.

The youthful zvaayungu are the only postcolonial spirits to arrive at Horus Farm. While each of the other categories of madhlozi spirit can have a ceremony all to itself, this doesn't seem to apply to the zvaayungu.[5] They are far from ubiquitous in the Chipinge region and hold a tenuous, controversial, and ambiguous place in local cosmology. Few doubt their presence, but many doubt their legitimacy. They delicately embody an intersection of Europeanness along with Shona-ness, both of which are external to an Ndau identity framework, though in very different ways. Definitions of *zvaayungu*, impressions of their existence, and judgments of their value vary from person to person depending on place of residence, age, and professional or spiritual role. In each case, zvaayungu are explicitly associated with Europeans and with Zimbabwe's colonial past because they first began appearing at Ndau ceremonies after Zimbabwe's independence in 1980. Many of the characteristics of the zvaayungu described above—the language, the clothing, and their consumption habits—are indexically associated with vayungu, or white people. The two clearest objects of the signs of zvaayungu presence for the Ndau are Shona Chimurenga soldiers and Europeans.

There are four general categories into which people's interpretation and understanding of the zvaayungu can be placed. First, as described above, is the view that they are genuine spirits of soldiers killed during the Second Chimurenga. In this view, the zvaayungu are the spirits of the Zimbabwean soldiers who died along the Zimbabwe-Mozambique border in the 1970s. This was certainly the orthodox position and general consensus among attendees at Horus Farm. At ceremonies during which zvaayungu appear there was general agreement that this was the case, but this conclusion is still being questioned and considered. Eddie Hlakama, a musician in Mt. Selinda, somewhat ambiguously told me that the zvaayungu are not *exactly* from the Chimurenga; they can even come from Angola.[6]

Khosanai Wilson Simango, a n'anga working at the Chipinge Musika market, insisted they are fakes; they lie; they can't be real: "Zvaayungu is a lie. There is no white person who wakes up in [possesses] a black person. It's all lies, lies!" He continued, "What I know is that there are people . . . telling lies to people because they want money. The thing they say is, the *chimurungu* [a person possessed by a white person], do you think it is a white person on his own, just as he is [referring to me], he will come and possess me, a black person, me? It cannot be. They are lies."

His dismissal implies that the zvaayungu present themselves as the spirits of white people, a claim supported by the indices they choose to represent themselves (in language, clothing, and consumption). Simango told me that young people likely purchase them in flea markets of the magical and supernatural in Soweto, South Africa, saying, "And they lie, seducing people with lies like this, and they lie praying now. They say, Firi firi firi firi, [imitating how the possessed people talk] as if they are white people. Do you think a white person speaks English like they [the chimurungu mediums] do, when they can speak it properly like they do in Johannesburg?" Another n'anga from Chipinge, Jabulani Mulambo, also denied their legitimacy, saying, "They are lying."

"Firi firi" works as an ideophone, conveying meaning through its sound qualities (Kohn 2005, 181), iconically capturing the nasality heard in all local mimicry of white English speech. It is iconic to British English, based on the indexicality of nasality with British speech, but also works to index foreignness, whiteness, and, for Simango, the explicit effort to mimic. He heard it as a dicent index of pretense.

Rodwell Muzite, the acting headman of Muzite, also fervently denied their legitimacy, adamant that these "spirits" are dangerous fakes. He told me, "I don't sanction them here. I don't even want to see them." He forbade them. By sitting in chairs, wearing caps, and smoking cigarettes, these spirits were trying to act European and, in his mind, this affront proved their illegitimacy. These choices defy common madhlozi norms. At best, they were shortcuts to the prestige associated with being a medium, at worst, the dangerous practices of witches intended to trick people. Further inland, no one is convinced that the spirits are real, and many have not even heard of them. In Bangwe and Tonhorai my questions were dismissed, met with confusion and surprise.[7]

Some zvaayungu do present themselves as the spirit of white people. Black soldiers as well as white ones suffered during the Second Chimurenga and were not properly buried, and their lives were transformed by the traumatic encounters of war. When James Mabuyawa was helping me with translation as I interviewed Ambuya Mazveshe, he seemed to agree in part with Muzite and the n'anga that I interviewed in Chipinge. He suggested that the zvaayungu were liars, but Ambuya Mazveshe interrupted him. "They don't lie," she said. "*Mabwacha* died at war. They say, I died at mountain so and so. They say the name they used in their youth. . . . I am so and so, I am so and so . . . with anger [fervor]." She accepted them at face value.

For some, the zvaayungu were Shona soldiers, for others they were white. For some they were genuine, for others they were spurious.

The most common response to my questions about zvaayungu identity was a simple acceptance of the unknown. It is hard to know who or what these spirits are. Even people like Masiza, who embrace their presence and participate in their ceremonies, concede a lack of certainty. When I turned to him at Horus Farm and asked, "Where do the zvaayungu come from?" Masiza turned to me, shrugged, and replied, "Ah, I don't know." When I asked Hlatywayo, who had been so helpful in elucidating my understanding of Muzite history, about the zvaayungu, he repeated Masiza's "I don't know."

It remains to be seen whether zvaayungu become more widely embraced or further marginalized. But everyone agreed that they began to arrive after independence and present themselves as the spirits of the Shona soldiers who died in the area during the second Chimurenga. The mediums for the zvaayungu are all "born-frees," born after 1980. They have no memory of the war but serve as mediums for the very fighters who helped achieve that independence and remember it viscerally.

I rarely encountered doubt in my fieldwork. In matters of spirituality and religion, almost everyone stood by their convictions without a second thought. But the most common responses to questions about zvaayungu identity—the spirits of Shona Chimurenga soldiers or fakes pretending to be possessed by white people—were often informed by doubt. The door was open, somewhat, to changing opinions, disagreement, and wonder. While both possibilities were part of an interpretive move as objects of the signs of possession, the effect of this signification differed depending on whether that object was understood to be an intended but false object (as in the spirit of white people), possible but uncertain, or actual and authentic.

I've intentionally avoided characterizing any of the views offered to me about spirits as belief. It is either dismissive or reductive to characterize knowledge as belief. But the relationship between the zvaayungu and the living opens that door somewhat. Masiza's answer implied a "yet," as in "I don't know . . . yet." The immediate interpretant to the zvaayungu, for Masiza, is uncertainty, but it is also cooperation. He trusts them, in part because of the habits built on years of experience with all of the madhlozi spirits and the accompanying joy and security that they bring. Habits shape belief (Peirce 1992, 129). Masiza does not yet *know* who the zvaayungu are, but he *believes* that learning it will be worthwhile. The truth of this encounter, the eventual interpretant of zvaayungu signs, is still to come. It is, perhaps, unsurprising that the people I spoke with who participated in zvaayungu ceremonies were open to them, whereas those who didn't engage with them dismissed them. There were no signs of authenticity to force that door open. Imagination and perception collide in ceremonial moments with the zvaayungu, shifting the perspective in terms of which actor is the primary agent of experience (Short 2007, 77). The instability of zvaayungu semiosis invited either openness to the possibility of new semiotic domains or resistance. The objects and interpretants of zvaayungu signs are neither stipulated nor assured.

Peircean theory accommodates both the possible and the actual. Music's potential "exceptionalism" emerges from its engagement with the possible and the actual simultaneously (Turino 2008, 16). The zvaayungu's role hinges to a significant extent on how this interplay is engaged. The possibilities inherent in zvaayungu's presence vary because much is unknown, and what is known is only occasionally understood as an authentic, dicent sign. The differences and shifts between rheme and dicent signs inform the kinds of continuities that are possible as the living grapple with the identity of the zvaayungu. Everyone I talked to interpreted the signs of possession in the zvaayungu as, at minimum, a rheme of a possessing spirit. Masiza wasn't sure whether the signs of a possessing soldier were *actually* connected to that soldier, but it was possible. Multiple indices of possession organized people's experiences, constrained the possibilities at hand, and forced open the door of such an interpretation, indices imbued with the presence of the zvaayungu and marking the here and now (haecceity), making them difficult to ignore. But Khosanai Simango, Mulambo, and Muzite doubted the possibility, interpreting such signs as dicents of deceit. Masiza and Mazveshe did not; they accepted the presence of the spirits and acted accordingly. There was anger in the words of Muzite, Simango, and Mulambo as they asserted the deception of these young tricksters, reflecting the tension between the indices of possession, the impossibility of *varungu* spirits, and the desire to root out such dangerous practices.

Encounter 2: Zvaayungu and Madzviti

The perspective of the spirits themselves should play an important role in people's understanding. When not possessing the living during ceremonies, madhlozi are bodyguards or soldiers liaising between Mwari and the ancestors, the midzimu. When trusted, as at Horus Farm, they have their own experiences that shape the goals of performance. The ceremony provides the spirits with positive experiences. Attendees become witnesses to spiritual encounters as much as they are participants in it. Because the zvaayungu are so young, Masiza said, they aren't really sure how to act. They are still learning, so they model their behavior on that of the madzviti elders in the spirit world, learning how to act and what to do by example. Because the madzviti were also soldiers and had been around for more than a century, the zvaayungu look up to them. The spirits interact with one another, protect the midzimu, intervene with Mwari, and reciprocate in kind for the participants' contribution of bodies in which to dance and the respect shown through ceremonial life. They learn during these interactions. This is perhaps most evident in the music, which is derived in part from madzviti drumming rather than the Shona music that one might have expected for Shona spirits but which also suggests the sonic impact of colonialism itself.

PERFORMING ZVAAYUNGU

Zvaayungu ceremonial performance is reminiscent of that performed for the spirits described previously; generally, each phase of the ceremony is similar. A small group of drummers supported by singers, primarily women, sing and play until the energy level is high enough for other participants to engage and for the dancers to really move. Sounds from the drums and voices contribute to a multisensory fabric designed for a specific purpose: to bring dancing spirits embodied in willing mediums. Multisensory semiotic density helps ensure positive experiences.

It doesn't matter much what kind of drum is played. Like zvipunha, zvaayungu spirits have no drum of their own, and performers tend to use a chigubhu, a deza from the mhongo ceremony, or both. One drummer plays the chigubhu using two sticks, and if a drum such as the chimudumbana or one from the mhongo mateza is available, a second drummer can play the main beat on that drum with either one hand or a stick. This drumming serves essentially the same purpose as do the makosho. Perhaps reflecting these spirits' youth, the drumming used to accompany the zvaayungu dance is comparatively simple. Unlike the varied rhythms used for the other spirits, which allow for greater density, a certain amount of variation, and improvisation, zvaayungu drumming, at least the playing that I've observed and that has been described to me, largely comprised a single rhythmic motif that occasionally was interrupted by timed stops coinciding with the steps of the dancing spirits (see figure 6.2). The only variations replace some strokes with muffled beats or silence.

FIGURE 6.2. A drummer (lower right) muffling the drum with his hand

It is striking that zvaayungu drum for themselves, something never seen among the other spirits. This may reinforce their ambiguity and confidence, but it is also a pragmatic choice for youthful spirits teaching attendees how events should unfold. Many people, including VaMasiza, asserted a similarity between madzviti and zvaayungu drumming, a similarity that is intentional on the part of zvaayungu spirits, who look to the madzviti as role models. Both are spirits who were caught in war and emerged from trauma.

Madzviti spirits are indexed by a driving duple rhythm on makandira frame drums and songs with lyrics in either Swazi or Zulu, languages of the Gaza Nguni soldiers they were in life. The zvaayungu employ similar rhythms clearly drawn from those used for the madzviti. Chonapi Gwenzi, among many others, explained to me that the music the spirits enjoyed in life should determine the music that can effectively invite them. Drum patterns aren't symbols; they rely on sign-object relations established in past instances, the ground of their significance, in order to work. The reliance of zvaayungu drumming on madzviti antecedents is surprising. But, while imitating madzviti rhythms could be evidence of duplicity for skeptics, Masiza's suggestion that the zvaayungu are basically learning how to be spirits from the madzviti is plausible. Both employ driving duple rhythms with little syncopation.

Whereas madzviti drumming utilizes different tones, accents, and timbres on multiple drums, zvaayungu drumming primarily relies on one timbre

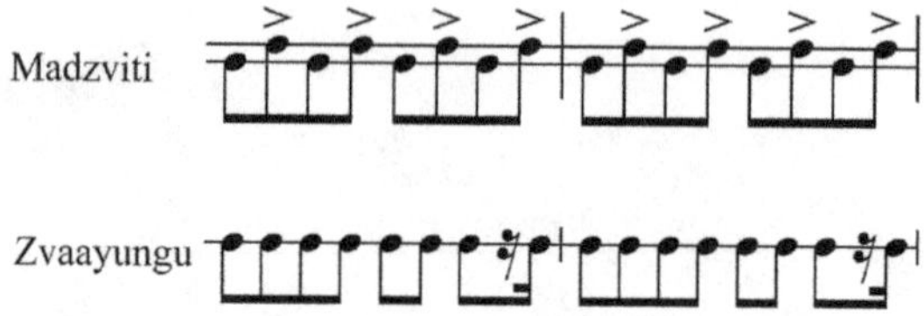

FIGURE 6.3. Madzviti and zvaayungu rhythms

but pauses briefly at the end of each cycle in a way that is actually iconic of mhongo patterns. It is significant that zvaayungu drummers also displace the last stroke, creating an audible difference that accentuates a strong initial beat rather than a seamless cycle of equal beats as found in madzviti drumming. There is a certain iconicity to European military drumming and the intersection of colonialism and modernity with whiteness. For one thing, only zvaayungu drumming employs a single tone. Perhaps this reflects the spirits' youth, but perhaps it is iconic of English itself, which is not a tone language. The pick-up note, rendered as a sixteenth note in figure 6.3, makes this pattern quite marchlike, with less metric ambiguity than those of the madzviti, zvipunha, and mhongo. The iconicity between zvaayungu drumming and the marchlike patterns of postcolonial military marches could also reflect the twentieth-century military training of the spirits. Like other signs of the zvaayungu, these patterns mark the spirits as the product of modernity and colonialism. They sound neither black nor white, traditional nor modern, but render the emerging intersection between these categories. They don't sonically prioritize either side of those binaries but perform the transformative emergence of their encounter, forming new continuities with their sonic in-between-ness.

ROOTS AND FRUITS OF PERFORMANCE SIGNS

Thinking of signs as processual rather than static representations requires attending to each component: sign, object, and interpretant. It is productive to think of semiotic objects as the roots and semiotic effects as the fruits of signification. Drumming (the fruits) results from the intent of inviting spirits to possess their mediums and dance (the roots). The conviction that happy spirits protect ancestors who protect the community provides the roots of that intention, which "represents its satisfaction conditions" (Kockelman 2011, 717). Each discrete sign is but one point on a continuous path of unfolding meaning.

At Horus Farm, after the ceremony turned in earnest to the dancing zvaayungu, one of the spirits settled at the chigubhu to start things off. He played the simple pattern shown in figure 6.3 as a man played a chimudumbana with his hand to strike the beat, four beats per cycle. The other zvaayungu and one or two others danced in the center as a crowd gathered around them. A few women played makosho, a few clapped, and the rest watched. The sun shone as we witnessed the zvaayungu's efforts; the late morning hour was rejuvenating as the cool of night faded after hours of ceremonial performance.

Determining the roots of this performance depends in part on the agent interpreting the signs. The spirits, the men, the women, and I would each participate in these processes in different ways. Several basic truths shaped the signs of performance that unfolded in multiple ways for multiple people throughout the morning. First, even for those who died in the twentieth century, it was now the twenty-first century. Our presence at Horus Farm was an acute reminder that we were performing during the days of fast-track land reform. My observations were filtered through the lens of my camera. For the spirits, one root is the desire to dance, the purpose of any madhlozi emergence. Dancing can't take place without the drum, so the spirit drums.

The index of this pattern to zvaayungu and possession is rooted in iconicity with both madzviti performance and previous ceremonial experiences. Thus, the indexicality of the here and now is also rooted in iconicity. Sign types are nested, icons within indices. Legisigns are also nested, zvaayungu drumming within madhlozi drumming within spirit possession drumming. The indexical specificities rooted in this experience and in the here and now begin with the generality of similarity. Some of these relations are conventional. People agree that this drumming is for the zvaayungu, but this convention does not make these symbols.

The core women quickly joined the drumming spirit in singing "*Zvamauya woye* (Now that you have come)." As with each preceding ceremonial phase, women bore the primary burden of singing. The spirits danced and played their whistles in the center. It was still early, and the playing was appropriate but low on energy. The performance was thus quite similar to the previous evening's zvipunha ceremony. Like the spirits, of ambiguous ontology and with unclear motives, the recurring phrase *Zvamauya woye* was incomplete, awaiting future resolution. "Now that you have come . . ." but then what? There was no clause to complete the thought, only the responding sound of anguish, *yowerere*. The conditions of war and modernity from which these spirits emerged remained seemingly unresolved, confusing, and traumatizing. Perhaps more than those of their spiritual predecessors, the zvaayungu's

FIGURE 6.4. "Zvamauya Woye"

deaths seem as incomplete and unresolved as their lives. The song performed this lack of resolution.

It was difficult to hear the call over the dense collective musical texture. To encourage participation, the spirit that was playing the drum joined in, loudly singing the response part with the women. A man to my left asked Masiza, "Have the [other] spirits emerged yet?" Masiza replied impatiently, "Not yet." A man took up the drum and immediately picked up the pace and varied the pattern with the displaced sixteenth note described above. The spirits clapped both with and at the other participants, gesturing for more energy, effort, and noise. As with the zvipunha, the new pace, an emphasis on the front of the beat, increased effort, and additional voices did the job. A dancing woman exhibited the telltale signs of possession less than a minute after the new drummer began, but there was still work to do. She fell entranced into the other spirit's arms and went limp. For the rest of the performance, the drumming accelerated, the pitch continuously rose, and the spirits danced with ever-increasing energy, jumping at timed pauses every fifteen to twenty cycles. Several minutes later, the spirit hadn't quite woken up. Masiza, disappointed, said, "It's not enough, it's not working." Less than ten seconds later, one of the dancing spirits started a new song, and everything began again.

The roots of success are many: experience, a desire to facilitate participation, habits learned by singing multiple genres for other madhlozi spirits, and a responsibility to sing (seemingly felt primarily by the women). The simplicity of zvaayungu drumming also has utility and reflects the values of ceremonial performance. The key variables in one's evaluation of the occasion as successful, effective, or good/beautiful (*kunaka*) are determined by its expected outcomes. Performances are judged by their impact. With ceremonial drumming, this effectiveness is based on a performance's ability to elicit the range of desired ceremonial outcomes such as dancing, spirit possession, and dancing spirits in possessed mediums.

The zvaayungu pattern can be played by anyone with minimal drumming competence; once the dominant spirit encouraged it, multiple people took turns playing the drum. Virtuosity can actually distract from the proceedings and defer possession.[8] Density of texture is ensured by other means: Women sing multiple parts in the call and response, dancing spirits blow their whistles as they dance with the apparent purpose of filling out the texture, drummers add variety and strength to their strokes over time, and makosho players cut through the building noise. This is one of the fruits of their initial effort, directly connected to it, an interpretant (effect) that is now an indexical sign of that effort and the latest link in a chain of causality (Kockelman 2011, 717).

The overall sound is simultaneously an interpretant of the work that preceded it (rooted in intent) and a sign leading to a new interpretant, a dancing spirit.

Zvaayungu just want to dance; it is the desired end to the performative means. That seems to be the main reason why they awaken at all. If the drum plays correctly and consistently and the participants are engaged with one another in an efficacious integration, then the performance is a success. It is these *effects* that determine one's judgment of the performance's quality. The zvaayungu are more proactive than their counterparts in ensuring "correctness."

The spirits' dancing reveals multiple roots as well. Zvaayungu dance with loose steps iconic to the madzviti but less aggressive. After dancing ten to twenty cycles of the basic pattern, drummers can shift and cue a pause in which the spirits jump up and down. The singers and makosho continue, and the drums and dancers wait briefly before starting again. In juxtaposing indices connected to the war of independence, the colonial legacy, and modernity against clear indices of Ndau spirituality and icons of the madzviti and other familiar spirits, the zvaayungu are semiotically complex, and they creatively index multiple histories. The sound of the drum emerges from encounters with madzviti spirits, extending an encounter with Gaza Nguni soldiers and the Portuguese during the nineteenth century. As they reach my ears, these interactions extend into a new encounter.

VaMasiza speculated to me that as the spirits mature and as the living grow more familiar with them, the drumming and dancing will become more complex, but that remains to be seen.[9] The zvaayungu's attraction to their spiritual elders, the madzviti, makes sense. The arrival of the madzviti in the Ndau communities of Chipinge is surprisingly iconic of that of the zvaayungu. Both groups are the spirits of foreign soldiers who fought and died in the area during a period of foreign control and subjugation. The fruit of the Gaza Nguni occupation, beyond the emergence of madzviti spirits, is a shared Ndau identity that is defined in part by that history. Zvaayungu reflect a similar history and perhaps suggest a similar legacy in which the spiritual modernity they signify embeds itself in local identities.

Spirits as Agents

Spirits are agents. Not only do they interpret signs during performance, deciding whether to wake up, to dance, or to engage with other living and dead participants, but they also signify themselves. In interpreting the signs around them, they make their own interpretants. These effects—waking up, drumming, and speaking—then become signs for the other participants to interpret, and on it goes. Madhlozi spirits are capable of being affected and capable of wielding signs as the means toward their own ends; they have the capacity to act, if subject to constraints, like all actors. If agency is defined by the capacity and the freedom to fulfill the ends one desires, then spirits are agents.

Biosemioticians, anthropologists enacting the ontological turn, and others looking to push the humanities and social sciences beyond the human understandably question the nature of agency, equating it with the making of interpretants. Kockelman (2011, 721) asserts that lawnmowers are agents, "not because they select per se but because they were selected." Stuart Kauffman applies agency to bacteria (2008, 78).[10] Tomlinson rightly resists this trend, arguing that granting agency to cells and bacteria erases the power of agency to address affect in the experiences of complex entities such as humans (2016, 158–59). Tomlinson's point pushes affect to the center of human experience and to agency itself.[11] The reduction of agency to a simple response to stimuli can be a powerful addition to theories of the inanimate, but it erases the utility of agency in studies of life. Drums, snuff, dirt floors, and human vocal cords can be the instruments of agency or affordances of agency, but not the agent itself (Kockelman 2011). The making of semiotic interpretants is not equivalent to all processes of thirdness.

The objects of performance signs, and the roots and fruits of semiosis, are determined and known via interpretation. Agents are necessary for semiosis. At Horus Farm, the spirits expected to be invited, fed, and engaged. Others expected their drumming to work, expected the spirits to wake up, and eventually expected them to leave. But possession isn't inevitable. Drummer and spirit each did what was felt to be necessary to ensure that these expectations were realized. Given that zvaayungu interpret signs in performance and respond with signs of their own, wielding them to enact their own desired ends explicitly confirms their agency.

It is curious that Mahmood (2009, 20) limits the capacity she associates with agency to the realization of one's interests against tradition or custom. The role of acting spirits and their relation to their living compatriots begs questions about the role of custom and tradition in these collective ceremonial experiences. Semiosis is grounded in habits shaped by previous semiotic encounters. It is a short step from habit to custom, yet even for scholars who value the habitus (Mahmood 2005), custom and tradition become stultifying constraints on the possibility of freedom.

Studies of trance and possession can shift to the possibility of measuring physiological data instead of purpose, the performative realization of purpose, or even spirituality. If biomechanics determines everything from one's pulse to one's desire for intimacy and one's reliance on spirits of the dead, the erasure of what is absent *absolves* inquiry about purpose or intention of the need to account for the "affective dimensions of experience." Deacon (2012b, 53) criticizes the biological sciences for relying on "homunculi" filling the gaps left by a narrow focus on the physiological. He also dismisses spirits and gods as homunculi, the pre-scientific explanations for meaning and agency. Diminishing spiritual explanations as illusory sources of meaning contradicts Ndau elisions between nature and culture. The ontology of Masiza and the spirits for whom he performs is as natural as the purposes for which they engage with one another. The zvaayungu are not an "absential relation," as Deacon describes meaning, purpose, and consciousness. "Like meanings and purposes," he writes, "consciousness may not be something *there* in any typical sense of being materially or energetically embodied, and yet may still be materially causally relevant" (12, emphasis in original). The spirits *are* embodied. Deacon argues that "despite the obvious and unquestioned role played by functions, purposes, meanings, and values in the organization of our bodies and minds, and in the changes taking place in the world around us, our scientific theories still have to officially deny them anything but a sort of heuristic legitimacy" (12). I would add the unquestioned roles played by spirits and God. In these communities, spirits also have more than "heuristic legitimacy."

Habits guide the interpretation of signs, as well as the selection of responses to those signs. These habits could be considered as part of the "black box" of habitus; they are the embodied accumulation of experience of past signs with evolutionary, historical, personal, and intersubjective dimensions (Kockelman 2011, 717). Habits are not always predictable, shared, or compatible. Thus, the zvaayungu may be a spirit conforming to habits of identifying madhlozi, they may be charms conforming to fears of witchcraft, or they may oppose habits of interpretation and remain unknown, confusing, even terrifying. Samson Mapfumo asserted the necessity of snuff in spirit possession.[12] Breathing snuff (*kubema forya*) arouses the spirit; it allows the spirit of the medium in question to wake up within them. But the zvaayungu spirits do no such thing. They abhor snuff, along with the seven-day ceremonial beer. Instead, they smoke cigarettes in straight-backed chairs, drinking brandy and bottled lager. In Mahmood's terms, their actions could be construed as realizations of zvaayungu interests against the weight of madhlozi tradition. Mapfumo and Muzite, members of the same local community, did not see those traditions as flexible, so they interpreted those signs as evidence of something more sinister. Zvaayungu practices seem to employ the instability of life to shape *new* habits and traditions rather than simply resist old ones.

For Horus Farm community members, the contradiction between spirit traditions and the evidence at hand, that zvaayungu spirits arrived without the need of snuff or the desire for homebrew, had the opposite effect. The actions of the spirits opened up the supposed boundaries placed by tradition. Their presence exposed and reaffirmed the dynamism of spirituality and tradition. Regardless of one's interpretation, the zvaayungu disrupt habits built up over decades of ceremonial interaction. There is a conflict between the known ceremonial world of midzimu and madhlozi and the implications of the zvaayungu's behavior. Now people must "create a new habit that will encompass this foreign habit and, in the process, remake [them]selves, however momentarily, anew, as one with the world around [them]" (Kohn 2013, 63). Habits such as this are rarely noticed as such, but when they clash with the signs at hand, the disruption is felt. It triggers an affective evaluation grounded in the body's habits, the sedimented tendencies rooted in past ceremonial experiences, personal desires, and social expectations; thus the anger of Headman Muzite, the frustration of the n'anga Wilson Simango, and the open chuckle of Davison Masiza in response to the zvaayungu's presence.

Affect is at the center of agency in action (Tomlinson 2016). It connects purpose to interpretation, shaping the self and its accompanying habits and values. Emotion is a by-product of these relational processes and part of the changing of habits, the emergence of meaning and experience, and the society in solution that make these processes central to life. In this way, zvaayungu spirits as agents contribute to social transformation. The conflict between a narrow interpretation of what is possible spiritually and what is evident ceremonially triggered anger for Headman Muzite. The affective dimensions of my questions about zvaayungu spirits affected him physically. The signs of anger seemed comparable to those in my experience as his voice rose in pitch and volume and his gestures of dismissal were an aggressive and emotive accompaniment to his words. For Masiza, the dimensions of possibility were more open, and thus the signs of zvaayungu presence were less threatening. He had less interest in controlling local events than the political headman and less expectation of having answers to these complex spiritual contradictions than the n'anga Simango. Thus the affective intensity of his response was more muted and manifest as bemusement. He laughed, an emotive of acceptance and wonder.

In the shared singing of "Zvamauya" there were several instances in which the spirits revealed their capacity to shape the experiences of those around them, wielding their power to signify for the sake of their specific goals: to dance, involve others, and wake up a fellow spirit. The zvaayungu initiated the drumming, they urged people to work harder by clapping, gesturing, and modeling energetic ceremonial behavior, and when the first song failed to fully bring the spirits that were anticipated, the spirits were the ones to quickly start again with a new song, singing for themselves and for the community that invited them.

Zvaayungu spirits, like all madhlozi spirits, are spirits of the other; they embody a certain epistemology about the other and inform ways of knowing the other. Therefore, their introduction of "foreign habits" is unsurprising, a part of their purpose as they eventually become spirits of a changing Ndau self. The disagreement about zvaayungu identity and ontology is a reminder that there are limits, profound limits, to what one can know about the other. Social engagement and interaction require knowledge of the other. Crapanzano writes, "We can never know the mind of the other, and yet we must act as if we do" (2014, 255). Even members of the Horus farm community like Masiza who invited them, drummed for them, and catered to their impetuous demands would admit that they aren't really sure who the zvaayungu are, but they do the best they can and display obvious trust. Authenticity and trust are key to the manner of their interpretation. Trust builds on expectation and opens habits of interpretation; authenticity speaks to the veracity of the sign-object connection. The zvaayungu's authenticity is somewhat under question, given the range of possible interpretations, but the trust, at Horus Farm at least, is apparent.

Despite their consistent presence in ceremonies and interaction with living participants, the zvaayungu remain partly unknown; their utility is accepted more easily than their ontology. From a certain perspective, such as Masiza's, in which the madhlozi are helpful and historically important, the arrival of the zvaayungu is easy to categorize. From a different perspective, such as Wilson Simango's and Rodwell Muzite's, in which local spirituality is entirely divorced from whiteness, European modernity, and the colonial encounter, the zvaayungu become a contradiction, impossible to accept and thus threatening.

In both cases, within each of these possible truths, the zvaayungu require local actors and participants in ceremonial life to account for their ambiguity and make decisions about how the colonial experience and the postcolonial present are dealt with in spiritual terms. The zvaayungu participate in these evaluations as agents of their own participation. They have an active presence in the proceedings. Via their own semiotic representations, they embody a modernity that is local and spiritually knowable. Within the terms of a modernist discourse the modern becomes, for the Horus Farm community, at least, a relatively new local tradition, historically rooted, enthusiastically performed, and collectively confronted. By inviting the zvaayungu and dancing with them, perhaps local communities can use their spiritual guidance to acquire some control over the conditions of modernity that inevitably shape their lives, making modern history work for them.

Encounter 3: Ndau and Chimurenga Soldiers

During ceremonial interactions, the living and the dead become creative actors in the making of local history and society. There is a powerful connection between the living and the dead, between the present and the past, that renders local historical understanding distinct from that found in societies in which historical awareness is based primarily on literacy or living memory. The Ndau need not rely on their memories of past struggles because they can revisit the actors from those eras when they return as madhlozi during a ceremony. The spirits embody the roots of their own emergence. In Ndau religious experience, spirit possession is a direct and embodied form of memory, a form of lived history that helps locals deal with strangers, deal with the other, and potentially deal with uncertainty. Communities thus have the opportunity to refine their relationships with influential actors long dead. The past becomes a dynamic part of the here and now and can be continually reexamined. When the young men and women of Horus Farm become possessed by the zvaayungu, they are possessed by history.

Key moments in the past exist in the present for the Ndau as madhlozi ceremonies move from one spiritual community to the next, reliving local history. Every significant era perdures in the present. The young mediums of Chipinge embody the spirits of soldiers who lived through the war that made Zimbabwe. In an almost literal sense, possession integrates the trauma of social encounters with the other into a dynamic sense of self for local people. Just as the living continue to negotiate the trauma of their Gaza Nguni past through a continuing engagement with the madzviti, locals like VaMasiza engage their personal memories of the war with the memories of the zvaayungu embodied in their children. These interactions, both during specific ceremonial experiences and over time, become the dominant mode of history for these Ndau communities, more powerful than books or the rhetoric of politicians. When the young zvaayungu spirit came to me with a smile and an accusation, he took control of a complex social relationship, redefining conflict in his own terms. By bringing me beer, taking control of our encounter, and doing so with magnanimity, the spirit and the community to whom he appeared were able to redefine and realign the inequality that led to his death. Our exchange gave this soldier a chance to show his former colonizer and enemy his humanity and provide an opportunity to reconsider their relationship. Like all spirits, he relies on the living in order to return, to dance, and to live again. The men who witnessed our exchange enjoyed it, smiling, laughing, and expressing their appreciation for the beer that was offered. Nobody seemed surprised. By providing the music and movement that invite the zvaayungu, participants collectively take control of their own history, validate their memory, and work toward a hopeful future.

A SPIRITUAL MODERNITY

As spirits of modernity, zvaayungu embody and perform the modern, engage with ideas of modernity historically and spiritually, and force the communities in which they emerge to confront these challenging historical issues while also affording them the opportunity to redefine what modernity can mean. They even indigenize its influence, subvert modernist discourse, and turn the modern into tradition. This is not an alternative modernity . . . yet. Following Ferguson and others, the material challenges facing communities such as this undermine any efforts to claim modernity. Participants in the zvaayungu ceremony "traditionalize" characteristics that are tied to the modern, which then tie the modern to the local.[13] It is a productive making of indexicality between tradition and modernity through mimesis, iconicity, and co-occurrence: the poiesis of interpretant-making.

These are the spirits of colonial encounter. Their preference for chairs and cigarettes is meaningful. The zvaayungu turn their back on many of the components of ceremony that have long defined local ritual life. Using snuff, brewing beer, and sitting respectfully on the ground have long been ways in which the living and the dead show respect, authority, and integrity to one another. Simply put, they are traditions, traditions that the zvaayungu reject or redefine in preference for indices of modernity. Their modernity is inextricably embedded in whiteness and the violence of colonialism. Their ambiguity exposes the intersection of black and white in recent history.

Modernity is an elusive term. Locally, it is part of a powerful indexical cluster combining ideas of the West, capitalism, financial well-being, and progress. It is oriented toward the future. Modernity is not something I employ theoretically but, rather, something I explore ethnographically. Within the unique conditions of colonial and postcolonial Zimbabwe, the terms, premises, and logic of modernity have become locally specific rather than broadly abstract. Of course, *modern* does not equal *Western*, but it is embedded materially within items emerging from and identified with the West. It is inextricably tied to British colonialism. This is perhaps truer in the circumscribed context of the ceremony than in everyday life. The signs of a zvaayungu ceremony index time and place in confusing, even paradoxical ways. Some elements, like the drum, cloth, and dance, mark the local but also mark the past—here and then. Other elements, like the cigarettes, chairs, button-down shirts, and displaced notes to conclude phrases, mark the foreign but also the present, the here and now, perhaps integrating the there and now with the here and then. Combining the terms of haecceity, the here and now, is a process that is still unfolding.

Modernity matters in this context because, in engaging with the zvaayungu, participants encounter modernity, historicize it, learn it as it is embodied in the spirits, and evaluate it. The spirits confront local expectations. The zvaayungu's attitude and presence force the living to confront the history they embody. From one point of view, each element of the zvaayungu's presence that breaks with tradition and distinguishes them from other madhlozi spirits is understood locally as modern. That was the word my interviewees used when I asked about the stools, the brandy, or the hats, at least when they weren't saying *Western*. These are the signs of the zvaayungu that led to angry denunciations from Simango, Mulambo, and Muzite. They are modern; they are foreign; they are things of the European.

I don't want to overlook the material dimension of modernity in Zimbabwe as people aspire to better lives and indices of achievement, a point taken from Ferguson (2012). But modernity is also about a sense of time that is both progressive and inevitable. In a community emerging from more than a century of colonial misrule, missionary zeal, postcolonial instability, and neoliberal degradation, the temporal narrative of modernity plays out in expectations of progress, Christian values, and material markers of success. Within such a framework the spirits are indices of the past and of pre-modernity. Modernity opposes tradition. As Judith Butler puts it, "Hegemonic conceptions of progress define themselves over and over against a pre-modern temporality that they produce for the purposes of their own self-legitimation" (2010, 102). My students from Zimbabwe (including Chipinge) have often been dismissive of "traditional" music and spirituality precisely because of its indexical connection to a past they would like to leave behind.

This disagreement about zvaayungu legitimacy and authenticity reflects two competing interpretations of the way modernity is understood geographically, historically, and personally. If the modern is equated with the West and an unprovincialized Europe, as in cosmopolitan Zimbabwe, then the zvaayungu don't make any sense. That is why Rodwell Muzite forbids them within his jurisdiction. They're threatening and incompatible with centuries of Ndau spirituality. If the modern is understood as locally emergent and authentic, however, then the zvaayungu are a consistent and welcome fit within the lineage of local spirits.

SYNECHISM: THE CONTINUITY OF EXPERIENCE

Zvaayungu are contested and distrusted in part because they are neither Shona nor European, black nor white, modern nor traditional. They are in between. They speak and act in ways that are in between. Indeed, their ambiguity may productively call into question the very categories they blur. The complexities behind local modernity and contemporary spirituality dialectically inform one another such that spirit possession becomes a performed, nondiscursive contributor to local understandings of modernity. To paraphrase James Ferguson (2012), local ceremonies are spaces in which people can experience their history but are also able to think about that history and play with what it means. Zvaayungu spirits are semiotically complicated and ontologically ambiguous. This has potentially dramatic implications for epistemology but also reflects the inherent flexibility of local spiritual life. Zvaayungu offer something to the future of these communities by changing what is possible and bringing those possibilities to life. Their presence is an interpretant of all that has happened before their appearance and a sign of what might happen next. In a way, this possible future, as telos, determines the course of the present as local actors interpret their past. Zvaayungu inevitably cause anxiety since nobody is exactly sure what that telos is for the spirits themselves. Why are they here? What is *their* purpose?

Perhaps the zvaayungu offer new continuities, reshaping old truths in order to undermine binaries otherwise accepted as oppositional. The zvaayungu are in between multiple dualities—past and present, black and white, modern and traditional, Shona and Ndau—in such a way that they expose these binaries as fictitious analytic impositions. Their between-ness reveals hidden continuities that connect seemingly oppositional forces. In connecting black to white and modernity to ritual tradition, they threaten long-established views. Spirits can't be white, as some locals said repeatedly, yet the zvaayungu exhibit a number of traits tied to Zimbabwe's history of white authority. Their respect for authority is less obvious, if it is there at all. Even the semiotic continuities that make madhlozi ceremonies such multisensory experiences are disrupted and challenged.

Temporal layers of historical moments and their communities are made manifest in the sequence of spirits who arrive to dance: nineteenth-century madzviti spirits, eighteenth-century zvipunha girls, and twentieth-century zvaayungu soldiers. In a ceremony, each of these historical times is revisited and potentially redefined. In the context of these competing temporal frameworks, the zvaayungu spirits are the most recent and unknowable. Their legacy and their role are still unfolding. All madhlozi spirits embody history; they are visitors from the past who can continue to shape people's memory. The zvaayungu embody a historical modern via their dress, language, and behavior. Modernity often implies a rupture with the past (Comaroff and Comaroff 2014), but in this case the past that is ruptured is a modern one. The modern becomes historical, and thus negotiable, through the zvaayungu's presence. The intersection of progressive time and the historical layering of the ceremony complicates and undermines the totalizing implications about progress implicit in discourses of modernity. The zvaayungu implicitly challenge those discourses.

Epilogue

My final hours at Samson Mapfumo's home in the hills of Muzite before heading back to Chipinge and eventually Illinois were bittersweet. I was leaving after more than two years of living and learning in Zimbabwe. Samson Mapfumo and his family had introduced me to mhongo, madzviti, the wonderful mbira playing and musicianship of Zombiyi Muzite Gwenzi, and some of the best cooking in Zimbabwe at this very spot. But I hadn't left yet; VaMapfumo, Moses Zharikira, Tendai Chitopo, and I were reliving some of our shared experiences of the past years, already nostalgic for a time that technically was not yet over. I spent a lot of time taking pictures, trying to capture every possible combination of friends and family. At their request, I took a photo with Mr. and Mrs. Mapfumo standing in front of their maize crop, of which they were justifiably proud. In a poor attempt to compliment his farming skills, I told VaMapfumo that his fields looked so great that none of my friends would believe there was hunger or drought in Zimbabwe. He immediately frowned and asked with concern whether that was really true. "Then don't show them to anyone," he said. I assured him that his great crops wouldn't convince anyone that everything was all right in Zimbabwe. He seemed relieved. He was proud of his field, after all, and we continued taking pictures. But he asked me again before I left to tell people the truth about Zimbabwe.

The challenges facing people in these communities remain as important now as at the time of Mapfumo's frustration. There have been ups and downs, but unemployment remains high, the essentials of daily life remain scarce, and ZANU-PF remains in power. Issues related to land reform, inequality, and distribution remain at the forefront of people's minds such that chimurenga (as an expression of struggle and resistance) remains a part of everyday discourse and of life itself (Maposa, Hlongwana, and Gamira 2010). Ferguson's (2006) frustration with the importance of avoiding a naïve kind of "Afro-optimism" or an unwarranted "Afro-pessimism" speaks well to my own experiences writing about life in Chipinge. State institutions have tightened their grip in Chipinge because ZANU-PF now wins local parliamentary seats that were unattainable while Ndabaningi Sithole was politically active. For many people, local traditions are losing their appeal as they are pushed further and further from the promises and aspirations of modernity. Local identity formations—ethnicity, language, religion, and nationality—are being continually redefined in the face of perpetually shifting geopolitical pressure. The future is unclear.

But for the people represented in these pages, spiritual relationships can help. Ceremonial traditions do not thrive simply because custom is resilient or because the so-called structures from which they emerge are fixed but, rather, because they provide hope; hope that people in the present can use the experiences of the past to make a better future (Rorty 1999), hope that makes new experiences possible (Crapanzano 2004, 101). Spirits fulfill that hope. Ceremonies shape the ways in which practitioners understand the world, the cosmos, their place in history, their role in the present, and their path moving forward. Practices in performance are profound means for locals to access these truths and learn, continue, and improve these "habits of action."

Masiza plays for his spirits, and Matabuka becomes possessed by them, largely because it is useful; it is a good thing to do; it feels good. When I asked someone who this particular spirit was, or why that particular spirit chose to possess the living and dance at ceremonies, the answer was often simply "Because they help us." Zvipunha help with childbirth and harvest, mhongo heal, madzviti protect the midzimu and the living, and the zvaayungu . . . well, for them, the jury is still out. But if the madzviti destroy culture, zvipunha nurture it, and mhongo preserve it, perhaps zvaayungu create culture, using their ambiguity to creatively respond to twenty-first-century dynamism. The duality of each allows Ndau identity to evolve and reflect the transformations of history. The madzviti are no longer Gaza Nguni soldiers, but they are not yet ancestors. The zvipunha are not yet mothers but are no longer childless. The mhongo are not mermaids but are more than VaDanda neighbors. The zvaayungu are not white but are not simply Shona. Each informs the way selves are known through their explicit otherness.

Dancing is central to these processes of assistance, and the living help their spirits do just that with musicking. Actors from the past can help protect and guide the living if they are respectfully engaged. People trust them. The dialogic and intersubjective nature of Ndau historical understanding that emerges from these relationships makes history a living practice. Spirit possession *is* history. Communities can literally interact with those who preceded them, invert asymmetrical historical power relations, and reconfigure themselves into positions of strength. It is a mutual process of assistance that, when played right, makes for a smoothly run and happily lived society: mutually assured construction.

Performing, playing, and doing are the means by which ideas and habits become action. They become social consciousness as they are lived (Williams 1977, 130). Moments in the here and now make pasts matter and futures possible. Timbres, tones, and rhythms potentially correspond with expectations and ideals of the dance, social cooperation, and appeasement of spirits. These connections are authentic in that they are understood, whether explicitly or not, to be real. In this way, ritual is transformative, turning possibility into actuality.

Performances help form, solidify, and embody the values of local communities, meaningfully generating habits and habitus. Knowing what is good and right, and effectively performing to those standards, not only makes for more entertaining performances, which matters, but allows for cosmological balance and emotional success. Values properly embodied in the steps of the madzviti, the density of mhongo drumming, or the modest singing of the zvipunha make people and their spirits happier, improving the communities involved. No one I spoke with framed these processes in this way, but when habits of doing, feeling, and being are so visibly and audibly embodied and realized, no one needs to explicitly state how and why. Language is secondary to these embodied thoughts.

But I don't want to suggest that the ceremonial space is a utopia. There is an ideal, one that may even match expectations, but countless influences sever these continuities and undermine the reliability of trusted processes. After centuries of marginalization and subservience to outside influences, it can be hard to trust age-old markers of authority. The variety of attitudes towards the Ndau cosmos held by people in Chipinge shows that not everyone finds the spirits to be the best guides to life. Political and economic insecurity serve as evidence for some that the spirits' power has waned. Money, jobs, school, debt, disease, political insecurity, and drought can all undermine continuity with spiritual reality; trust takes effort.

Ritual performance is not naïve, rote repetition. Circumstances of history, community, and cosmology all make the embodiment of ideals difficult to realize. Spirits can be vengeful, politicians corrupt, and parents jealous. But the best way for practicing Ndau adherents of the local cosmology to protect and prevent against the intrusion of these undesirable elements is to respect their spirits and keep them happy via the ceremonies in which they dance. The madhlozi use the lessons learned during their tumultuous pasts to guide the living through their troublesome present.

With spiritual guidance, it should not be a leap of logic to move from the minutiae of performance such as timbre or a shuffled dance step to the loftiest of cosmological and social ideals. Timbre can noticeably influence one's relationship with the spirits. When Masiza drummed well for the zvipunha, the spirits came, danced, and convinced the living that they would have their protection in the months to come. When Ambuya Mazveshe replaced the mateza drums with zvigubhu jerry cans, the shifting timbre and erasure of spiritual indexicality opened up entirely unexpected possibilities for performance. The values of society, the guidance of history, the relationships of the cosmos, and the emotional responses to all of those signs shape the ways in which contemporary Ndau confront the world they live in.

Music, emotion, experience, purpose, and spirituality are all notoriously difficult to capture with language. The ways in which each is meaningful can be hard to put into words or generalize with symbols. The knowledge of experience and music is only partly compatible with the knowledge of language (Seeger 1977). Perhaps we should accede to Samuels's urge that we abandon our "fetishization of meaning" (Samuels 2006) and defer to Glissant's admonition that we grant people the right to "opacity" (Glissant 1997), but I would counter that the inclusive approach to meaning offered in these pages illuminates what is possible to know in the experience of another without presuming that it is easy, predictable, linguistic, or comprehensive and without slipping into solipsism (Crapanzano 2014). Much remains opaque, although hopefully relying so openly on the very tools through which I have thought and learned about these issues allows my own method to be as transparent as possible and suggests a path forward. Semiotics can help overcome Seeger's dilemma.

The model presented here is a tool for understanding meaning and experience as felt in lived moments and for making that leap from the minute to the magnificent. Signs initiate complex processes of perception, interpretation, and experience that both distinguish self from other and integrate self with other. The semiotic transitions of emotional processes—from the indeterminacy of affect and the embodiment of emotion-appraisals to the recognition of feelings and expression of emotives—judge the relations between the sensory world, the habits and values of the self, and the goals for the future perceptually, physiologically, culturally, and publicly in relation to personal and collective well-being.

All interpretation relies on models, whether explicitly or not. Mine is semiotic. Begin with the sign: listen, look, feel. What are the effects of those signs—tears, smiles, guilt, dance, possession? What objects, histories, and purposes behind those signs led to those effects? How do people's habits, values, and senses of who they are in relation to the living and the dead around them (as subjectivity, intersubjectivity, and identity) lead people to interpret those sign-object and sign-interpretant relations as they do? What becomes possible through these associations? What becomes real? What inspires the signs and interpretants that people use and create? Semiotic terms allow for ever greater precision when approaching these questions. When considering firstness, the whole phenomenon (in this case, the ceremony), use the thirdness of signs to learn the relations of secondness that matter. If signs are dismissed as mere signification, as representation, it is worth remembering that representations can cause real facts. Playing drums, singing, shouting, possessing, and moving: Reality is made in such ways.

The goal is understanding not only the ceremonial practices at the heart of this text but the means by which I've come to understand them. Peircean theory disciplines my thinking. These are the tools I used to reach what little understanding and clarity I have achieved and to put into words what has little need of them in people's lives: musical meaning. In this model emotion is semiotic, spirits are agents, and the future is, in part, made via signs. The potentially daunting terminology used in Peircean semiotics has little to do with the continental traditions that have most informed recent social theory and can be compromised by the association. The "phenomenological movement" and post-Saussurean structuralism are other models that have been widely used to generalize from instances and capture what otherwise seems ineffable, but they have also led to umbrella dismissals of sign studies as static, product-oriented taxonomies removed from the experiential and the phenomenological.

The point of clarifying the different relations behind signs as opposed to interpretants, indices as opposed to symbols, or rhemes as opposed to dicents is precisely process and experience, not product or structure. Life never holds still, and tools that allow insight into the dynamism of process and the seeming ineffability of experience are essential to understanding why musicking and ritual matter. To be alive is to be semiotic. Like signs, we are little more than our relations. There is an irony in using a model so rich with new terminology to combat criticisms of taxonomy, but there is value as well, in escaping discourses I prefer not to employ, un-writing symbolocentric legacies, and encouraging analytical precision when addressing ephemeral experiences like spirit possession and emotion. The tools I use are not ends but means. Peirce (2008, 304) calls theory and practice the two great tasks of humanity. Ndau practitioners put the theories and philosophies engrained through experience and biocultural evolution into practice, whereas I use my observations and lessons learned to generalize purposes and consequences, putting practice into theory.

Experiences like the madhlozi ceremony are moments when the relations that matter in twenty-first-century Chipinge are formed, reformed, or questioned. The objects of history and purpose with which I examined Madzviti practices in Chapter 3 have analogues in other spiritual performances. Zvipunha, mhongo, and zvaayungu have their own histories and reasons for awakening. Similarly, the subtlety of specific musical signs and their resonant effects among listeners in Zvipunha drumming, explored in Chapter 4, suggests the importance of musical skill for other spirits. In order to be effective, every spiritual performance should generate an experiential focus on the here and now. The range of consequences for different semiotic interpretations in the mhongo performances described in Chapter 5 demonstrate that every ceremony is unique and unpredictable. Goals are not always realized. Tradition only takes one so far. This becomes even more apparent in the ambiguous agency of the zvaayungu, detailed in Chapter 6, which forcibly brings the complexities of multiple pasts to bear on impending futures, making past continuous with future, black with white, Shona with Ndau, and modern with traditional, here with there and now with then.

The continuity explored in that chapter should be extended beyond the continuity of objects, signs, and interpretants. The individuals and communities they create are continuous with one another through their shared experiences, the intersubjectivity of their lives. They are continuous with me via my research and ongoing efforts to understand my experiences with them. And they are now continuous with you, as readers of this book, which is just one particular perspective on the lives represented here.

Most important, participants are continuous with their spirits, not merely in the most obvious way, spirit possession, but in their shared projects of shaping a future together. For the participants in ceremonial life, spirits are real. They participate in daily life and cause ceremonial action. Everyone works together towards common purposes by brewing beer, playing drums, preparing food, dancing, singing, and acknowledging the spirits by means of performance. These shared experiences reaffirm relationships that have consequences for social life beyond the frame of the ceremony. The living and the dead have a responsibility to one another that relies on a delicate balance. Events have causes; thus, actions have consequences. Behavior in the here and now can influence the future for generations to come. The very bodies of musicians, mediums, and other participants are continuous with spiritual realms via the spirits resident within them.

If emotion is an embodied, physiological process grounded in biocultural evolution, how does it account for these kinds of continuities? The ontological turn that questions nature itself, opening up unexpected possibilities, becomes continuous with the semiotic turn I employ to engage with an affective turn that wrestled with the gaps of recent discursive turns. The continuities of these spinning epistemological frameworks run headlong into the ontological givens of spirits and selves in places like Chipinge, complicating music's relation to sound through dance and undermining meaning's distinction from affect.

The collapse of the economy, rule of law, and food security in Zimbabwe have made planning for the future important but unpredictable and scary. Many in Chipinge have been losing hope, growing disenchanted, and working hard to flee the country. But others, perhaps with a long-term view confirmed by their continued relationships with actors from eras throughout history, remain patient. So many of the people mentioned in these pages are gone now, having either fled for the possibilities offered elsewhere in Zimbabwe or in South Africa, Mozambique, the United Kingdom, or the United States or passed away during the struggle of the intervening years, that I feel compelled to offer this text as a testament to their generosity in the face of hardship. When Samson Mapfumo trusted me simply because of copper and rain, he was actually trusting his spirits. I was an unwitting means to an end: a sign. For VaMapfumo, the spirits were communicating directly with him through those beads and raindrops. He ignored the signs that made many of his neighbors wary: my white skin, tape recorder, notebooks, and questions. He ignored the worsening odds facing his community's flourishing and simply helped. In the face of those same worsening odds, Vhukani Muzite seemed relaxed, exhibiting the patience born of experience. He told me not to worry because President Mugabe couldn't live forever and, besides, the spirits know what is best and will guide them through. Masiza always referenced his spirits when difficult journeys, purchases, and other events went well. He confronted the challenges of the here and now head-on via the haecceity of ceremonial performance and collective musicking, bringing past realities and future possibilities to the immediate present.

Masiza and his cohorts rely on the spirits for survival itself. Families like his can now drum and sing for their spirits with beer they brew themselves on good land they farm for themselves. Sometimes, things were hard and weren't going as he hoped. Usually, at those times, he would respond as so many others did in his village at Holland Farm, at Muzite, along the Mozambique border, or in Bangwe, near the Save River's dusty banks. He would hold a ceremony and get those spirits to dance. That always helped.

APPENDIX A

ChiNdau Glossary

ChiNdau orthography follows standard English pronunciation, with some exceptions. There is no *l* sound in standard Shona, but the influence of Nguni languages has led to a sizable vocabulary of words using *l* in ChiNdau. Other exceptions include the following (Hannan 1987, 753):

b	implosive
d	implosive
dy	pronounced as *jigga* in ChiShona and as *rdya* in ChiNdau
hl	an Nguni-derived sound that doesn't appear in English
n'	pronounced as *ng* in *sing*
sv	pronounced as *sh* simultaneously with *f*
zv	pronounced as *zh* simultaneously with *v*

ChiNdau includes two unmarked tones (high and low) that can affect meaning. Infinitive verbs begin with *ku-* (as in *kubuda*) and are marked with a dash below.

ambuya	Grandmother.
baba	Father.
-bema	To ingest tobacco.
-bikira	To cook for or brew beer for someone or something.
-buda	To emerge.

-budira	To possess, literally, "to emerge upon." To be possessed is the reflexive form, *-budirwa.*
-chaya	To play an instrument.
chigejo	Madzviti skirt.
chigubhu	Cylindrical drum or large container for liquid. Also called *tangi.*
Chilapalapa	Pidgin language that emerged when colonial settlers began communicating with their local workers. Also called *fanagalo.*
chimudumbana	Small cylindrical drum used in muchongoyo. Plural, zvimudumbana. Also the small drums of the mhongo mateza. In some areas called *katenha* or *chiyamudumbu.*
Chimurenga	Struggle. The label for the Zimbabwe's major local conflicts.
Chingotoro	Language of the zvipunha that is an old form of ChiNdau.
chingunda	Wig made of plant fibers worn by mhongo mediums. Also called *ngundu* or *chingunde.*
chipfuko	Water container used by madzviti. Also called *katende kemvura.*
chipunha	Madhlozi spirit of a young girl from the early Ndau period. Plural, *zvipunha.* Also called *chisora* and *chinyasikana.*
chirombo	Spirit a person is born with that shapes certain skills and personality traits. Plural, *zvirombo.*
chisena	Madhlozi spirits from Mozambique.
chisora	See *chipunha.*
-da	To want.
dhlozi	Outsider spirit, non-ancestral spirit. Plural, madhlozi or mashave. Also called *shave.*
doro	Beer.
dzinza	Family lineage through the father.
dzviti	Madhlozi spirit of a warrior from Gaza-Nguni, either Zulu or Swazi. Plural, madzviti.
forya	Tobacco. Also called *fodya.*
gandira	Frame drum played with sticks for madzviti spirits. Plural, *makandira.*
-gaudza	The sound people make when becoming possessed.
gondo	Spear used by madzviti. Plural, makondo.

gosho — Gourd or can rattle. Plural, makosho. Also called *hosho*.

hondora — Male equivalent of *chipunha*.

kanyi — Rural home. Plural, makanyi. The Shona term *kumusha* is also used.

katende kemvura — See *chipfuko*.

madanda — Mhongo spirits from the Danda region of Mozambique. Also *manyanga*.

madhlozi — See *dhlozi*.

madzviti — See *dzviti*.

mambo — Chief, lord, or god.

maoko — Hands, used to refer to clapping during performances. Also called *maboko*. Singular, *ruoko* or *boko*.

mapenzi — Madhlozi spirit of fools. Singular benzi.

mapunha — Mediums for zvipunha spirits.

marozvi — Madhlozi spirits from the Rozvi kingdom.

mashayi — See *dhlozi*.

matende — Madhlozi spirits of baboons.

mateza — Set of four or five kettle-shaped drums played for mhongo. Singular, *deza*. The three large drums played by the main drummer are called *muryi*, *mukati*, and *muoshwe* (left, center, and right). The smallest are *zvimudumbana*.

mazinda — Madhlozi spirits from Mozambique related to mhongo. Rennie (1973, 100) calls them spirits of cannibals.

mbira dzaVaNdau — Ndau lamellaphone. Locally known as *mbira*.

MDC — Movement for Democratic Change.

mhatso — House. The Shona term *imba* is also used.

mhondoro — Territorial lion spirits in ChiShona; the spirits of chiefs. Often simply called *midzimu* in ChiNdau.

mhongo — Dhlozi spirit, often a person from Danda. Often supported by *nzuzu*.

midzimu — See *mudzimu*.

mubereko — Cloth used by a woman to carry a child on her back.

mudzimu — Ancestral spirit. Plural, *midzimu* or *vadzimu*.

-mukira — To possess. Specifically used in Ndau, this literally

	means "to awake upon." To be possessed is *kumukirwa*.
munhu	Person. Plural, *vanhu*. Also *muntu*.
mutupo	Totem. Plural, *mitipo*.
muroyi	Witch.
mweya	Spirit, air, breath.
Mwari	God.
muyungu	Person of European descent. Plural, vayungu. Also *mungezi* or *murungu*.
ndonga	Walking stick. *Tsvimbo* in Shona. Ndabaningi Sithole chose *ndonga* as the name for his political party.
n'anga	Indigenous doctor and herbalist. Plural, either n'anga or dzin'anga.
ngoma	Song. *Ngoma* does not usually mean "drum" as it does in standard Shona.
ngozi	Aggrieved spirit, one who hasn't become an ancestor owing to some slight or crime on the part of the living.
ngundu	See *chingunda*.
nheni	Nanny. Plural, manheni. Used as a synonym for *zvipunha*.
njuzu	See *nzuzu*.
nyamusoro	Healer who relies on spirit possession for diagnosis and treatment.
nzuzu	Mermaid spirit; also *njuzu*.
-ombera	Ritual clapping.
sekuru	Grandfather or maternal uncle.
Sope	Distilled spirits used recreationally and during ceremonies. Also called *kachasu*.
-svikira	To possess. More common in Shona, it literally means "to arrive on." To be possessed is *kusvikirwa*.
svikiro	Shona for "spirit medium."
-tamba	To play or dance. Also used in theNdau greeting *Munotamba here?* This literally means "Do you play?" but suggests "How are you?"
tangi	See *chigubhu*.
-tsutsa	To possess, specifically for a *shayi* or dhlozi spirit.
unhu	Being. A moral sense of personhood (Kyker 2016).

uroyi	Witchcraft.
ZANU-PF	Zimbabwe African National Union—Patriotic Front.
ZANLA	Zimbabwe African National Liberation Army.
ZAPU	Zimbabwe African People's Union.
zenda	Sometimes used to refer to male mhongo spirits. Plural, mazenda. See *mazinda*.
ZIPRA	Zimbabwe People's Revolutionary Army.
zvaayungu	Madhlozi spirits of soldiers from the Second Chimurenga. Also *zvemakuru*.
zvipunha	See *chipunha*.

APPENDIX B

Semiotic Glossary

The model employed in this book relies on the extensive semiotic vocabulary devised by C. S. Peirce. It integrates this vocabulary with other terms from affect theory and the anthropology of identity. This appendix is meant to mitigate the initially daunting task of keeping track of these interrelated theoretical tools and terms.

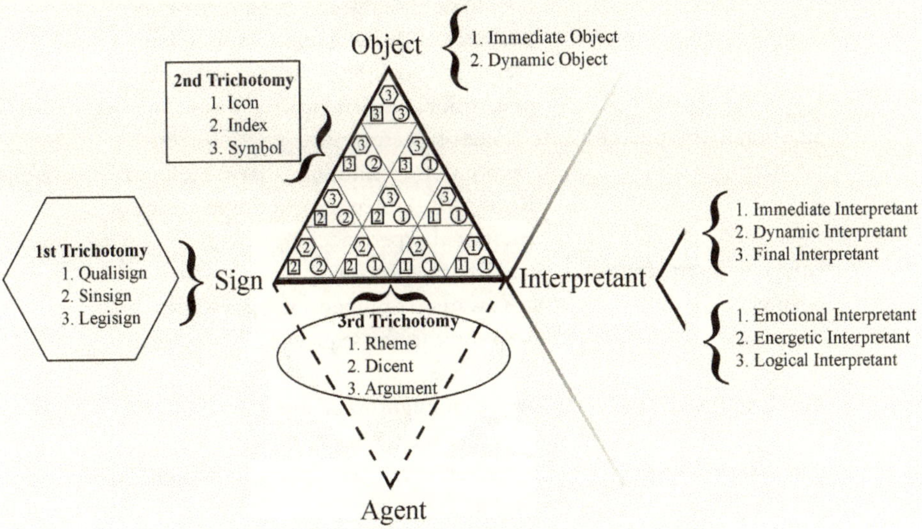

FIGURE A.1. Visual representation of the complexity of the tripartite sign, according to C.S. Peirce

affect	The emergent aspect of all experience that engages and initiates emotional processes. Step one in the sequence of emotional experience.
argument	"A sign which, for its Interpretant, is a sign of law" (Peirce 1998, 292).
degenerate index	An indexical sign that refers to secondness as reference only (Peirce 1998, 274).
deictic	The first index. Represents its object by directing attention to it. A genuine index.
dicent	A sign interpreted as *actually* being connected to its object.
dimension of value	An open axis of interpretation along which a sign's relation to purpose is understood.
dynamic interpretant	The actual effect of a sign in an interpreter (Peirce 1998, 498).
dynamic object	The "real object" (Peirce 1998, 409) or the mediate object (480).
emotion	A process of response to and appraisal of signs that signify objects of value and thus effect changes in the body and habits of the self.
emotion-appraisal	The specific embodied moment when signs are physiologically evaluated relative to purposes of thriving and surviving (see Damasio 2003). Step two in the sequence of emotional experience.
emotional interpetant	An affective interpretant.
emotive	An expression of emotions that are felt (see Reddy 2001). Step four in the sequence of emotional experience.
energetic interpretant	An active interpretant.
feeling	One's awareness of emotion-appraisals. Step three in the sequence of emotional experience.
final interpretant	How a sign ought to be interpreted given enough time (Peirce 1998, 498).
first trichotomy	The trichotomy of the sign: (1) qualisign, (2) sinsign, (3) legisign.

firstness — "That which is such as it is positively and regardless of anything else" (Peirce 1998, 267).

genuine index — An indexical sign in existential relation to its object (Peirce 1998, 274).

habit — A tendency to respond to circumstances and stimuli on the basis of similar circumstances or stimuli in the past (Turino 2008, 95).

haecceity — An index that forcibly draws attention to the immediate here and now. The second species of indexical now. The absence of generality, pure secondness (Short 2007, 50).

icon — Sign of resemblance, representing objects "only insofar as they resemble them themselves" (Peirce 1998, 460).

identity — A representation of the self, whether self-selected or not; a partial selection of habits employed to represent ourselves to the world around us (Turino 2008, 102).

immediate interpretant — The "interpretability" of the sign (Peirce 1998, 498).

immediate object — Semiotic objects only as they are represented by signs (Short 2007, 196).

index — A sign of contiguity, representing objects "only by virtue of a real connection with them" (Peirce 1998, 460).

indexical nows — (1) "Dramatic pointing indices that . . . produce heightened attention to the object" (Turino 2014, 214). (2) Indexes with immediate proximity to the here and now, pointing unequivocally to "this moment" (see *haecceity*).

interpretant — That which a sign determines in its interpreter (Peirce 1998, 409).

intersubjectivity — Subjectivity as informed by the lived engagement with others in real time, shaping future relationships and their accompanying habits.

legisign	A type or law that is a sign.
logical interpretant	Symbolic interpretant.
metonym	The second index. Represents its object via an associated characteristic.
object	That which is stood for by something (sign) to some effect (interpretant).
qualisign	"A quality which is a sign. It cannot actually act as a sign until it is embodied" (Peirce 1998, 291).
replica index	The third index. Represents its object by serving as the token of a type (or sinsign of a legisign) with the purpose ofreplicating that type.
rheme	A sign that is interpreted as *possibly* being tied to its object.
second trichotomy	The trichotomy of the sign-object relationship: (1) icon, (2) index, (3) symbol.
secondness	"That which is such as it is as being Second to some First, regardless of anything else" (Peirce 1998, 160).
self	One's physical body and all of one's habits of thinking, doing, feeling, and being (see Turino 2008).
sign	"Anything which is determined by something else, called its Object, and so determines an effect upon a person, which effect I call its Interpretant, that the latter is mediately determined by the former" (Peirce 1992, 478).
sinsign	"An actual existent thing or event which is a sign" (Peirce 1998, 291).
subjectivity	The partial and immediate selection of habits and physical capacities engaged in the here and now.
symbol	A sign of stipulation, representing objects "because dispositions or factitious habits of their interpreters insure their being so understood" (Peirce 1998, 460).
synechism	"The tendency to regard everything as continuous" (Peirce 1998b, 1).

third trichotomy — The trichotomy of the sign according to its interpretant: (1) rheme, (2) dicent, (3) argument.

thirdness — "That whose being consists in it bringing about a secondness" (Peirce 1998, 267). Representation is thirdness.

Notes

Prologue: Music, Experience, Meaning

1. Muchongoyo is a local Ndau form of secular dance/drumming popular in Zimbabwe and Mozambique (Perman 2010, 2017).

2. Sithole also founded the party that eventually would rule the country, the Zimbabwe African National Union, before being replaced by Robert Mugabe (M. Sithole 1999).

3. *Muyungu* (or *murungu)* is the local term for a person of European descent. It originally specified English people but now means anyone who is white or acts like someone who is white.

4. Samson Mapfumo was by no means the only local elder who aided my research. Vhukani Muzite, in particular, was instrumental in opening doors among local elders.

5. In this case I refer to the mbira dzavadzimu, a focal point of my research in Harare. The spirit told me not to be timid about my research, to thank my teachers, and to learn about instruments other than the mbira, assignments I'm still trying to live up to.

6. Regardless of one's stance regarding its morality or legitimacy, fast-track land reform's devastating impact on local food security is irrefutable (Alexander 2006; Zamchiya 2011, 2013b).

7. Christopher Small's (1998) term "musicking" is the most effective English translation for the performance practices that might otherwise be called music.

8. As in much of Zimbabwe, many people in Chipinge are devout churchgoers who never associate with spirits.

9. Both projects perhaps owe a debt to the work of John Blacking (1995), who similarly asked about music's experiential value.

10. In my application of Peirce I am particularly indebted to Turino (1999), Peirce (1998), and Short (2007) but have been inspired by others as well (Kockelman 2011; Kohn 2013; Tomlinson 2015).

11. Peirce replaced the term *phenomenology* with *phaneroscopy* to distinguish his approach from that of Husserl and others (Short 2007, 61). Peirce's phaneron is "the collective total of all that is in any way or in any sense present to the mind, quite regardless of whether it corresponds to any real thing or not" (1931–58, 1:284). Harris Berger takes Turino to task for claiming Peircean phenomenology as an alternative to what Turino calls "continental phenomenology" and what Berger calls "the phenomenological movement, to which Peirce is an outsider" (2015, 39). As an advocate for Peircean thought who has rarely relied on the texts at the core of this movement, I understand Berger's point, but no single approach to phenomenology is scriptural. As long as a qualifier is added, there should be little confusion between the expansive and influential "phenomenological movement" and the Peircean phaneroscopic variant.

Chapter 1. Introduction: Finding *Madhlozi* in Chipinge

1. The Rhodesian government's draconian Land Apportionment Act of 1930 evicted farmers from the fertile plateau and forcibly resettled them on arid, marginal land (Maposa, Hlongwana, and Gamira 2010, 192). In 1925, D. M. Stanley told the Lands Commission, "It is impossible for natives to work there between 10 A.M. and 3 P.M. Otherwise a couple of days sees them crippled. It is malarious and the general climatic conditions are not favourable to the propagation of the Nordic European race" (cited in Moyana 1984, 109).

2. The name *Gazaland* refers to the Chimanimani and Chipinge Districts, where Zimbabwe's Ndau population lives (Moyana 1984).

3. I spent time working in several other communities along the road mentioned above that play little direct role in this book.

4. The Shona form of *makosho, hosho*, is sometimes used as well. In ChiNdau, the singular is *gosho*.

5. This version is called the mbira dzaVaNdau.

6. Simango studied at the mission school at Mt. Selinda before arriving at the Hampton Institute in Hampton, Virginia, where he became a source for Natalie Curtis, Melville Herskovits, and Franz Boas, with whom he studied. He eventually came into contact with Paul Robeson and W. E. B. DuBois before returning to Mozambique and eventual anonymity in Ghana (Columbus Simango 1919; Curtis 1920; Boas 1920, 1922a, 1922b, Boas and Simango 1922; Herskovits 1923; Andrade 1989; Spencer 2013; Perman 2015).

7. Interview with Jabulani Chinengawo Mulambo, Khosanai Wilson Zunzu Simango, and Joseph Mutwanha at the Chipinge Market on August 17, 2005. All further quotations from Jabulani Mulambo, Wilson Simango, and Joseph Mutwanha are from this source.

8. A few articles are "Zimbabwe: Death and the Fear of Witchcraft" (Nzenza 2015), "Finding the Hub of Zim Witchcraft" (Chara 2015), and "Zimbabwean Mother Kills Son to Sell Ear to Witch Doctor" from *The Telegraph* (Laing 2010).

9. Viveiros de Castro (2005) keeps the nature-culture divide but inverts it. Nature becomes subjective and variable, whereas culture is shared.

10. Mpande Chikumbo, a civil servant in the municipal government, apostolic minister, and former mhongo medium, has a unique perspective on the potential intersection of spirit-based and Christian understandings in Chipinge:

> Lord Jesus Christ . . . told me that all these spirits we call sekurus, ambuyas, they know witches. The sekurus, n'angas, and varoyis, they're all under one spirit. He actually told me that there is a spirit which was here in Zimbabwe called Mwari whose headquarters was at Matebeleland. He came and he destroyed it. . . . He said all spirits report to a spirit whose headquarters is somewhere in the center of Africa. And it's a second headquarters which is here in Zimbabwe. So all these sekurus, these ambuyas, these chiefs you may research, they report to a spirit called Bakubwe. . . . It is that spirit which is worshipped by the Nigerians. They are all fighting against God. No matter how sweet the tongue of a n'anga can be he will not tolerate Jesus Christ, he will never. He may say, God, God, God because God is for all of us, but he will never utter the word of Jesus. He will not. So if you want to understand very well that [be sure] to analyze the spirits and [if] they fail to do it as they would do, they would go and report to Bakubwe. And Bakubwe in all his might will come and face him. . . . They failed to kill me because of the presence of Lord Jesus. Whenever they came, those healers with their things, and when vakuru came, they immediately saw that he appeared and started crying. And they don't cry with two eyes, but with one, tears on the left eye. So all these spirits you are investigating, they're all under Bakubwe. They are all under the influence of Satan. They are all under the same host, saka they are the same. There is no difference. (Interview with Mpande Chikumbo in Chipinge on May 24, 2005. All further quotations from Mpande Chikumbo are from this source.)

Chikumbo's Christian perspective found space for God, Mwari, Allah, Buddha, and all the spirits. In November, when there are no ceremonies, all these deities attend a meeting. For Chikumbo, they all serve Satan, whether knowingly or not. The collapse of Zimbabwe, the rise of Europe and the United States, and the tumult in the Middle East only confirm for him that most of the world's divine figures have lost their power. In a Nietzschean twist, Mwari is dead.

11. I admire Carin Vijfhuizen's (2002) book *The People You Live With*, which concerns life, gender, power, agriculture, and belief in the Mutema chieftaincy, but her focus on the dangerous ways in which n'angas and spirit mediums exploit their spirits for personal gain overshadows the good they can do in people's lives.

12. Interview with A. Mhlanga at Daisy Hill, Chipinge, on February 16, 2005.

13. In a similar vein, a young woman named Patience told me that the "modern" headmaster at her sister's boarding school ignored the spiritual significance of the area where the school had been built. As Patience told it, strange things began to happen; ghosts (*zvipoko*) appeared. Once the headmaster relented and the ritual advised by a n'anga was performed, the unusual activity stopped. Patience related another story in which someone stole maize from a n'anga where she lived. Although the n'anga did nothing, when the thief brought the maize to be milled, it turned into cement. Interview with Patience in Mudanda on May 30, 2004.

14. There are synonyms for *mwari* in the literature (Wilder 1907a; Gelfand 1962; Bourdillon 1987; Vijfhuizen 2002), but I never heard them during my research.

15. *Midzimu* and *vadzimu* are both plural forms of the singular *mudzimu*. *Vadzimu* is more common in standard Shona, but I heard both forms equally in Chipinge (see Hannan 1987).

16. In Shona practice *mhondoro* (lion spirits) are the powerful spirits of former chiefs. Their ceremonies and performance practices are quite separate from those of the vadzimu. In Ndau spiritual life, ancestral spirits of chiefs are simply midzimu. Mhondoro, as a separate category, doesn't exist. Compare the differing descriptions of royal, or chiefly, ancestral spirits in Vijfhuizen (2002) and Lan (1985) for their differing descriptions of royal, or chiefly, ancestral spirits.

17. *Guwa*, or *guva*, means "grave." *Kurova guwa* means "to beat the grave" (Kyker 2009), and *kusemendera guwa* means "to cement the grave" (Muyambo and Maposa 2013).

18. Shona *bira* ceremonies for vadzimu spirits are communal events that are well attended and dominated by complex music on either drums or mbira (see Berliner 1993; Fry 1976; Gelfand 1962; Lan 1985).

19. The prefix "Va-" is a polite form of address for men. VaMasiza is thus akin to Mr. Masiza.

20. Some mhongo spirits *choose* to leave the lineage for personal reasons, however.

21. The prefix "Chi-" indicates the spoken language; thus ChiNdau is the Ndau language, ChiShona the Shona language.

22. The terminology suggested by John Keith Rennie (1973, 1985) and Charles Blakney (1969, n.d.) seem to match exactly yet is different in numerous ways from that used by other scholars or in my own work (see Vijfhuizen 2002; MacGonagle 2007). Rennie acknowledges Blakney for sharing his materials, which perhaps accounts for this similarity. Likewise, I am extremely grateful to Charles Blakney for sharing his unpublished work on spirits in Gazaland.

23. In an article based on his conversations with C. Kamba Simango, Franz Boas writes, "If a mulungu has no more relatives and his memory has been forgotten, or if it goes to a strange line in which it has no relatives or friends, it wanders around groaning and becomes a chilombo (pl. zilombo) or a dzoka (from kudzoka). It makes a rattling noise in the throat, because a person groans when possessed by a dzoka for the first time. A synonym for the latter is zinthiki (pl. manthiki[,] normally in

the meaning of a ceremonial song; compare kunthikinya[,] to strangle, to tie up the throat). The Zulu call the chilombo idlozi (pl. amadlozi), a word that has taken the form dlozi in Chindau" (1920, 2).

24. Interview with Ambuya Mazveshe in Muzite on October 2, 2005. All further quotations from Ambuya Mazveshe are from this source.

25. Interview with Ngarife Matabuka and Pileni Dube in Muzite on October 4, 2005. All further quotations from them are from this source.

26. A man interviewed by MacGonagle in Mozambique claimed that Ngungunyane's mother was a Ndau woman, perhaps bringing the connections between Nguni and Ndau communities closer than it might otherwise appear (2008, 38).

27. The prefix *ma-* is a common marker for the plural. One dzviti becomes several madzviti; one bodyguard becomes several mabodyguard.

28. The following spirits mentioned in the literature and in my interviews did not appear during ceremonies I attended. *Marozvi* spirits come from the Rozvi kingdom of Changamire (MacGonagle 2007, 45). *Zvisena* spirits come from Sena-speaking Mozambique. Joseph Mutwanha, a n'anga in Chipinge, described them as similar to mhongo, but Mudiwa told me that these spirits sit in chairs, drink clear beer like lager, and eat rice, just as zvaayungu do (see also Junod 1934a, 276; Blakney 1969, 100; Shoko 2006, 5). The *mapenzi* are the spirits of fools (Wilder 1907; Junod 1934a), the *matende* are the spirits of baboons, and the *mazinda* are, according to Rennie, "cannibals from Marorwe, that is[,] from the Mkondo Mine area" (1973, 100). His description contradicts one given by Mutwanha, who said, "When I say zinda, they are children of mbongo, meaning that they are friends of the mbongo. . . . You are not from here, you, you are not a Danda, but it [the zinda] will say, I used to live in Mozambique but my home was so and so; then you know that it is a zinda." Mudiwa also describes mazinda spirits from Mozambique (see also Blakney n.d.; MacGonagle 2007). *Madzimba, madanda, manyanga, manhiki, chinoreni,* and *jukwa* are all either associated with mhongo spirits or considered kinds of mhongo. In an interview in Muzite on October 5, 2005, Ambuya Mazveshe said, "They [madzimba] have a relationship with the mermaid and the mbongo" (see also Junod 1934a). Madanda are spirits from the Danda-speaking region of Mozambique (MacGonagle 2007, 87). *Chinoreni* and *jukwa* are synonyms for mhongo given by Mudiwa and Mpande Chikumbo respectively. Finally, *zvisora* and *zvinyasikana* are synonyms for *zvipunha*, whereas hondora are seemingly rare male versions of the zvipunha (Rennie 1973; Blakney n.d.). I never met anyone who used the term.

29. *Muroyi* is the singular term for "witch"; *varoyi* is the plural.

30. John Keith Rennie refers to the spirits of witches or suicide victims as *pfukwa* (1973, 101).

31. Given the remoteness of the school and the unreliability mobile networks at the time, the only telephone available was in the headmaster's office.

32. Interview with Mudiwa at Buffelsdrift on May 12, 2005. All further quotations from Mudiwa are from this source.

33. She used the word *amadhlozi*, reflecting a Nguni influence on pronunciation.

34. Interview with Patience in Mudanda on May 30, 2004.

35. This graph was inspired by the imagery of the ethnomusicologist Richard Wolf (2001, 398).

36. Multiple military bodies worked along the Zimbabwe-Mozambique border in the 1970s. In Zimbabwe, the Zimbabwe African National Liberation Army (ZANLA) was the military wing of the Zimbabwe African National Union (ZANU), and the Zimbabwe People's Republican Army (ZIPRA) was the armed wing of the Zimbabwe African People's Union (ZAPU). In Mozambique, the Mozambique Liberation Front (FRELIMO) became the ruling party after independence, whereas the Mozambican National Resistance (RENAMO) was the opposition force, which was heavily populated by Ndau. All passed through Chipinge.

37. Henry Moyana (1984), John Keith Rennie (1973, 1985), and Elizabeth MacGonagle (2007) provide important exceptions to this tendency.

38. The orthodox history of Chipinge and the Ndau was largely written in the 1970s and 1980s and thus relied on the historicist writing strategies common at that time.

39. Like other autochthonous communities transplanted by the eventually dominant population, Manyakadzivuta are often viewed as primitives who rightly lost their place to the flow of history and their more advanced successors.

40. The Portuguese referred to everyone who was under the control of the Monomutapa and who spoke what is now a version of Shona as the Karanga. Those outside their control were called Tonga (Rennie 1985, 166).

41. Rennie (1973, 62) suggests that Changamire is a version of Changa we Mbire (Changa from Mbire), but there is no consensus. I attended the installation of a new Chief Mutema in 2005 near Ngaone, where new chief installation ceremonies are still held.

42. This region of Mbire should not be confused with the region near Dande in the north, also known as Mbire (Beach 1994, 115).

43. Interview with Vhukani Muzite in Muzite on August 23, 2005. All further quotations from Vhukani Muzite are from this source.

44. Interview with Enos Simango and Julia Chigamba in Harare on February 1, 2004. All further quotations from Enos Simango are from this source.

45. Rennie suggests that this supposed founding by sons of Monomutapa was a legitimizing device connecting these young polities to the power of the Monomutapa Empire (1985, 172). These theories of Sanga's origin also seem to conflate the Mutapa and Changamire states. Beach relates numerous versions of the story specific to different times and places. The only consistency in these stories is that some or all of these secondary states are thought to have been founded by sons of either Monomutapa or Changamire (Beach 1980, 162–63).

46. Many publications identify the Danda population as Ndau. MacGonagle distinguishes Danda as a "political" ethnic marker, whereas Ndau is a more general term (2007, 49).

47. The Moodie family alone owned more than 108,000 acres (Moyana 1984, 112).

48. Moyana argues that "in Gazaland as in other parts of the country the farm labourer was deprived of his rights as a human being and existed only as an object of abuse and exploitation. The exaction of high rents and taxes not only filled the coffers of the settler with a handsome income but destroyed any prospects of escape by the African from dehumanizing labour contracts, which resulted from the artificial creation of poverty in the African areas by the Land Apportionment Act" (1984, 120).

49. Numerous outstanding texts provide greater detail about this period than is possible to discuss here. See, e.g., Shamuyarira 1965; Sithole 1999; Martin and Johnson 1981; Astrow 1983; Bhebe 1989; Turino 2000; Msindo 2007; Raftopoulus and Mlambo 2009; Ndlovu-Gatsheni 2013; Tavuyanago 2013.

50. For different accounts of the power struggle between Mugabe and Sithole, compare that written by Sithole's brother, Masipula Sithole (1999), to that by Martin and Johnson (1981).

51. Sabelo Ndlovu-Gatsheni (2015) refers to the ambitions and projects related to the tenure of Robert Mugabe as Mugabeism, which has informed all aspects of life in Zimbabwe. See also Perman (2017).

52. Kyker cites evidence that inflation reached the ludicrous figure of 650 million googol percent by the end of 2008 (2016, 234; see also Hanke and Kwok 2009).

Chapter 2. Moving Signs: The Experience of Affective Semiosis

1. In 1888 Peirce said, "First is the beginning, that which is fresh, original, spontaneous, free. Second is that which is determined, terminated, ended, correlative, object, necessitated, reacting. Third is the medium, becoming, developing, bringing about" (Peirce 1992, 280).

2. In "On Phenomenology" Peirce outlines three essential faculties that align with his basic categories: observation, discrimination, and generalization (1998, 147).

3. Turino (2014) provides a more complete discussion of Peirce's categories and their specific utility for understanding musical experience.

4. Deacon refers to the tendency to focus too much on a fixed connection between a sign and its objects as the fallacy of "misplaced concreteness" (2012b, 12).

5. For further biographical information about Enos Simango, see Kariamu Welsh Asante's book *Zimbabwe Dance* (2000).

6. The anthropologist Saba Mahmood separates habitus from mere habits, saying, "Habitus—unlike habits—once acquired through assiduous practice, takes root in one's character and is considered unchangeable" (2005, 136). I agree with Turino's critique that it is more productive to think of habits along a continuum rather than think of a binary of habits and habitus (pers. comm.). All habits can change, regardless of how deeply rooted.

7. Although I am indebted to Turino's (2008) model of self and identity, I include subjectivity as an essential Second, which is especially salient during the ongoing present.

8. I use *Ndau* as shorthand to cover the various uses of the word in the Ndau language. More specifically, ChiNdau refers to the language, MuNdau to a single person, and VaNdau to Ndau people collectively.

9. In Zimbabwe, Ndau is officially a dialect of Shona. In Mozambique, it is often listed separately (Katupha 1994; Gadelii 2001).

10. ChiNdau is hardly a unified dialect; it shows disparities across chieftaincies, geographical barriers, and the shifting borders of the Gaza state, the British and Portuguese colonial maps, and the independent Zimbabwean and Mozambican boundaries (Bortland 1984; Junod 1934b, 18).

11. Translating from Ndau to Shona (and English), Sithole is Mwoyo (heart), Muyambo is Dziva/Mvuu (pool/hippopotamus), Mhlanga is Mbizi (zebra), Sigauke is Mhumhi (wild dog), Moyana is Gwai (sheep), Dhliwayo is Ishwa (flying ant), Hlatywayo is Nungu (porcupine), Nyoni is Shiri (bird), and Simango is Shoko (monkey).

12. There are divergent theories of ethnicity in Zimbabwe. The well-known historian Terence Ranger famously placed responsibility for tribal and ethnic distinctions at the feet of colonialism, arguing that "there existed no intermediate concept of ethnicity" (Ranger 1989, 120). The historian Elizabeth MacGonagle, who wrote the most important recent work on Ndau identity, disagrees with Ranger's conclusions, arguing that ethnicity's origins rest in the pre-colonial period (MacGonagle 2007).

13. Because the habits of intersubjectivity are always embodied, I elide the anthropologist Thomas Csordas's distinction between intersubjectivity and intercorporeality into the single term *intersubjectivity* (Csordas 2008).

14. This also recalls Durkheim's "collective effervescence," during which people may feel, think, or act in concert (1915, 226). Thanks to Stefan Fiol for bringing this to my attention.

15. Blakney translates *kumukira* as "to rise in" (1969, 99).

16. Think of Maya Deren's "divine horsemen" (1953).

17. The missionary George Wilder described this aspect of Ndau spirituality as follows: "These are called Rombos. Nobody knows their origin. They simply are at hand to possess the body of every infant. . . . They remain in the person until death, when they leave and become Dzimus, as above. The Rombos and the Dzimus are evidently one and the same. . . . The Dzimu, moreover, being free from bodily limitations, has power over the Rombo in the living person" (1907b, 161–62).

18. Ahmed traces this legacy to Aristotle (2004, 5). Martha Nussbaum's (2001) philosophical approach to emotion is explicitly rooted in the work of Aristotle, to very different ends than those of anthropology.

19. Tomlinson complains, rather colorfully, that "musicking attracts affect theorists like moths to a candle, usually because they think it accommodates their vague ideas of intensities unfettered by sign, meaning, and agency" (2016, 166).

20. To offer just two examples, Tomlinson recognizes "the alliance of feelings and meaning in all signs" (2016, 148) and the clinical psychologist Diana Fosha says, "Subjectively, the experience of affect . . . gives meaning to our lives" (2000, 14).

21. Massumi's autonomous affect recalls an autonomous art that undermines the centrality of cultural determinism, the necessity of ethnographic insight, and even human diversity.

22. Thus emotives are interpretants of feelings that are interpretants of emotion-appraisals that are interpretants of affect. For Peirce, all interpretants function as signs (1998, 497).

23. Despite never-ending attempts to break down the mind-body distinction credited to Descartes, its resolution is elusive. Mind and body are often used to represent culture and nature in analysis as analogous categories. I resist efforts to treat them as separately operative. Both mind and body are involved; each informs the other; collectively they inform and are informed by one's sense of self and the habits that comprise it.

24. I previously labeled this step "perception" (Perman 2010, 434).

25. Moods, "the sustaining of a given emotion over long periods of time" (Damasio 2003, 43), could be characterized as states, but the process of emotion need not be quick. Stasis is an illusion.

26. In explaining the interpretant in 1907, Peirce argued that "there is something which the sign in its significant function essentially determines in its interpreter. I term it the 'interpretant' of the sign. In all cases, it includes feelings; for there must, at least, be a sense of comprehending the meaning of the sign" (1998, 409).

27. Damasio provides a thorough account of problems in James's approach and ways to overcome them without undermining James's overall contribution (Damasio 2004, 2010).

28. Peirce himself was concerned that feelings (what I call affect) are not actually semiotic. "It may possibly be," he wrote, "for example, that I am taking too narrow a conception of the sign in general in saying that its initial effect must be of the nature of feeling, since it may be that there are agencies that ought to be classed along with signs and yet that at first begin to act quite unconsciously" (1998, 409). If body is in mind, my tear ducts know what they are doing.

29. The physiology involved is complex and understood only in part, despite dramatic recent advances. Huron, (2011) for instance, provides compelling evidence for the role of prolactin in the pleasure experienced with sad music.

30. As Hesmondhalgh (2013, 29) points out, Nussbaum's (2001) sense of "appraisal" is contemplative, whereas Damasio's is narrowly physiological. I integrate them because contemplation is also within the body. Thus, unlike Nussbaum and Hesmondhalgh, I agree with Damasio (2010) that the body is always involved.

31. The Shona equivalent *kunzwa* is also common in Ndau-speaking Zimbabwe.

32. For Austin, constatives are speech acts that describe something and performatives are speech acts that *do* something, that can change the world. Saying "They are

married" simply describes a fact. Saying "I now pronounce you man and wife" changes a fact (changes the world). Adding emotives adds the possibility that saying "I love you" changes the self (see Austin 1962; Reddy 2001).

33. The legacy of emotion studies in ethnomusicology is also rooted in the Pragmatist tradition. Working at the University of Chicago under Dewey, Leonard Meyer (1956) developed a groundbreaking theory that explored the way habits of musical expectation are thwarted or realized in order to elicit emotional response. His student Charles Keil (1966, 1987, 1995) brought similar sensibilities to the "discrepancies" of live performance, challenging Meyer's approach while simultaneously applying a similar logic to participatory practices.

Chapter 3. Late Afternoon: *Madzviti* and the Foundation of Interpretation

1. Masiza played the mbira commonly called *mbira dzaVaNdau* (Perman 2015).

2. Even my first meeting with Masiza was shaped by ZANU-PF interest. I had arranged to meet with a local muchongoyo group led by Mai Matiti for a demonstration. Because of my interest in the mbira, she brought VaMasiza along as well. Members of the ZANU-PF youth brigade happened to pass by and questioned my recording activities. Luckily, I had my research permit with me and they let us continue. They even danced along as they drank, making their presence felt at all times. Mai Matiti was visibly shaken by their threatening manner.

3. Peirce (1988, 120) refers to purpose as a form of final cause.

4. In *A Million Years of Music* Tomlinson (2015) asserts that the capacity for making music does not rely on linguistic precursors; music is not epiphenomenal.

5. Etherington suggests that Shaka forced Zwide north in 1819 (2013, 113–14).

6. From another point of view, perhaps my presence was initiated when the kingdom of Mbire collapsed and Rozvi communities moved into the Chipinge region, eventually to be identified as Ndau (Maposa, Hlongwana, and Gamira 2010, 192), or when Cecil Rhodes's Pioneer Column arrived to initiate the theft of land whose eventual resettlement provided the stage for the ceremony described herein, or it could be my parents' participation in the Peace Corps in Kenya in the 1970s, which likely inspired my interest in African music and politics.

7. These events are often described from a Zulu-centric point of view and defined as the Mfecane, a word invented by E. A. Walker in 1928. The historian Julian Cobbing adamantly rejects the term and concept of mfecane (1988, 519), arguing that "Mfecane theory suggests that Shaka's military innovations and his brutal quest for expansion decimated the region to 'near genocidal effect'" (487), paving the way for colonial expansion and justifying apartheid policies. The historian Sabelo Ndlovu-Gatsheni supports Cobbing's conclusions, arguing that white scholars helped justify colonial settlement by blaming the Zulu for regional devastation (Ndlovu-Gatsheni 2016, 3). This narrative gives Shaka, the young Zulu king, most of the credit or blame for the events that followed.

8. Nxaba Msane arrived in Chisanga in 1828, ending the independence of the Chisanga chieftaincy. He was driven out by Soshangane (Rennie 1978; Liesegang 1967, 1970, 1983).

9. Soshangane named his roving capital Mandhlakazi (MacGonagle 2008, 36).

10. Wilson Mhlanga, a member of the Mapungwana family born in the Chipinge highlands before Mzila arrived, claims that Mawewe was the victor in this war and forced Mzila into the Chipinge highlands (Mhlanga 1948, 71).

11. MacGonagle (2008, 51) cites locals who describe Ngungunyane's "exodus" back to Mozambique as a "death march" in which thousands migrated and many were killed.

12. After a political void was left by the loss of Gaza rule, the Ndau-speaking area, which straddled present-day Zimbabwe and Mozambique, was divided between the British South Africa Company and the Companhia de Moçambique (Alexander 2006, 19). British and Afrikaner farmers soon filled the void.

13. This nickname comes from a local greeting given when someone visits another's home. The host responds to the guest with "*Ndauwe* [it is you]." Junod gives a darker reading of this origin, tying it to a prostrate greeting to the Gaza king to remind people that "they were slaves" (1934b, 17).

14. MacGonagle argues that assimilation was more common for Ndau men than for women (2008, 45).

15. The name *Gaza* lives on as the largest high-density township in Chipinge and as the name of the province in Mozambique where most Mozambican Ndau now live.

16. When people say Swazi, it is possible that they mean Ndwandwe, whose original homeland was quite close to contemporary Eswatini (Aldridge 2015).

17. Interview with Hlatywayo Matakura in Muzite on September 9, 2005. All further quotations from Hlatywayo Matakura are from this source.

18. Interview with Chief Rodwell Muzite in Muzite on September 20, 2005. All further quotations from Chief Muzite are from this source.

19. Lobola, called "bride-price" or "bride wealth" in English, *roora* in ChiShona, and *pfuma* (which also means "wealth") in ChiNdau, is a series of fees paid by a prospective husband to the father of his bride-to-be as compensation for the loss of future labor, as a gesture of sincerity, and for many other complex reasons (Vijfhuizen 2002, 27).

20. Although Ngungunyane led for only a few years, many Ndau associate him with the worst of Gaza rule (MacGonagle 2007, 2008).

21. Tonya Taylor (2010) has published an excellent article about a n'anga who relies on both a mudzimu and a dzviti in his healing practice.

22. Although I never heard the term used by anyone else, the n'anga Mutwanha calls the dzviti shield a *dava*. There is an entire vocabulary for the weaponry of the madzviti.

23. This last one is only hypothetical since I'm not sure I've ever heard of the spirits' making mistakes.

24. Becker (2004) emphasizes that trance possession is a learned skill, one that people can get better at with practice.

25. Kyker (2016) provides an excellent explanation of husahwira in her book about Oliver Mtukudzi.

26. This stomp is the signature move in muchongoyo (this term being derived from an old word meaning "to stamp one's feet," *kuchongoya*), the most important secular form of Ndau dance (Perman 2010, 2017). These similarities are unsurprising given that the Gaza Nguni who eventually became madzviti spirits were the ones who developed muchongoyo as a training exercise.

27. A similar frame drum is used in Tsonga (Shangaan) communities in Mozambique and South Africa. Kirby refers to these in *The Musical Instruments of the Native Races of South Africa* as *mantshomane* (1934, 41), whereas Johnston calls them *ncomane* (1972, 10). This term is similar to *chingomana*, which is often used in Chipinge for the smaller muchongoyo drum otherwise known as *katenha*, *chinyamudumbi*, or *chimudumbana*. Enos Simango calls all muchongoyo along Chipinge's northern border with Mozambique chingomana. Musical and cosmological practices among Ndau and Tsonga communities are closely related and intimately tied to their shared history with the Gaza Nguni.

28. As is done elsewhere in Chimanimani, Ambuya Jaisi used a clay drum for the madzviti rather than a wooden frame drum. Her hakata included seashells, nut shells, coins, beads, and other small items.

29. Although these comparisons are obviously cursory, the Zulu drumming transcribed by Meintjes (2004, 186) is similarly duple, transcribed in 4/4 with little syncopation. The texture is dominated by eighth notes and their subdivision into sixteenth notes. The mandhlozi songs that Thomas F. Johnston describes and transcribes from the Tsonga community in Mozambique are especially similar (Johnston 1972). As Johnston describes it, the term *mandhlozi* is for "undesirable Zulu spirit" (10), which gives these spirits quite a different presence and value than in the Ndau communities in which I worked.

30. For instance, Matabuka translates the lyrics that open this chapter into Ndau and then into English.

31. Mthethwa is a Zulu totem. It is also the name of the army originally defeated by the Ndwandwe state whose members formed much of the fleeing Gaza Nguni army after Shaka's military successes.

32. I should note that this respect is nothing like the reverence that one finds at many church services. During one ceremony, as one dzviti spirit was dancing his farewell song in preparation for departing his host's body, Mapfumo started dancing extremely aggressively, ending with a humorous pose that elicited laughter from everyone watching. He then strutted around pretending to be possessed. No one took offense. Perhaps they were as amazed as I was that this man in his late seventies could dance so expertly and powerfully.

33. As mentioned above, he thinks of Zulu, Swazi, and Ndebele as basically the same when it comes to madzviti spirits.

34. Peirce describes different kinds of interpretant. Briefly, three interpretants, nested from first to third, include (1) emotional interpretants, which are feelings for Peirce,

affect for me; (2) energetic interpretants, which involve "effort," as I refer to here with "action-oriented" effects; and (3) logical interpretants, which are thoughts (Peirce 1998, 409). All energetic interpretants contain emotional components, and all thoughts contain energetic interpretants.

Chapter 4. Evening: *Zvipunha*, Signs, and Transformative Experience

1. Zivanai is a pseudonym.

2. Of course, they are not important to *all* local events such as this. Christian communities do *not* rely on zvipunha spirits.

3. Thanks to Jennifer Kyker for suggesting the phrases "outsider mothers" or "other mothers."

4. According to the literature, these include farming spirits (Taylor 2010, 306), rain spirits (Vijfhuizen 2002, 198), peripheral women's spirits (Rennie 1985, 180), the spirits of infants (Shoko 2006, 5), spirits of the VaKaranga (Junod 1934, 280), nuisance spirits (Mandondo 1997, 358), and the spirits of unwed girls (Blakney 1969, 101). They also include the female spirits of girls who died without having married (Mpande Chikumbo), *vasikana*, or girls (Ambuya Mazveshe), *madzitete*, or elder aunts (Mulambo); *manheni* or *vasikana vanosenza*, or nannies or housemaids (Enos Simango), and *vana vadiki*, or little children (Mutwanhi) according to my field notes.

5. Early researchers such as Bullock dismissed them as "a mere innovation of no historical standing" reflecting a "regrettable tendency shown by the younger generation of the Mashona" (1928, 147).

6. Mpande Chikumbo also describes an equivalent male spirit called *zvingwaringwari* who behaves in much the same way. Rennie (1973) and Blakney (1969) mention *hondora*, described as a male chipunha.

7. *Mapendji* is an alternative spelling for *mapenzi* (*benzi* means "fool"), another category of spirits that can include baboons. Nobody associated mapenzi with zvipunha in my research. Midozo is another spelling of midonzvo (walking sticks).

8. Not everyone labels their speech as Chingotoro. They are sometimes so child-like that they barely speak.

9. This was translated by Mpande Chikumbo during the interview.

10. Ngarife Matabuka said very much the same thing. His dzviti was not an ancestor but was still related.

11. This is both iconic of children's eating habits and indexical of bad manners. Wild derere is called *gusha*.

12. Blakney notes, "It is said that they [zvipunha] died of hunger when they were still young. During the starvation times, they would go about in small hills looking for crabs under rocks to live on" (n.d., 4).

13. Women also played the drums and the makosho and led the singing during madzviti ceremonies.

14. This is also true of the powerful *nzuzu* mermaid spirits.

15. This idea was brought home to me in conversation with Julia Chigamba during my interview with Enos Simango in 2004. Simango said, "Right. They are the ones who made this dance, so they played and distracted children, looking for things to distract children with so that the children wouldn't cry for their mothers."

16. Juju has become a common borrowed synonym for witchcraft (uroyi).

17. Much of the musical analysis to follow comes from my article "The Ethics of Ndau Performance: Questioning Ethnomusicology's Aesthetics" (Perman 2011b).

18. In muchongoyo, drummers carry the chigubhu on a strap over the shoulder and play both drumheads with sticks (Perman 2010).

19. The chimudumbana is a small drum used primarily for other purposes.

20. Daisy Hill lies approximately twenty kilometers south of Chipinge, close to Holland Farm.

21. Kohn (2013) expands Peirce's original to include nonhumans as well.

22. The role of touch is taken even further when musicians literally beat madzviti rhythms onto the heads of mediums.

23. The word is also spelled "fodya," which is a more common Shona spelling. Although smell as a sensory experience is not part of the conversation concerning forya, the fact that ingesting it through the nose is the one essential sensory experience for spirit possession suggests the centrality of this olfactory experience.

24. *Mubereko* stems from the verb *kubereka*, or "to carry on the back like a child." Enos Simango called this *chiapron*, from the English word *apron*.

25. Turino outlines four functions of icons: form recognition, token-type relations, the "inkblot" function encouraging imaginative interpretation, and the rendering of imagination in perceivable form (2014, 192–194).

26. This may be a space for aesthetics as the giving of coherence and form to disparate signs. Shaping multiple potential signs into a single knowable and interpretable sign is central to many expressive and artistic practices. This precedes judgment, which, I have argued, must not be detached from ethical considerations (Perman 2011). Aesthetics as the judgment of form and semiotic coherence is rooted in Peirce's thinking (Peirce 1992; Short 2007; Kockelman 2016, 4)

27. Peirce eventually modified this as a distinction between designators and reagents. Designators "merely stand for things or individual quasi-things with which the interpreting mind is already acquainted," he writes, whereas reagents "may be used to ascertain facts" (Peirce 1931–58, 8:368n23). Martin Lefebvre further delineates the difference as one between "indirect indexical relations" and "direct indexical relations" (2007, 390n35), which is similar to my own distinction between deixis and metonym. Replica indices add purpose to indexicality.

28. This is much like Peirce's distinction between three nested kinds of iconicity: image, diagram, and metaphor (1992, 273).

29. Peirce's genuine indices are solely deictic.

30. Turino (2014) advocates using P-symbol as an explicitly Peircean version, in order to avoid confusion between the colloquial symbol and Peirce's symbol.

31. Cumming credits David Lidov (1999).

32. My interpretation of *haecceity* follows a semiotic chain based on Short's use of Peirce's reinterpretation of Dons Scotus's original term *haecceity*.

33. There seems to be a possibility of fruitful theoretical overlap between this kind of haecceity and Heideggerian being-in-the-world (Berger 2015).

34. VaMasiza's efforts to keep me informed could have undermined his contribution to the success of the ceremony, pulling him out of the here and now and into the reflective "aboutness" of symbolic thought.

35. One could equate "ultimate purpose" with Peirce's final interpretant. Peirce distinguishes the dynamical interpretant, or "the actual effect that is [the sign] has on me," from the final interpretant as "the purpose" (1992, 498). The final interpretant is "that which would finally be decided to be the true interpretation if consideration of the matter were carried so far that an ultimate opinion were reached" (496). In this way, Peircean semiotics becomes teleological. The purpose is the telos.

36. As Turino also suggests, repetition in formalized ritual like this also connects an individual's life experiences and provides security (pers. comm.).

37. I would identify this particular sign as a rhematic indexical legisign that ties the drumming pattern to the possibility of spirits, not a dicent. Rhemes represent possibility, whereas dicents represent actuality.

38. It does this as a rhematic indexical legisign.

39. In an earlier article (Perman 2011a) I criticized approaches to mimesis for eliding iconicity with a neglected indexicality, but Taussig's (1993) approach to mimesis is important precisely because it accounts for this transformation of iconicity into indexicality, although it does so with theoretical language that has nothing to do with Peirce. My article's critique was incorrect.

40. Although critical of "symbolocentric" accounts of meaning, I am aware that a similar charge of what Gary Tomlinson (2015, 206) calls "unjustified indexicocentrism" could be made for an overemphasis on the indexical. Despite this, I can't help but grant most of the value of "optimal experiences" to indexicality.

41. Turino (2014) emphasizes the "reality function" of indices.

42. I rely on four beats per cycle and two subdivisions per beat.

43. This isn't fixed or true for everyone. Just as outsiders would likely only think of the most general of types, insiders would focus on the narrowest of types.

44. Thanks to Tom Turino for pointing out this important component.

45. The translation is by Mpande Chikumbo.

Chapter 5. Overnight: *Mhongo* and the Effects of Performance

1. Madzitya is a pseudonym.

2. Qualisign-sinsign-legisign is the first trichotomy, icon-index-symbol is the second trichotomy, and rheme-dicent-argument is the third.

3. Synthesizing the affects of recent affect theory with Peirce's explanations of signs and interpretants provides a way of connecting the disparate contributions to emotion studies from multiple disciplines. Many would disagree, however. It is hard to reconcile narrowly physiological measurements of so-called universals (Damasio 2003) with socially constructed feelings (Abu-Lughod and Lutz 1990) and pre-personal intensities (Massumi 1987).

4. *Mateza* is the plural form, *deza* the singular. They are also called *matedze* if plural, *dedze* if singular (Muchuri 2015).

5. The beat is subdivided into three pulses.

6. Mhongo from Danda are also called *manyanga* (Blakney 1969, 100). Ambuya Mazveshe mentions related spirits called *madzimba* that are separate from the Va-Danda spirits. Chikumbo and Mutwanha also describe a category of related spirits called *mazenda* that mediate between the mhongo and the midzimu.

7. Rennie suggests that this supposed foundation by sons of Monomutapa was a legitimizing device connecting these young polities to the power of the Monomutapa Empire (Rennie 1985, 172).

8. Rennie uses *mhongo* as a general term, much as I use *madhlozi*. He describes spirits who originate on the Mozambique coast as *madanda* or *manhiki* (1973, 100). I use *mhongo* because that was overwhelmingly the preferred term during my research.

9. Nzuzu can also live in the mountains (Vijfhuizen 2002, 198).

10. He was referring to a man who, through illness, is preparing to become a medium.

11. A healer is often called a *nyamusoro*, which means "at the head" because the spirit possesses the head and shoulders of the healer (Rennie 1973, 95).

12. This episode appeared on the front page of the *Manica Post*, a weekly regional newspaper, later that month.

13. Madzviti, zvipunha, and zvaayungu spirits emerge for two or three hours at a time.

14. The song "Makwitika" (the name of the mateza) shown in figure 5.7 was performed for me in Muzite, Mozambique, outside the ceremonial context, which perhaps liberated the playfulness of the performers to demonstrate more virtuosity. This song introduces this set of drums, which is named Makwitika, honors the spirits being summoned by acknowledging their home (in the mountains), and sets the stage for the ceremony to follow. The lyrics are Makwitika waunza makwitika ndiani?(Makwitika, who is it that brought Makwitika?) / Iyeye-ye, Makwitika ndiye wabarwe mhute mugomo (Hey, it is Makwitika that was born in the mist of the mountains.) / Gongo kuruma shondo (The vagina bites the penis.).

15. Following Small (1998), musicking includes dancers and listeners.

16. There are exceptions to this rule, but Ambuya Mazveshe was a particularly conservative devotee of her spirits.

17. The word for the jerry can is *chigubhu*, just like the barrel drum used in muchongoyo and for the zvipunha and zvaayungu spirits.

Chapter 6. Early Morning: *Zvaayungu* and the Shaping of Ndau Modernity

1. Each category of spirit exhibits its own tendencies, and every spirit has a unique personality, but some generalizations can apply. While the madzviti are aggressive, the mhongo comparatively quiet, and the zvipunha childlike, each of these accompanies a reserved respect for the living participants exhibited through greetings and offerings.

2. Interview with Chonapi Gwenzi at Buffelsdrift on May 12, 2005. A multi-instrumentalist, Gwenzi plays mbira dzaVaNdau, *chimazambi*, and guitar.

3. While presumably unrelated, I am reminded of the opening line of a folk tale that C. Kamba Simango told Franz Boas while studying at Columbia University. In the "Lion and the Hare" he opens with "Nge imge nshiku mphontholo yakavona shulo ikati, 'Ehe, ndiwe, iwewe wakavulaya vana vangu'" (Boas and Simango 1922, 170) (One day Lion saw Hare, and said, "Yes, you are the one who killed my children") (1922, 175).

4. I rarely heard *zvemaguru* in the Holland Farm area south of Chipinge, where Masiza lives. The term means "things of the big, important people." Ambuya Mazveshe and her family said *mabwacha* was a translation of *zvivarungu*.

5. I can only rely on my own experience, but nobody ever mentioned an instance in which the zvaayungu were given a ceremony of their own, unlike any of the other spirits mentioned thus far.

6. Jennifer Kyker suggested that these spirits could be identified as "Frontline spirits" of the soldiers from the Frontline States who died in one of several related anticolonial wars in the region, including those in Angola, Botswana, Mozambique, Tanzania, Zambia, and Zimbabwe (email to the author, August 27, 2018).

7. It's possible, of course, that people here simply didn't want to tell me.

8. The only ceremonial drumming in which I ever saw someone reprimanded for being too elaborate was mhongo drumming.

9. Interview with Davison Masiza at Tongogara Village, Holland Farm, on May 13, 2005.

10. I encountered Kauffman's claim in an article by Gary Tomlinson, who quotes it from an article by William Connelly (Tomlinson 2016, 158; Connelly 2011, 793).

11. Biosemioticians have controversially freed semiosis from this kind of rigid understanding of agency (Hoffmeyer 2009; Kockelman 2011), granting semiosis and agency to bacteria. Short and Tomlinson are justifiably suspicious of such efforts (Short 2007; Tomlinson 2016). In his discussion of purpose, Short (2007, 177) argues that extensions of agency like this undermine its value and diminish its explanatory utility. My focus on humanity should not be seen as a critique of work that attributes semiosis

and agency to nonhumans (Kohn 2013). It could, however, be seen as resistant to work that attributes semiosis and agency to the nonsentient.

12. Interview with Samson Mapfumo Muzite on September 29, 2005.

13. The complex dynamics between tradition and modernity obviously unfold in diverse ways around the world (Ferguson 2006; Comaroff and Comaroff 2014; Perman 2017).

Bibliography

Abu-Lughod, Lila, and Catherine A. Lutz. 1990. "Introduction: Emotion, Discourse, and the Politics of Everyday Life." In *Language and the Politics of Emotion*, edited by Catherine A. Lutz, and Lila Abu-Lughod, 1–23. Cambridge: Cambridge University Press.

Agawu, Kofi. 2016a. *The African Imagination in Music*. Oxford: Oxford University Press.

———. 2016b. "Tonality as a Colonizing Force in Africa." In *Audible Empire: Music, Global Politics, Critique*, edited by Ronald Radano and Tejumola Olaniyan, 334–56. Durham, NC: Duke University Press.

Ahmed, Sara. 2004. *The Cultural Politics of Emotion*. London: Routledge.

Alexander, Jocelyn. 2006. *The Unsettled Land: State-Making and the Politics of Land in Zimbabwe, 1893–2003*. Oxford: James Currey.

Alonso, Ana Maria. 1988. "The Effects of Truth: Re-Presentations of the Past and the Imagining of Community." *Journal of Historical Sociology* 1 (1): 33–57.

American Board Mission. 1915. *Chindau-English and English-Chindau Vocabulary*. Binghampton, NY: Kennedy Morris.

Andrade, Mario Pinto de. 1989. "Proto-Naciolismo Em Moçambique: Um Estudo De Caso; Kamba Simango (c. 1890–1967)." *Arquivo: Boletim do Arquivo Historico de Mocambique* 6: 127–48.

Astrow, Andre. 1983. *Zimbabwe: A Revolution That Lost Its Way?* London: Zed Press.

Austin, J. L. 1962. *How to Do Things with Words*. Cambridge, MA: Harvard University Press.

Barthes, Roland. 1964. *Elements of Semiology*. New York: Hill and Wang.

Beach, D. N. 1980. *The Shona and Zimbabwe, 900–1850: An Outline of Shona History*. London: Heinemann.

———. 1984. *Zimbabwe Before 1900*. Gweru, Zimbabwe: Mambo Press.

———. 1994. *A Zimbabwean Past: Shona Dynastic Histories and Oral Traditions*. Gweru, Zimbabwe: Mambo Press.

Becker, Judith. 2004. *Deep Listeners: Music, Emotion, and Trancing*. Bloomington: Indiana University Press.

Berger, Harris M. 2009. *Stance: Ideas About Emotion, Style, and Meaning for the Study of Expressive Culture*. Middletown, CT: Wesleyan University Press.

———. 2015. "Phenomenological Approaches in the History of Ethnomusicology." Oxford Handbooks Online. Retrieved September 26, 2019, from https://www.oxfordhandbooks.com/view/10.1093/oxfordhb/9780199935321.001.0001/oxfordhb-9780199935321-e-30.

Berliner, Paul. 1993. *The Soul of Mbira: Music and Traditions of the Shona People of Zimbabwe*. Chicago: University of Chicago Press.

Bhebe, Ngwabi. 1989. "The Nationalist Struggle, 1957–1962." In *Turmoil and Tenacity: Zimbabwe, 1890–1990*, edited by Canaan S. Banana, 50–109. Harare, Zimbabwe: College Press.

Bigheno, Michelle. 2008. "Why I'm Not an Ethnomusicologist: A View from Anthropology." In *The New (Ethno)musicologies*, edited by Henry Stobart. Lanham, MD: Scarecrow.

Blacking, John. 1995. *Music, Culture, and Experience*. Chicago: University of Chicago Press.

Blakney, Charles P. 1969. "Chipunha, a Rhodesian Cult." *Practical Anthropology* 16: 98–108.

———. n.d. "Spirits Worshhipped in Gazaland." Manuscript.

Boas, Franz. 1920. "Der Seelenglaube Der Vandau." *Zeitschrift für Ethnologie* 52 (1): 1–5.

———. 1922a. "Der Verwandtschaftssystem Der Vandau." *Zeitschrift für Ethnologie* 54 (1): 41–51.

———. 1922b. "The Avunculate Among the Vandau." *American Anthropologist* 24 (1): 95–97.

———. 1923. "Ethnographische Bemerkungen Über Die Vandau." *Zeitschrift für Ethnologie* 55 (1): 6–31.

Boas, Franz, and C. Kamba Simango. 1922. "Tales and Proverbs of the Vandau of Portuguese South Africa." *Journal of American Folklore* 35 (136): 151–204.

Bortland, C. H. 1984. "Conflicting Methodologies of Shona Dialect Classification." *South African Journal of African Languages* 4 (1): 1–12.

Bourdieu, Pierre. 1977. *Outline of a Theory of Practice*. Cambridge: Cambridge University Press.

———. 1990. *The Logic of Practice*. Stanford: Stanford University Press.

Bourdillon, Michael. 1987. *The Shona Peoples*. Gweru: Mambo Press.

Bullock, Charles. 1928. *Mashona (the Indigenous Natives of Southern Rhodesia)*. Westport, CT: Negro Universities Press.

Butler, Judith. 2010. *Frames of War: When Is Life Grievable?* London: Verso.

Buzuzi, Stephen, and Michael Bourdillon. 2001. "Traders and Trees in Nyanyadzi." In *Women, Men and Work: Rural Livelihoods in South-Eastern Zimbabwe*, edited by Paul Hebinck and Michael Bourdillon, 81–102. Harare, Zimbabwe: Weaver Press.

Chakrabarty, Dipesh. 2000. *Provincializing Europe: Postcolonial Thought and Historical Difference*. Princeton, NJ: Princeton University Press.

Chara, Tendai. 2015. "Finding the Hub of Zim Witchcraft." *Sunday Mail* (Harare), April 12. Accessed August 2, 2017. http://www.sundaymail.co.zw/finding-the-hub-of-zim-witchcraft/.

Charumbira, Ruramisai. 2015. *Imagining a Nation: History and Memory in Making Zimbabwe*. Charlottesville: University of Virginia Press.

Chikowero, Moses. 2015. *African Music, Power, and Being in Colonial Zimbabwe*. Bloomington: Indiana University Press.

Clayton, Martin, Byron Dueck, and Laura Leante, eds. 2013. *Experience and Meaning in Music Performance*. Oxford: Oxford University Press.

Cobbing, Julian. 1988. "The Mfecane as Alibi: Thoughts on Dithakong and Mbolompo." *Journal of African History* 29 (3): 487–519.

Comaroff, Jean, and John L. Comaroff. 2014. *Theory from the South: How Euro-America Is Evolving Toward Africa*. Stellenbosch, South Africa: Sun Press.

Comaroff, John L., and Jean Comaroff. 1992. *Ethnography and the Historical Imagination*. Boulder, CO: Westview Press.

Connelly, William E. 2011. "The Complexity of Intention." *Critical Inquiry* 37 (4): 791–98.

Crapanzano, Vincent. 2004. *Imaginative Horizons: An Essay in Literary-Philosophical Anthropology*. Chicago: University of Chicago Press.

———. 2014. "Must We Be Bad Epistemologists? Illusions of Transparency, the Opaque Other, and Interpretive Foibles." In *The Ground Between: Anthropologists Engage Philosophy*, edited by Veena Das, Michael Jackson, Arthur Kleinman, and Bhrigupati Singh, 254–78. Durham, NC: Duke University Press.

Csikszentmihalyi, Mihaly. 1990. *Flow: The Psychology of Optimal Experience*. New York: Harper and Row.

Csordas, Thomas J. 2008. "Intersubjectivity and Intercorporeality." *Subjectivity* 22(1): 110–21.

Cumming, Naomi. 2000. *The Sonic Self: Musical Subjectivity and Signification*. Bloomington: Indiana University Press.

Curtis, Natalie. 1920. *Songs and Tales from the Dark Continent*. New York: G. Schirmer.

Damasio, Antonio R. 2003. *Looking for Spinoza: Joy, Sorrow, and the Feeling Brain*. New York: Harcourt.

———. 2004. "William James and the Modern Neurobiology of Emotion." In *Emotion, Evolution, and Rationality*, edited by Dylan Evans, 3–14. Oxford: Oxford University Press.

———. 2010. *Self Comes to Mind: Constructing the Conscious Brain*. New York: Vintage.

Deacon, Terrence W. 2012a. "Beyond the Symbolic Species." In *The Symbolic Species*

Evolved, edited by Theresa Schilhab, Frederik Stjernfelt, and Terrence Deacon, 9–38. Dordrecht, The Netherlands: Springer.

———. 2012b. *Incomplete Nature: How Mind Emerged from Matter*. New York:Norton.

Deleuze, Gilles. 1978. "Gilles Deleuze, Lecture Transcripts on Spinoza's Concept of Affect." http://www.webdeleuze.com/php/sommaire.html.

Deleuze, Gilles, and Felix Guattari. 1987. *A Thousand Plateaus: Capitalism and Schizophrenia*. London: Continuum.

Deren, Maya. 1953. *Divine Horsemen: The Living Gods of Haiti*. Kingston, NY: McPherson.

Descola, Phillipe. 2013. *Beyond Nature and Culture*. Chicago: University of Chicago Press.

Dewey, John. 1894. "The Theory of Emotion: (I.) Emotional Attitudes." *Psychological Review* 1: 553–69.

———. 1895. "The Theory of Emotion: (II.) The Significance of Emotions." *Psychological Review* 2:13–32.

Doke, Clement M. 1931. *A Comparative Study in Shona Phonetics*. Johannesburg: University of the Witwatersrand Press.

Durkheim, Emile. 1915. *The Elementary Forms of the Religious Life*. New York: Free Press.

Earthy, E. Dora. 1925. "On Some Ritual Objects of the Vandau in South Chopiland Gaza, Portuguese East Africa." *Annals of the Transvaal Museum* 11 (2): 125–28.

———. 1931a. "Note on the 'Totemism' of the Vandau." *Bantu Studies* 5 (1): 77–79.

———. 1931b. "The Vandau of Sofala." *Africa* 4 (2): 222–30.

Eldredge, Elizabeth A. 1992. "Sources of Conflict in Southern Africa, c. 1800–30: The Mfecane' Reconsidered." *Journal of African History* 33:1–35.

———. 2015. *Kingdoms and Chiefdoms of Southeastern Africa*. Rochester, NY: University of Rochester Press.

Emoff, Ron. 2002. *Recollecting the Past: Musical Practice and Spirit Possession on the East Coast of Madagascar*. Middletown, CT: Wesleyan University Press.

Engelke, Matthew. 2007. *A Problem of Presence: Beyond Scripture in an African Church*. Berkeley: University of California Press.

Etherington, Norman. 2004a. "A Tempest in a Teapot? Nineteenth-Century Contests for Land in South Africa's Caledon Valley and the Invention of the *Mfecane*." *Journal of African History* 45:203–19.

———. 2004b. "Were There Large States in the Coastal Regions of Southeast Africa Before the Rise of the Zulu Kingdom?" *History in Africa* 31:157–83.

———. 2013. *The Great Treks: The Transformation of Southern Africa, 1815–1854*. London: Routledge.

Eyre, Banning. 2015. *Lion Songs: Thomas Mapfumo and the Music That Made Zimbabwe*. Durham, NC: Duke University Press.

Feld, Steven. 1974. "Linguistic Models in Ethnomusicology." *Ethnomusicology* 18 (2): 197–217.

———. 1984. "Communication, Music, and Speech About Music." *Yearbook for Traditional Music* 16: 1–18.

———. 1990. "Wept Thoughts: The Voicing of Kaluli Memories." *Oral Tradition* 5 (2–3): 241–66.

Ferguson, James. 2006. *Global Shadows: Africa in the Neoliberal World Order*. Durham, NC: Duke University Press.

———. 2012. "Theory from the Comaroffs, or How to Know the World Up, Down, Backwards and Forwards." *FieldSights: Theorizing the Contemporary, Cultural Anthropology*. https://culanth.org/fieldsights/theory-from-the-comaroffs-or-how-to-know-the-world-up-down-backwards-and-forwards.

Fontein, Joost. 2015a. "Rain, Uncertainty, and Power in Southern Zimbabwe." *Critical African Studies* 8 (1): 47–74.

———. 2015b. *Remaking Mutirikwi: Landscape, Water and Belonging in Southern Zimbabwe*. Woodbridge, UK: James Currey.

Fosha, Diana. 2000. *The Transforming Power of Affect: A Model for Accelerated Change*. New York: Basic Books.

Friedson, Steven. 1996. *Dancing Prophets: Musical Experience in Tumbuka Healing*. Chicago: University of Chicago Press.

———. 2009. *Remains of Ritual: Northern Gods in a Southern Land*. Chicago: University of Chicago Press.

Fry, Peter. 1976. *Spirits of Protest: Spirit-Mediums and the Articulation of Consensus Among the Zezuru of Southern Rhodesia (Zimbabwe)*. Cambridge: Cambridge University Press.

Gadelii, Karl Erland. 2001. "Languages in Mozambique." *Africa and Asia* 1:6–12.

Gelfand, Michael. 1962. *Shona Religion: With Special Reference to the Makorekore*. Cape Town: Juta.

Gill, Denise. 2017. *Melancholic Modalities: Affect, Islam, and Turkish Classical Musicians*. Oxford: Oxford University Press.

Glissant, Edouard. 1997. *Poetics of Relation*. Ann Arbor: University of Michigan Press.

Hall, Margaret. 1990. "The Mozambican National Resistance Movement (Renamo): A Study in the Destruction of an African Country." *Africa* 60 (1): 39–68.

Hamilton, Carolyn, ed. 1995. *The Mfecane Aftermath: Reconstructive Debates in Southern African History*. Johannesburg: University of the Witwatersrand Press.

Hanke, S. H., and A. K. F. Kwok. 2009. "On the Measurement of Zimbabwe's Inflation." *Cato Journal* 29 (2): 354–64.

Hannan, M. 1987. *Standard Shona Dictionary*. Harare:, Zimbabwe: College Press.

Harries, Patrick. 1983. "Slavery Amongst the Gaza Nguni: Its Changing Shape and Function and Its Relationship to Other Forms of Exploitation." In *Before and After Shaka*, edited by J. B. Peires, 210–29. Grahamstown, South Africa: Institute of Social and Economic Research, Rhodes University.

Hemmings, Clare. 2005. "Invoking Affect: Cultural Theory and the Ontological Turn." *Cultural Studies* 19 (5): 548–67.

Herskovits, Melville. 1923. "Some Property Concepts and Marriage Customs of the Vandau." *American Anthropologist* 25 (3): 376–86.

Hesmondhalgh, David. 2013. *Why Music Matters*. West Sussex, UK : Wiley-Blackwell.

Higgins, Kathleen Marie. 2012. *The Music Between Us: Is Music a Universal Language?* Chicago: University of Chicago Press.

Hoffmeyer, Jesper. 2009. *Biosemiotics: An Examination into the Signs of Life and the Life of Signs.* Scranton, PA: University of Scranton Press.

Hofman, Ana. 2015. "The Affective Turn in Ethnomusicology." *Muzikologija* 18:35–55.

Holbraad, Martin. 2009. "Ontography and Alterity: Defining Anthropological Truth." *Social Analysis* 53 (2): 80–93.

Holleman, J. F. 1953. "Accommodating the Spirit Amongst Some North-Eastern Shona Tribes." In *The Rhodes-Livingstone Papers*, no. 22. Oxford: Oxford University Press for the Rhodes-Livingston Institute.

Hugo, H. C. 1935. "The Mashona Spirits." *NADA: The Southern Rhodesia Native Affairs Department Annual* 13: 52–58.

Huron, David. 2011. "Why Is Sad Music Pleasurable? A Possible Role for Prolactin." *Musicae Scientiae* 15 (2): 146–58.

———. 2015. "Affect Induction Through Musical Sounds: An Ethological Perspective." *Philosophical Transactions of the Royal Society of London B: Biological Sciences* 370 (1664): 2014.0098.

James, Robin. 2012. "Affective Resonance: On the Uses and Abuses of Music in and for Philosophy." *PhaenEX* 7 (2): 59–95.

James, William. 1884. "What Is an Emotion?" *Mind* 9: 188–205.

Jankowsky, Richard C. 2010. *Stambeli: Music, Trance, and Alterity in Tunisia.* Chicago: University of Chicago Press.

Johnston, Thomas F. 1972. "Possession Music of the Shangana-Tsonga." *African Music* 5 (2): 10–22.

Junod, Henri Philippe. 1934a. "Les Cas Possession et L'exorcisme Chez Les Vandau." *Africa: Journal of the International African Institute* 7 (3): 270–99.

———. 1934b. "A Contribution to the Study of Ndau Demography, Totemism, and History." *Bantu Studies* 8 (1): 17–37.

Kapchan, Deborah. 2017. "The Splash of Icarus: Theorizing Sound Writing/Writing Sound Theory." In *Theorizing Sound Writing*, edited by Deborah Kapchan, 1–22. Middletown, CT: Wesleyan University Press.

Katupha, J. M. M. 1994. "The Language Situation and Language Use in Mozambique." In *African Languages, Development and the State*, edited by Richard Fardon and Graham Furniss, 89–96. London: Routledge.

Kauffman, Stuart. 2008. *Reinventing the Sacred: A New View of Science, Reason, and Religion.* New York: Basic Books.

Keil, Charles. 1966. "Motion and Feeling Through Music." *Journal of Aesthetics and Art Criticism* 24 (3): 337–49.

———. 1987. "Participatory Discrepancies and the Power of Music." *Cultural Anthropology* 2 (3): 275–83.

———. 1995. "The Theory of Participatory Discrepancies: A Progress Report." *Ethnomusicology* 39 (1): 1–20.

Kirby, Percival R. 1934. *The Musical Instruments of the Native Races of South Africa.* London: Oxford University Press.

Kisliuk, Michelle. 2017. "Writing the Magnified Musicking Moment." In *Theorizing Sound Writing*, edited by Deborah Kapchan, 86–113. Middletown, CT: Wesleyan University Press.

Kleinman, Arthur. 2014. "The Search for Wisdom: Why William James Still Matters." In *The Ground Between: Anthropologists Engage Philosophy*, edited by Veena Das, Michael Jackson, Arthur Kleinman, and Bhrigupati Singh, 119–37. Durham, NC: Duke University Press.

Kockelman, Paul. 2005. "The Semiotic Stance." *Semiotica* 157 (1–4): 233–304.

———. 2011. "Biosemiosis, Technocognition, and Sociogenesis: Selection and Significance in a Multiverse of Sieving and Serendipity." *Current Anthropology* 52 (5): 711–39.

———. 2013. *Agent, Person, Subject, Self: A Theory of Ontology, Interaction, and Infrastructure.* Oxford: Oxford University Press.

———. 2015. "Four Theories of Things: Aristotle, Marx, Heidegger, and Peirce." *Signs and Society* 3 (1): 153–92.

———. 2016. *The Chicken and the Quetzal: Incommensurate Ontologies and Portable Values in Guatemala's Cloud Forest.* Durham, NC: Duke University Press.

Kohn, Eduardo. 2005. "Runa Realism: Upper Amazonian Attitudes of Nature Knowing." *Ethnos* 70 (2): 171–96.

———. 2013. *How Forests Think: Toward an Anthropology Beyond the Human.* Berkeley: University of California Press.

———. 2015. "Anthropology of Ontologies." *Annual Review of Anthropology* 44:311–27.

Kramer, Fritz. 1993. *The Red Fez: Art and Spirit Possession in Africa.* London: Verso.

Kyker, Jennifer. 2009. "Carrying Spirits in Song: Music and the Making of Ancestors at Zezuru Kurova Guva Ceremonies." *African Music* 8 (3): 65–84.

———. 2016. *Oliver Mtukudzi: Living Tuku Music in Zimbabwe.* Bloomington: Indiana University Press.

Laing, Aislinn. 2010. "Zimbabwean Mother Kills Son to Sell Ear to Witch Doctor." *Telegraph* (London), July 1. Accessed August 2, 2017. http://www.telegraph.co.uk/news/worldnews/africaandindianocean/zimbabwe/7866744/Zimbabwean-mother-kills-son-to-sell-ear-to-witch-doctor.html.

Lambek, Michael. 2002. *The Weight of the Past: Living with History in Mahajanga, Madagascar.* New York: Palgrave MacMillan.

———. 2016. "On Being Present to History: Historicity and Brigand Spirits in Madagascar." *HAU: Journal of Ethnographic Theory* 6 (1): 317–41.

Lan, David. 1985. *Guns and Rain: Guerrillas and Spirit Mediums in Zimbabwe.* London: James Currey.

Lefebvre, Martin. 2007. "The Art of Pointing: Peirce, Indexicality, and Photographic Images." In *Photography Theory*, edited by James Elkins, 220–44. New York: Routledge.

Leys, Ruth. 2011. "The Turn to Affect: A Critique." *Critical Inquiry* 37 (3): 434–72.

Lidov, David. 1999. *Elements of Semiotics*. New York: St. Martin's Press.

Liesegang, Gerhard. 1967. "Beiträge Zur Geschichte des Reiches der Gaza Nguni im Südlichen Mocambique, 1820–1895." PhD, University of Cologne.

———. 1970. "Nguni Migrations Between Delagoa Bay and the Zambezi, 1821–1839." *African Historical Studies* 3 (2): 317–37.

———. 1983. "Notes on the Internal Structure of the Gaza Kingdom of Southern Mozambique, 1840–1895." In *Before and After Shaka*, edited by J. B. Peires, 178–209. Grahamstown, South Africa: Institute of Social and Economic Research, Rhodes University.

MacGonagle, Elizabeth. 2007. *Crafting Identity in Zimbabwe and Mozambique*. Rochester, NY: University of Rochester Press.

———. 2008. "Living with a Tyrant: Ndau Memories and Identities in the Shadow of Ngungunyana." *International Journal of African Historical Studies* 41 (1): 29–53.

Mahmood, Saba. 2005. *Politics of Piety: The Islamic Revival and the Feminist Subject*. Princeton, NJ: Princeton University Press.

———. 2009. "Agency, Performativity, and the Feminist Subject." In *Pieties and Gender*, edited by Lene Sjørup and Hilda Rømer Christensen, 13–46. Leiden: Brill.

Mandondo, Alois. 1997. "Trees and Spaces as Emotion and Norm Laden Components of Local Ecosystems in Nyamaropa Communal Land, Nyanga District, Zimbabwe." *Agriculture and Human Values* 14 (4): 353–72.

Mangena, Tendai, and Sambulo Ndlovu. 2013. "Implications and Complications of Bride Price Payment Among the Shona and Ndebele of Zimbabwe." *International Journal of Asian Social Science* 3 (2): 472–81.

Manzungu, Emmanuel. 2004. "Environmental Impacts of the Fast-Track Land Reform Programme: A Livelihoods Perspective." In *Zimbabwe: The Past in the Future*, edited by David Harold-Barry, 53–68. Harare, Zimbabwe: Weaver Press.

Maposa, Marshall Tamuka. 2012. "A Loud Silence: The History of Funeral Dress Among the Ndau of Zimbabwe." In *Was It Something I Wore? Dress, Identity, Materiality*, edited by Relebohile Moletsane, Claudia Mitchell, and Ann Smith, 148–61. Cape Town: Human Sciences Research Council Press.

Maposa, Richard S., James Hlongwana, and Daniel Gamira. 2010. "'Aluta Continua': A Critical Reflection on the Chimurenga-Within-Third Chimurenga Among the Ndau People in Chipinge, District, Southeastern Zimbabwe." *Journal of African Studies and Development* 2 (6): 191–200.

Marashe, Joel. 2014. "The African Traditional Religious Landscape: An Examination of the Role of Traditional Leaders in the Fight Against HIV and AIDS in Chipinge, Zimbabwe." *Verbum et Ecclesia* 35 (1): 1–8.

Martin, David, and Phyllis Johnson. 1981. *The Struggle for Zimbabwe*. New York: Monthly Review Press.

Martin, Emily. 2013. "The Potentiality of Ethnography and the Limits of Affect Theory." *Current Anthropology* 54 (S7): 149–58.

Martinez, Jose Luiz. 1996. "Musical Semiosis and the *Rasa* Theory." In *Musical Semiotics in Growth*, edited by Eero Tarasti, 99–128. Bloomington: Indiana University Press.

Masquelier, Adeline. 2001. *Prayer Has Spoiled Everything: Possession, Power, and Identity in an Islamic Town of Niger*. Durham, NC: Duke University Press.

Massumi, Brian. 1987. "Notes on the Translation and Acknowledgments." In *A Thousand Plateaus: Capitalism and Schizophrenia*, edited by Gilles Deleuze and Felix Guattari, xvi–ix. London: Continuum.

———. 1995. "The Autonomy of Affect." *Cultural Critique* 31: 83–109.

Mate, Rekopantswe. 2012. "Youth Lyrics, Street Language, and the Politics of Age: Contextualising the Youth Question in the Third Chimurenga in Zimbabwe." *Journal of Southern African Studies* 38 (1): 107–27.

McAllester, David. 1954. *Enemy Way Music*. Cambridge, MA: Harvard University Press.

Meintjes, Louise. 2004. "Shoot the Sergeant, Shatter the Mountain: The Production of Masculinity in Zulu Ngoma Song and Dance in Post-Apartheid South Africa." *Ethnomusicology Forum* 13 (2): 173–201.

Meredith, L. C. 1925. "The Rain Spirit of Mabota Murangadzwa, Melsetter District." *NADA: The Southern Rhodesia Native Affairs Department Annual* 3: 77–81.

Meyer, Leonard B. 1956. *Emotion and Meaning in Music*. Chicago: University of Chicago Press.

Mhlanga, Wilson. 1948. "(1) The Story of Ngwaqazi. (2) The History of the Amatshangana." *NADA: The Southern Rhodesia Native Affairs Department Annual* 25: 70–73.

Moore, Donald S. 2005. *Suffering for Territory: Race, Place, and Power in Zimbabwe*. Durham, NC: Duke University Press.

Moyana, Henry Vusso. 1984. *The Political Economy of Land in Zimbabwe*. Gweru, Zimbabwe: Mambo Press.

Msindo, Enocent. 2007. "Ethnicity and Nationalism in Urban Colonial Zimbabwe: Bulawayo, 1950 to 1963." *Journal of African History* 48 (2): 267–90.

Muchuri, Tinashe. 2015 (October 23). "Re-Enforcing Ndau Cultural Rights." *Panorama Magazine*.

Museka, Godfrey, Darmarris Kaguda, and Onias Matumbu. 2016. "Sounds of 'Death': The Adaptation of Madzviti-Muchongoyo Music in Silencing Dissenting Voices in Chipinge (Manicaland-Zimbabwe, 2002–2008)." In *Sounds of Life: Music, Identity and Politics in Zimbabwe*, edited by Fainos Mangena, Ezra Chitando, and Itai Muwati, 114–26. Newcastle: Cambridge Scholars Publishing.

Muyambo, Tenson M., and Richard S. Maposa. 2013. "The Post-Burial Rites of *Kusemendera Guwa* in the Indigenous Ndau Culture in Zimbabwe: Insights on Enculturation Theology." *Journal of Emerging Trends in Educational Research and Policy Studies* 4 (4): 589–93.

Nancy, Jean-Luc. 2000. *Being Singular Plural*. Stanford: Stanford University Press.

Ndlovu-Gatsheni, Sabelo J. 2013. "Zimbabwe and the Crisis of *Chimurenga* Nationalism." In *Coloniality of Power in Postcolonial Africa: Myths of Decolonization* by Sabelo J. dlovu-Gatsheni, 179–236. Dakar, Senegal: CODESRIA.

———. 2015. "Introduction: Mugabeism and Entanglements of History, Politics, and Power in the Making of Zimbabwe." In *Mugabeism? History, Politics, and Power in Zimbabwe*, edited by Sabelo J. Ndlovu-Gatsheni, 1–25. New York: Palgrave Macmillan.

———. 2016. "Nguni Empires." In *The Encyclopedia of Empire*, edited by John M. MacKenzie, 1–9. London: Wiley-Blackwell.

Ndumeya, Noel. 2018. ""Limiting the Domination": Anti-Colonial African Protests in South Eastern Zimbabwe, 1929–1940s." *Journal of Black Studies* 50 (2): 1–24.

Nussbaum, Martha. 2001. *Upheavals of Thought: The Intelligence of Emotions*. Cambridge: Cambridge University Press.

Nzenza, Sekai. 2015. "Zimbabwe: Death and the Fear of Witchcraft." *Herald* (Harare), October 7. Accessed August 2, 2017. http://www.herald.co.zw/death-and-the-fear-of-witchcraft/.

Oosterom, Marjoke A., and Lloyd Pswarayi. 2014. "Being a Born-Free: Violence, Youth, and Agency in Zimbabwe." IDS Research Report 79. Brighton: Institute of Development Studies

Orner, Peter, and Annie Holmes, eds. 2010. *Hope Deferred: Narratives of Zimbabwean Lives*. San Francisco: McSweeney's.

O'Sullivan, Simon. 2001. "The Aesthetics of Affect: Thinking Art Beyond Representation." *Angelaki* 6 (3): 125–35.

Parmentier, Richard J. 2016. *Signs and Society: Further Studies in Semiotic Anthropology*. Bloomington: Indiana University Press.

Peirce, Charles S. 1931–1958. *Collected Papers of Charles Sanders Peirce*. 8 vols. Edited by Charles Hartshorne, Paul Weiss, and Arthur Burks. Cambridge, MA: Harvard University Press.

———. 1955. *Philosophical Writings of Peirce*. New York: Dover.

———. 1982–2010. *Writings of Charles S. Peirce: A Chronological Edition*. 6 vols. Bloomington: Indiana University Press.

———. 1992. *The Essential Peirce: Selected Philosophical Writings; Volume 1 (1867–1893)*. Bloomington: Indiana University Press.

———. 1998. *The Essential Peirce: Selected Philosophical Writings; Volume 2 (1893–1913)*. Bloomington: Indiana University Press.

Perman, Tony. 2010. "Dancing in Opposition: *Muchongoyo*, Emotion, and the Politics of Performance in Southeastern Zimbabwe." *Ethnomusicology* 54 (3): 425–51.

———. 2011a. "Awakening Spirits: The Ontology of Spirit, Self, and Society in Ndau Spirit Possession Practices in Zimbabwe." *Journal of Religion in Africa* 41 (1): 59–92.

———. 2011b. "The Ethics of Ndau Performance: Questioning Ethnomusicology's Aesthetics." *Journal of Musicological Research* 31 (2): 227–52.

———. 2015. "A Tale of Two Mbiras." *African Music* 10 (1): 102–26.

———. 2017. "Muchongoyo and Mugabeism in Zimbabwe." *African Studies Review* 60 (1): 145–70.

Pinker, Steven. 1997. *How the Mind Works*. New York: Norton.

Raftopoulos, Brian. 2009. "The Crisis in Zimbabwe, 1998–2008." In *Becoming Zimbabwe: A History from the Pre-Colonial Period to 2008*, edited by Brian Raftopoulos and Alois Mlambo, 201–32. Harare, Zimbabwe: Weaver Press.

Raftopoulos, Brian, and Alois Mlambo, eds. 2009. *Becoming Zimbabwe: A History from the Pre-Colonial Period to 2008*. Harare, Zimbabwe: Weaver Press.

Ranger, Terence. 1989. "Missionaries, Migrants and the Manyika: The Invention of Ethnicity in Zimbabwe." In *The Creation of Tribalism in Southern Africa*, edited by Leroy Vail, 118–50. Los Angeles: University of California Press.

Reddy, William M. 2001. *The Navigation of Feeling: A Framework for the History of Emotions*. Cambridge: Cambridge University Press.

Rennie, John Keith. 1973. "Christianity, Colonialism and the Origins of Nationalism Among the Ndau of Southern Rhodesia, 1890–1935." PhD diss., Northwestern University.

———. 1978. "From Zimbabwe to a Colonial Chieftaincy: Four Transformations of the Musikavanhu Territorial Cult in Rhodesia." In *Guardians of the Land: Essays on Central African Territorial Cults*, edited by J. M. Schoffeleers, 257–85. Gweru, Zimbabwe: Mambo Press.

———. 1985. "Ideology and State Formation: Political and Communal Ideologies Among the South-Eastern Shona, 1500–1890." In *State Formation in Eastern Africa*, edited by Ahmed Idha Salim, 162–94. New York: St. Martin's Press.

Rice, Timothy. 2001. "Reflections on Music and Meaning: Metaphor, Signification and Control in the Bulgarian Case." *British Journal of Ethnomusicology* 10 (1): 19–38.

Rorty, Richard. 1999. *Philosophy and Social Hope*. New York: Penguin.

Rosaldo, Michelle. 1984. "Toward an Anthropology of Self and Feeling." In *Culture Theory: Essays on Mind, Self, and Emotion*, edited by Richard A. Shweder and R. LeVine, 137–57. Cambridge: Cambridge University Press.

Rouget, Gilbert. 1985. *Music and Trance*. Chicago: University of Chicago Press.

Sakakeeny, Matt. 2015. "Music." In *Keywords in Sound*, edited by David Novak and Matt Sakakeeny, 112–24. Durham, NC: Duke University Press.

Samuels, David. 2004. "Language, Meaning, Modernity, and Doowop." *Semiotica* 149:297–323.

———. 2006. "Bible Translation and Medicine Man Talk: Missionaries, Indexicality, and the 'Language Expert' on the San Carlos Apache Reservation." *Language in Society* 35 (4): 529–57.

Saussure, Ferdinand de. 1966. *Course in General Linguistics*. New York: McGraw-Hill.

Scherzinger, Martin. 2012. "Harmonic Fractals in the Music of the Lamellaphone." *Critical Interventions* 6 (1): 84–105.

Scott, David. 1999. *Refashioning Futures: Criticism After Postcoloniality*. Princeton, NJ: Princeton University Press.

Seeger, Charles. 1977. "Speech, Music, and Speech About Music." In *Studies in Musicology, 1935–1975*, edited by Charles Seeger, 16–30. Berkeley: University of California Press.

Shamuyarira, Nathan M. 1965. *Crisis in Rhodesia.* New York: Transatlantic Arts.
Shoko, Tabona. 2006. "'My Bones Shall Rise Again': War Veterans, Spirits, and Land Reform in Zimbabwe." Leiden: African Studies Center. ASC Working Paper no. 68.
Short, T. L. 2007. *Peirce's Theory of Signs.* Cambridge: Cambridge University Press.
Simango, Christine. 1969. "From Gold Coast to Mozambique: The Story of Christine Simango, Told by Herself." In *Daughters of Africa*, edited by Margaret Busby, 95–102. New York: Negro Universities Press.
Simango, Columbus K. 1917. "The African and Civilization." *Southern Workman* 46:552–55.
———. 1919. "A South African's Story." *Southern Workman* 48:268–70.
Sithole, Masipula. 1999. *Zimbabwe: Struggles Within the Struggle.* Harare, Zimbabwe: Rujeko.
Sithole, Masipula, and John Makumbe. 1997. "Elections in Zimbabwe: The Zanu (Pf) Hegemony and Its Incipient Decline." *African Journal of Political Science* 2 (1): 122–39.
Sithole, Ndabaningi. 1977. *Roots of a Revolution: Scenes from Zimbabwe's Struggle.* Oxford: Oxford University Press.
Small, Christopher. 1998. *Musicking: The Meanings of Performing and Listening.* Middletown, CT: Wesleyan University Press.
Spencer, Leon P. 2013. *Toward an African Church in Mozambique: Kamba Simango and the Protestant Community in Manica and Sofala, 1892–1945.* Luwinga, Malawi: Mzuni Press.
Stewart, Kathleen. 2007. *Ordinary Affects.* Durham, NC: Duke University Press.
Stoller, Paul. 1995. *Embodying Colonial Memories: Spirit Possession, Power, and the Hauka in West Africa.* New York: Routledge.
Taussig, Michael. 1993. *Mimesis and Alterity: A Particular History of the Senses.* New York: Routledge.
Tavuyanago, Baxter. 2013. "The 'Crocodile Gang' Operation: A Critical Reflection on the Genesis of the Second Chimurenga in Zimbabwe." *Global Journal of Human Social Science* 13 (4): 27–36.
Taylor, Tanya N. 2010. "'Because I Was in Pain, I Just Wanted to be Treated': Competing Therapeutic Goals in the Performance of Healing HIV/AIDS in Rural Zimbabwe." *Journal of American Folklore* 123 (489): 304–28.
Tolbert, Elizabeth. 2001. "Music and Meaning: An Evolutionary Story." *Psychology of Music* 29 (1): 84–94.
Tomlinson, Gary. 2015. *A Million Years of Music: The Emergence of Human Modernity.* New York: Zone Books.
———. 2016. "Sign, Affect, and Musicking Before the Human." *Boundary 2* 43 (1): 143–72.
Turino, Thomas. 1999. "Signs of Imagination, Identity, and Experience: A Peircian Semiotic Theory for Music." *Ethnomusicology* 43 (2): 221–55.

———. 2000. *Nationalists, Cosmopolitans, and Popular Music in Zimbabwe*. Chicago: University of Chicago Press.

———. 2008. *Music as Social Life: The Politics of Participation*. Chicago: University of Chicago Press.

———. 2009. "Four Fields of Music Making and Sustainable Living." *World of Music* 51 (1): 95–117.

———. 2014. "Peircean Thought as Core Theory for a Phenomenological Ethnomusicology." *Ethnomusicology* 58 (2): 185–221.

———. 2016. "Music, Social Change, and Alternative Forms of Citizenship." In *Artistic Citizenship: Artistry, Social Responsibility, and Ethical Praxis*, edited by David J. Elliott, Marissa Silverman, and Wayne D. Bowman, 297–312. Oxford: Oxford University Press.

Turner, Victor. 1969. *The Ritual Process: Structure and Anti-Structure*. Ithaca, NY: Cornell University Press.

———. 1974. "Liminal to Liminoid in Play, Flow, and Ritual: An Essay in Comparative Symbology." In *The Anthropological Study of Human Play*, edited by E. Norbeck, 53–92. Houston: Rice University Studies.

Vijfhuizen, Carin. 1997. "Rain-Making, Political Conflicts and Gender Images: A Case from Mutema Chieftaincy in Zimbabwe." *Zambezia* 24 (1): 31–50.

———. 2002. *'The People You Live With': Gender Identities and Social Practices, Beliefs, and Power in the Livelihoods of Ndau Women and Men in a Village with an Irrigation Scheme in Zimbabwe*. Harare, Zimbabwe: Weaver Press.

Vijfhuizen, Carin, and Locadia Makora. 1998. "More Than One Paramount Chief in One Chieftaincy? The Gender of Maintaining Worlds." *Zambezia* 25 (1): 59–81.

Vines, Alex. 1996. *Renamo: From Terrorism to Democracy in Mozambique*. Amsterdam: Eduardo Mondlane Foundation.

Viveiros de Castro, Eduardo. 2004. "Exchanging Perspectives: The Transformation of Objects into Subjects in Amerindian Cosmologies." *Common Knowledge* 10 (3): 463–84.

———. 2005. "Perspectivism and Multinaturalism in Indigenous America." In *The Land Within: Indigenous Territory and Perception of the Environment*, edited by Alexandre Surrallés and Pedro García Hierro, 36–75. Copenhagen: International Work Group for Indigenous Affairs.

Welsh Asante, Kariamu. 2000. *Zimbabwe Dance: Rhythmic Forces, Ancestral Voices; An Aesthetic Analysis*. Trenton, NJ: Africa World Press.

Wheeler, Douglas L. 1968. "Gungunyane the Negotiator: A Study in African Diplomacy." *Journal of African History* 9 (4): 585–602.

Wilder, George A. 1907a. "The Ndau Religion." *Hartford Seminary Record* 17 (1): 52–57.

———. 1907b. "Ndau Religion, Part II." *Hartford Seminary Record* 17 (2): 159–68.

Williams, Raymond. 1977. *Marxism and Literature*. Oxford: Oxford University Press.

Wolf, Richard K. 2001. "Emotional Dimensions of Ritual Music Among the Kotas, a South Indian Tribe." *Ethnomusicology* 45 (3): 379–422.

Zamchiya, Phillian. 2011. "A Synopsis of Land and Agrarian Change in Chipinge District, Zimbabwe." *Journal of Peasant Studies* 38 (5): 1093–1122.

———. 2013a. "The MDC-T's (Un)seeing Eye in Zimbabwe's 2013 Harmonized Elections: A Technical Knockout." *Journal of Southern African Studies* 39 (4): 955–62.

———. 2013b. "The Role of Politics and State Practices in Shaping Rural Differentiation: A Study of Resettled Small-Scale Farmers in South-Eastern Zimbabwe." *Journal of Southern African Studies* 39 (4): 937–53.

Index

TONY PERMAN is an associate professor of music at Grinnell College.

The University of Illinois Press
is a founding member of the
Association of University Presses.

Composed in 10.5/13 Adobe Garamond Pro
with Scala Sans display
by Jim Proefrock
at the University of Illinois Press
Cover designed by Jim Proefrock
Cover image: Tapera Chingodza plays
ngoma drums. Photo by Jennifer W. Kyker.

University of Illinois Press
1325 South Oak Street
Champaign, IL 61820-6903
www.press.uillinois.edu